Teaching and Learning in Virtual Worlds

D1742037

Teaching and Learning in Virtual Worlds

Edited by

C.A. DeCoursey and Shana Garrett

Inter-Disciplinary Press

Oxford, United Kingdom

The *Inter-Disciplinary Press* is part of *Inter-Disciplinary.Net* – a global network for research and publishing. The *Inter-Disciplinary Press* aims to promote and encourage the kind of work which is collaborative, innovative, imaginative, and which provides an exemplar for inter-disciplinary and multi-disciplinary publishing.

British Library Cataloguing in Publication Data. A catalogue record for this book is available from the British Library.

Inter-Disciplinary Press, Priory House, 149B Wroslyn Road, Freeland, Oxfordshire. OX29 8HR, United Kingdom.
+44 (0)1993 882087

ISBN: 978-1-84888-231-7
First published in the United Kingdom in Paperback format in 2014. First Edition.

This book is dedicated to Eric, Owen and Elizabeth

Table of Contents

Acknowledgements

The editors are grateful to those who have assisted in producing this volume on the use of virtual worlds in educational contexts. This project required a constellation of skills, efforts and minds. C.A. DeCoursey is grateful to her colleagues in the Department of English and the English Language Centre, at the Hong Kong Polytechnic University for their experience and assistance in this process, especially Dean Gui. She would also like to thank Christian M.I.M. Matthiessen, Head of the Department of English, for his support. Shana Garrett would like to thank her colleagues at Colorado Technical University for their support in allowing her the time and encouragement to continue her passion in working in the distance education field as well as the pleasure of working with such dedicated professionals. She would also like to thank her husband Bob for his amazing love and support during this time.

This volume is a result of the Inter-Disciplinary.Net conference 'Experiential Learning in Virtual Worlds,' held in Prague, Czech Republic, March 12-14, 2010. This conference was, and remains, an exceptionally dynamic event, with a diverse and committed group of presenters who together provide a springboard for inquiry into this relatively new field, and will continue to do so in the future. It is our pleasure to thank Jim Gritton, who remains a driver of research into virtual worlds and their uses. He is also a force in organising the conference annually, in mentoring young scholars, in providing feedback and facilitating future planning.

The work of assembling, editing, collating and tracking changes across pages and versions is onerous, and requires eyes and minds both detail-oriented and theoretically capable. We have been fortunate to be able to call on support from the people at Inter-Disciplinary.Net for assistance in producing the volume.

It has been a pleasure to work with colleagues from many different locations and backgrounds on this project. We look forward to many more interesting years of ELVW conferences and volumes, and to working with an expanding circle of those interested in researching the use of virtual worlds in education.

C.A. DeCoursey
The Hong Kong Polytechnic University

Shana Garrett
Colorado Technical University

Introduction

C. A. DeCoursey

Virtual worlds have grown in social and educational significance since the 1990s. They combine opportunities educators are quick to appreciate, and providers cannot ignore. In the same way that online communities bring together people from many locations, vocations and perspectives, virtual worlds assemble learners and practitioners, offering them ways of generating, discussing and disseminating content. Virtual worlds allow these communities to do a great deal more than exchange information. The graphical user interface, with its topography and synchronicity, underpins the avatar's sense of presence in-world. The removal of the procedural architecture found in fantasy and game worlds invites communities to detail their locations and interactions to suit their own particular needs. Such constructions offer learning communities unique opportunities. Educators can now guide learners through hands-on simulations of facilities, equipment, situations and processes which are actually available to few, yet necessary to a conceptual and practical grasp of a field. Neither traditional print materials nor financially-strapped institutions can give students such a range and particularity of experiences. And virtual worlds achieve a kind of social levelling that invites a breath of participants into the experience, and the conversation. It is no wonder, then, that over the past decade virtual worlds have been eagerly taken up across a great range of educational fields and contexts.

As a vehicle for research, virtual worlds are well-suited to our increasingly connected world. In this volume, nineteen contributors from Europe, north America and Asia explore issues of virtual subjectivity, experiential and distributed learning. The relevance of such work, and its implications for the future of global education, cannot be doubted. Mid-twentieth century, less than 10% of the population in developed countries attended university. A few decades on, we live in a world where exclusion on the grounds of identity is unacceptable, access is a right honoured in principle where it cannot be financially supported, and the pace of change drives a demand for lifelong learning. Twenty-first century business, administrative, and educational organisations across the globe share educational needs and modalities for its delivery. Traditional methods of tertiary teaching and research, physical meeting based in real-time, are increasingly unsustainable. Experiential learning in virtual worlds is destined to grow, and to some degree replace the classrooms, collectivities and pedagogies of the past.

Virtual subjectivity has been an area of sustained academic interest. Early writers speculated that the virtuoso technical affordances of virtual worlds would yield a fragmented plurality rather than a true self. But self has had a long history of being multiple. The virtual self extends and projects human sensibilities in ways not too different from physical senses. Most obviously, virtual subjects are visually tailored according to users' tastes. Users to customise their gender, age, ethnicity, height, facial and body traits, allowing exploration of basic elements of identity. These experiences feed back to the self at the keyboard, provoking questions, thoughts and further experiments. That is, avatar presence feeds back on users' private self-awareness of emotions, values and attitudes, assisting learning. This cycle is basic to researchers' and educators' understanding of virtual worlds as environments suitable for teaching and learning. Avatar subjectivity is also mediated textually in synchronous chat, though the use of paralinguistic expressions of personality such as gestures make the visual and textual difficult to separate. Users tend to treat virtual interactions as they do exchanges in real social environments. They ascribe social conventions to themselves and other avatars in synchronous interactions, interpreting appearance and interactions in ways similar to daily life. This visual stereotyping becomes communicative, operationalising the fit-to-context judgments through which users orient themselves in new situations. Educators can assume these in structuring activities, projects and assessments.

Three chapters in this volume explore how avatar subjectivity underwrites opportunities for training and research into human social processes and therapeutic interventions. Paul Jerry and Nancy Tavares-Jones raise questions about virtual identity in the first chapter. Their ethnographic study of avatar-use employs theories of mind to explore questions of embodiment, immersion, relationships and suggestibility. This work suggests educators need awareness that the persistence and consistency of the virtual self requires time to develop, and an appreciation of virtually immersible students as compared with those less engaged in the medium. In the next chapter, Thomas Edwards and Michael Walker offer a carefully constructed pedagogical framework for setting ethical and transformative learning into virtual contexts, and explores the ramifications in terms of technical affordances for paralinguistic and kinesic communication, as well as action learning and problem-based learning. It is a truism, that new media replicate older forms, at least in the early stages. Edwards and Walker point to a need for more careful virtual instructional design, rather than merely adapting face-to-face classroom activities in virtual contexts. Similarly, C. A. DeCoursey uses computational sentiment analysis to map lexico-grammar for affect, judgment and appreciation in students' reports of their off-task virtual sexual experiences. Using a long-standing psychological model of the multiple self, she attaches attitudinal lexis to the virtual avatar, the person at the keyboard, and the imagined successful self, in order to explore intra-psychic processes of learning in an area which remains somewhat proscribed in Chinese society.

Virtual frameworks and affordances make a habit of improving. For the educator, their interest has often focused on technical questions about the spaces where students engage in and represent their learning, in discussions of issues like scalability, information richness and object interrogation. For the learner, authentic presence has been greatly replaced by the mechanics of transportation. These discussions have been stimulated by and connected to the more philosophical affordances of virtual worlds—areas such as the socially constructed nature of understanding, personalisation, immersion, authenticity, and the role of narrative and reflection in representing what has been learned.

In the next three chapters, discussions centre on the ways in which virtual worlds support experiential and distributed learning. Virtual worlds engage and motivate learners. They replace conventionally passive and stationary classroom learning with cycles of exploration, performance and construction, replicate difficult but realistic situations and simulate professional applications, elicit and showcase user-generated content, and facilitate problem-based and task-based learning. The rapid expansion and uptake of virtual worlds in education fuels the on-going discussion about instructional design and new research potentials. Virtual worlds are well-suited to constructivist learning approaches yet challenges persist. Problem areas include itemising task typologies, structuring reusable in-world learning tasks, making full use of social and dialogic dimensions of virtual interactions between pedagogic agents and environments, and devising assessments to reflect situated cognition.

These issues are highlighted in by Yvonne Masters, Sue Gregory, Torsten Reiners, Vicki Knox and Barney Dalgarno, reporting on a pilot project exploring potential uses of virtual classrooms in preparing pre-service teachers. They outline an Australian example of a virtual practicum which combines live role-play with synchronous bot-scripted 'children' and machinima exemplars. These structure simulations approaching the complexity of real classrooms, thus making the virtual practicum realistic and useful. These authors demonstrate the value of virtual worlds in professional training, particularly in situations and contexts where 'real' experience is difficult to attain. Next, Eero Palomäki and Emma Nordbäck analyse of Finnish students' responses to learning chemistry vocabulary. They note the motivating impact of a playful virtual environment, one which does not resemble the normal classroom visually or in terms of interactions and functions, and its potential to support students through authentic work tasks. They also note the time an processes required for mature institutional support of virtual training courses to develop. Audrey Aronowsky, Beth Sanzenbacher, Johanna Thompson and Krystal Villanosa examine the use of simulations, game structures and digital technologies as instructional tools and in informal and experiential science learning. They identify a blended-learning approach which combines virtual science, for example geological digs and coral reef conservation, with blogging and other content-creation tools, and real-time contact through satellite calls, to make science real and interesting to teens.

The rapid uptake of virtual environments in education has created a demand for strategic approaches to managing experiential learning in virtual environments. Educational endeavours are increasingly global, and its modalities increasingly distributed. Course designers are reshaping learning objectives to focus on learners' process of acquiring them, taking up collaborative learning activities, and enhancing the role of simulation with its demand for perception and accuracy in the use of classroom input. Virtual learning instructional designs are increasingly focused on the processes, both in terms of graphic visualisation and content base that accompany tasks and activities, such that users' continuous choices for movement and interaction increase their exposure, experience, and retention.

Audrey Aronowsky, Beth Sanzenbacher, Johanna Thompson and Krystal Villanosa, highlight how virtual worlds support global community-building through a complex interplay of the ethical, social and technological dimensions of virtual learning. They indicate how the study of real and virtual marine ecosystems brought together teens and experts, field trips and distance-learning, science and conservationism. This paper indicates methods of handling virtual logistics when building global teams. Shana Garrett explores community creation in the virtual environment, the importance of communication and approaches to establishing communities are based on a creative vision of constructing a virtual environment that is dynamic and engaging in an effort to establishing and developing a positive working relationship for the online student.

The dispersed nature of contemporary education is made apparent by authors Clara O'Shea and Marshall Dozier. They consider the role of virtual presence and in-world activities in creating community. For graduate dissertation students from various European countries, peer interactions are difficult to organise, yet contribute vitally to dissertation completion and learner satisfaction. Taking a socio-material approach to the affordances of the virtual world, Dozier and O'Shea evaluate the case of a dissertation festival, where participants attended synchronously, and commented on each other's work through chat and by posting comments to boards. In the final chapter, Anna Peachey, Greg Withnal and Nicholas Braithewaite consider the potential of virtual worlds for generating knowledge. They address the need to develop approaches, problems and supporting materials, that make use of the Newtonian physical properties structured into virtual environments. Clearly, these may be exploited for the purposes of practical science, in areas such as measurement, gravity and momentum. At the same time, student responses to these learning approaches need to be explored. And while this chapter presents a study of a small number of participants, it represents a step forward in what virtual worlds may be used for, and how.

This volume contributes to our understanding of the ways technology drives the changes taking place in higher education, in its relations with society. Transnational flows of people and goods bring state-of-the-art practices and understandings to regions with varying abilities to fund and equip learners. The multimodal, temporally and visually dynamic information displays that effectively represent the intertextualities and polyphonies of our social interactions are increasingly used to support workplace job training and performance. The associated technical skills have become integral to functional literacy, and are common tertiary learning objectives and expected graduate attributes. Virtual worlds help make it possible for people across the world to connect to communities or practise and learning, meaning that individuals from all regions can experience, explore, and gain confidence as well as conceptual and practical proficiency. The roles and functions of teachers as mediating agents, and learners as content generators, are being rewritten by technology as much as by demand. As globalisation reshapes the delivery of education, virtual worlds have much to offer researchers, teachers and learners.

Part I:

Virtual Subjectivity

Reflections on Identity and Learning in a Virtual World: The Avatar in *Second Life*

Paul Jerry and Nancy Tavares-Jones

Abstract
Participation in learning in a virtual world requires the use of an avatar. An avatar is a representation of the learner in the virtual environment and varies in complexity depending on the virtual space. Our experience using *Second Life* informs this discussion of the nature and evolution of identity in or with an avatar. Necessarily, in a complex virtual world, an avatar becomes a virtual embodiment of an individual's identity. Some individuals spend time developing and evolving their avatar while others seem content to use a default setting in favour of completing whatever task has been set for them in the virtual world. Our interest lies with the experience of those individuals for whom the avatar becomes a significant extension of their off-line selves. Methodologically we have approached an understanding of identity and avatar using an ethnographic perspective. We draw on multiple data sources including reflections on personal immersion, as well as interview data with *Second Life* residents both new and old. Conceptually, we have approached our understanding of identity and avatar using Mann's (1994) theory of selfhood. Mann proposes that our sense of self is composed of three dimensions – time, embodiment, and relation (which is grounded in reflexivity.) Using this conceptualization to frame the development and evolution of an individual's identity as an avatar, we also examine psychological constructs such as theory of mind and the individual's experience of immersion and its potential relationship to the trait of suggestibility. While the implications of having multiple identities in online and off-line contexts are far-reaching, we focus our discussion of these implications for when a virtual world is used for educational purposes.

Key Words: Identity, learning, education, self, *Second Life*, virtual world, immersion.

*****

1. Introduction

As each new medium of human expression emerges, educators, among other groups, turn their attention to the possibilities the new medium presents for the enterprise of learning. *KZero Worldswide* estimates that as many as 1 billion virtual world registrations currently exist.[1] Bell defines a Virtual World (VW) as 'A synchronous, persistent network of people, represented as avatars, facilitated by networked computers.'[2] An example of a VW that educators have found to be fertile ground for creating learning experiences is *Second Life*[3] and this VW is the focus of the current study.

2. Second Life

Second Life (*SL*) is a virtual world where individuals navigate a virtual reality using an avatar. It is a persistent 3-D environment where residents are free to build, create, interact and live. There are few restrictions placed on everyday behaviour by the owner, Linden Labs. An individual wishing to enter this virtual world first creates an account, chooses a basic avatar which they will use to navigate in-world, and downloads a viewer that allows them access to both their avatar and the virtual world. Once logged in, an individual uses their avatar to navigate a 3-D environment. At the time of writing, the breakdown of the top 50 sims (places to go/things to do) in *Second Life* was 58% moderate, 32% adult, and 8% PG, proportions that have not changed substantially in the past year.[4]

Explorations of the use of virtual worlds in education often seem to focus on the nature of the medium and its potential uses and less so on the nature of the individuals who engage and involve themselves with the medium.[5] Developers of virtual worlds tend to focus on the 'user experience' and spend time and money on the interface with the virtual world (for example, simplifying the *SL* viewer),[6] the 'immersiveness' of the virtual space (i.e., how easily does it draw the attention of the individual to the exclusion of other competing stimuli), and in some contexts, the reality of the game-play and the believability of the non-player characters (NPCs). If there is a study of the users of virtual worlds, especially from the perspective of VW designers, it is often in the form of typical market analyses that address questions like 'who is our customer, how old are they, what is their gender, and perhaps most importantly, what is their level of income and how many hours (and dollars) are spent in-world per day/week/year?'[7] Less common in the literature is an exploration of the individual psychologies of the people who spend time in virtual worlds.[8]

In examining the intersection of the constructs of avatar and identity, we explore individuals who choose to enter virtual worlds, proposing possible theoretical and empirical considerations for continued research.

3. Identity and Self: Mann's Theory

Mann's approach to the self pre-dates the advent of virtual worlds. He was mainly concerned with a theory that would ground his work with psychopathology. Mann's model of human identity is formulated on three domains of experience – embodiment, time and reflexivity.

Mann's description of embodiment outlines humans as physical beings, comprising of a physical entity which takes up physical space.[9] Embodiment further describes the ability for humans to understand and develop their own experiences and limits to their physical existence. In addition to embodiment, Mann describes time as being an essential part of human identity. Humans, by their very nature, are comprised of a past, a present, and a future. People exist within a plane of time that is historical, continuous and can be planned for into the future.[10]

Lastly, Mann describes the concept of reflexivity as the third part of the human condition. Reflexivity comprises of a person's level of personal reflection and consciousness. How an individual interacts within the world around them, and how they process their experiences through self-reflection are key facets to the idea of reflexivity.

Mann's model has provided an interesting launch-point for exploring human experience in VWs. If, as he presumes, human beings have an identity that is grounded in embodiment, time, and reflexivity, then many aspects of the experience of VWs challenge these notions.[11] As an individual develops his or her identity to include an avatar, he or she is faced with Mann's categories of experience. Significant work has been done on the nature of embodiment represented by an avatar. Human form avatars have been shown to elicit human behaviour in VWs. For example, Yee and colleagues have noted that individuals will navigate their avatar in a virtual space as if it were in a real space, including respecting norms about personal space and nonverbal gestures.[12]

The concept of time, according to Mann, is also an essential part of the human condition. Humans exist within a plane of time that is both 'memoried and futured.'[13] With avatars, their existence ceases as soon as the VW participant goes off-line. Avatars may choose to occupy VW homes, and participate with other VW on-line avatars, however, when the participant terminates their experience in the VW, the avatar no longer exists. This directly challenges Mann's concept of time, as an avatar's time existence is sporadic, limited and not necessarily future oriented. At the same time, in spite of the seeming 'reality' of these virtual interactions, an avatar is not always a direct representation of the individual using it. A recent poll noted that close to half of avatar users change their appearance, primarily to be slimmer and younger, although some also change ethnicities.[14]

4. Castranova and the 'Bubble'

Castranova's exploration of Virtual Words began with his examination of the economics of virtual worlds and virtual goods.[15] He became interested in the phenomenon of goods and currency making the transition from VW to real world (RW). He noted that virtual goods were being traded both inside a VW using RW currency, or that virtual goods were being traded outside the boundaries of the VW they came from. He also noted that VW currency itself was being traded as if it were RW currency, with exchange rates that fluctuated with observable market forces.[16] His observations led him to consider the boundaries of VWs and their apparent permeability. As one author has stated elsewhere, Castranova invokes the notion of the magical circle (bubble?) where 'Individuals engage, for a period of time, in a specific place, an activity that is bounded by rules and everyone engages with the game as a meaningful but bounded event. When applied to virtual worlds, the magical circle is presented as a kind of membrane (bubble?) that encapsulates the game experience, bounding it in a kind of 'magical' place and time that exists for the participant.'[17] At the same time, there are many examples of the deliberate violation of the bubble. In televised media, we have the notion of the fourth wall, the idea that the television screen is like the fourth wall looking in to a typical three-walled set stage.[18] 'Breaking the fourth wall' is a dramatic technique of deliberately violating the fiction that the fourth wall is invisible to the actors. For example, in *Ferris Beuler's Day Off*[19] the main character routinely pauses the action and turns to address the audience. A similar phenomenon exists in Virtual Worlds with individuals making use of environments that were designed for gaming for other purposes such as machinima[20] and meetings.

In terms of avatar and identity, the challenge comes when an individual's avatar identity is challenged by others (or by circumstance) to break the fourth wall. When conversing with another avatar (and in turn with the person who is represented by that avatar), that fourth wall is inherently challenged. Which 'identity' does a VW participant embody? The avatar or themselves? Who is 'speaking'? How much of the 'real' person is revealed to the other avatar (and person it is representing?).

5. Theory of Mind and Avatar

Operationalizing Mann's notion of reflexivity poses an interesting challenge. The reflective nature of data generation in ethnography (see below) constitutes one means of engaging reflexivity as a method. Theory of mind (TOM) is a concept that may have applicability in considering the connection between an individual and his or her avatar. Philosophically, we are challenged by the existence of others and their 'knowability.' Descartes laid the groundwork for this issue.[21] Asking (essentially) 'what is knowable and how is it known', we are faced with the question of how it is that we know others – their existence, their thoughts, feeling and intentions. The modern response is that we build a 'theory of mind', a working model based on the assumption that others do exist and that they have thoughts and feelings they engage in, in a predictable manner. (Interestingly, off-line, we rarely question someone's existence. This can be problematic in a VW with non-player characters (NPCs) and chatbots populating the landscape.) The notion of predictability derives from the theory that we build about the person, how they typically respond to us and so on. When we interact with others, we call on this implicit theory of (their) mind and anticipate how they may respond to our interaction.

Theory of mind appears to rely on several things that may hold value for living in a VW. First, there is some element of cognitive TOM in any VW interaction. As we participate with others virtually, we continue to generate a TOM about the other avatars. If the avatar is a NPC, sophisticated gamers appear to build two theories – one that allows them to relate to the NPC as it is designed (i.e., they relate to the NPC as the NPC) and one that is really a 'theory of algorithm', trying to anticipate the finite loops of 'behaviour' programmed into the NPC. Second, there is some element of affective TOM. As we participate with others virtually, we also generate a TOM based on the apparent mood or affective valence of the other. In the absence of voice that carries key affective indicators, an individual may combine the visual presentation of the avatar[22] along with the textual nuances of typed communication (thinking in terms of *SL* chat) to develop a sense of the avatar's mood, building an affective TOM and constructing responses accordingly. In a related vein but beyond the scope of this project, we are considering the construct of hypnotic susceptibility[23] and its relation to empathy and affective TOM with the potential of examining a person's 'buy in' to a VW and their consideration of others/avatars as 'real' as a function of these measurable constructs.

6. Measuring Theory of Mind in Virtual Spaces

Measuring TOM is not an easy task. On the one hand, the notion that we build a predictive cognitive model for everyone we meet and spend time with suggests that measuring or demonstrating TOM should be a simple task. However, it becomes an issue of definition and measurement, each often defining the other in a circular manner. In this context, we use TOM to refer to the social psychological phenomenon of social perception of the presumed knowledge and beliefs about others' perceptions. Originally, this involved examining an individual's understanding of deception.[24] Empirically, this is done in two ways. The first is a false-belief task and the second is an appearance-reality task. Each is really a variation on the other. In both cases, they involve asking a subject to speculate on the choice another individual would make given a set of circumstances. In each scenario, the subject has information about the context that the other would not. For example, the subject might be told that a box contained candy and that the other individual knows this. The other individual then leaves the room, and during their absence, the candy is substituted for something else, like coins. The individual returns and the subject is asked what they think the individual will think is in the box. A correct answer is 'candy' because that is what the individual knew to be the case before they left the room. An incorrect response is 'coins'. A subject giving this answer would be considered to not have taken into account that their own knowledge changed but the subject's did not.

Formal assessment of TOM takes a number of forms including story boards that involve deception, multiple character perceptions, false-belief and appearance-reality tasks. Surprisingly, given the centrality of this concept to autism research and assessment, less than and handful of psychometrically validated tools exist for the assessment of TOM. One often-used example is the NEPSY-II[25] which includes a subtest called *Theory of Mind*. This subtest includes 16 items designed to tease out the various sub-facets of TOM including spontaneous imitation, false belief, deception and double deception scenarios and so on. The difficulty with all of the currently available normed assessments of TOM is that they involve the visual (and visual-motor) presentation of stimuli (including an actual double box stimulus like the candy-coin example above) to a subject. Administering these in *SL* is certainly possible but to date, there has not been an effort to translate these to virtual stimuli. What remains for us in assessment of TOM in *SL* is the thick descriptions of avatar identity that come from interaction and interview and self-report.

7. Ethnography and Methods

Ethnography is a broad term referring to a set of approaches to the understanding of a phenomenon, usually one of lived experience.[26] Post-modern evolution of traditional ethnography divides it into two streams, one being a 'quest to understand different lived worlds'.[27] The other is a deconstructive approach to expose the political and social discourses that mediate our experience of reality. In the first case, we seek to understand and depict – to the extent possible given our own on the phenomena we study – an accurate description of a lived experience. In the second, we seek to expose and critique the often implicit assumptions and practices of institutions as they form our experience of culture. In our exploration of identity in *SL*, we have employed several methods that fall loosely under the rubric of the first form, that of seeking to understand.

The post-structuralist ethnographic approach virtually (pardon the pun) demands that the observer be immersed in the phenomenon being explored. Historically rooted in the qualitative versus quantitative debate[28] the notion of the researcher being anything but detached from his or her work was considered a violation of the validity of the project. The evolution of mixed methods[29,30] and the critique of the discourse of science have led to the consideration that it might be necessary to live the experience being studied, giving a unique access to the nuances that might be missed in more traditional observational or interview/survey methods.

In the work partially represented by this contribution, the authors reflect on their experience of being avatars involved in a VW, viewing the experience through several lenses. One author (PJ) presents a view of longer-term residency (over 2 years) while the other author (NTJ) presents a view of shorter-term residency (less than 1 year). Further, both make use of self-reflection (including unstructured field notes) and chat interactions with longer-term residents as source data for these observations.

8. Avatar in *Second Life*: Observations[31]

I (NTJ) was first introduced to the *SL* virtual world in the summer of 2011 by the lead author, PJ. I downloaded a *SL* viewer, and the program requested that I choose a 'beginner' avatar. I had a very difficult time making a decision on my beginner avatar, despite assurances from PJ and the *SL* viewer prompt that I could alter my avatar's representation at a later date. Upon reflection, this was the first instance I began to question the importance and meaning of my avatar. I wondered about her (my?) appearance and how I wanted to be represented to others in the virtual world.

Learning about and refining my online avatar (according to Mann, my 'embodiment') required a considerable amount of time. After choosing an original avatar, completing the introductory tutorials, I began transforming the appearance of my avatar. After much consideration, I chose to alter most of my avatar's original appearance. I spent many hours in various in-world stores, and I ultimately chose to represent myself as an individual I wanted to resemble in 'real life'. I elected to 'purchase' additions such as red hair, jewelry, and dimples to complete the look I desired. I found this process extremely time consuming, and one which required much patience and meticulous attention to detail. I was (and continue to be) fascinated by the variety of items available for purchase.

After settling on an avatar appearance, I began venturing through different locations within *SL*. My first interactive sim was created as a fancy dress, dancing ballroom which contained approximately 20 other avatars at the time. I ventured out into the open area, and began to wonder how to interact with the others. I was unsure how one initiates conversations and interactions with others, especially since many of the participants were conversing in a seemingly free-flow and pre-acquainted manner.

As I began to meet others through open dialogue and personal in-world chat sessions, I became challenged by residents who held 'traditional social' conventions. One man stated that he did not appreciate being approached directly by a woman, as he preferred to do the 'approaching'. I felt that *SL* was a place where traditional social conventions could be challenged or changed, however, in my experience, many still held onto RW beliefs in the *SL* VW.

My experience within this sim allowed me to formulate an understanding of etiquette and other nuances that inherently come with learning any new culture.[32] I learned in-world topics such as *SL* terminology, dress codes for different locations and appropriate navigation procedures within sims (i.e. walking around, dancing, etc.).

Physical avatar mannerisms also became an interesting point of contention for me. Avatars would walk around, bump into, and push my avatar out of the way while navigating in-world. This type of behaviour would obviously not be tolerated in a traditional physical sense. This traditional sense of personal space was also challenged when discussing with others in the VW's. Many avatars would approach you and chat with you within a very close VW space. I found myself becoming uncomfortable when people would speak to me so closely – however this was being done in a VW, not a physical one. It raises the question about why I was so uncomfortable if it was not 'me' in the physical sense, but a representation of me as an avatar.

Along with these mobile avatar issues, a fellow resident introduced to me interpersonal avatar actions. The resident introduced me to sim related movements, such as dancing with other avatars. These in-world dancing movements resembled similar to 'real' world dancing, where traditional gender roles were maintained. Avatars selected their dancing role according to their avatar's gender, and chose their dance sequence of choice. Despite these dance movements, I felt uncomfortable being 'close' with another avatar and dancing with a virtual (pardon the pun) stranger.

I was also introduced to other avatar interpersonal movements (such as hugs and 'pounces') which required some background file management. As the name of their movements suggest, these movements included avatar 'physical' interaction. I felt very uncomfortable with most of these actions, as were completed without any permission (implicit or otherwise) of the other avatar. After questioning some residents about being hugged or pounced, I was often met by scorn and outbursts 'that it was fine to hug and pounce others as it was not "real".'

As I continued to venture through the ballroom sim, a resident approached me and began to strike up a conversation with a 'newbie'. He stated that I had a few clear signs that I was new to *SL*, and suggested that I seriously change my appearance past the 'superficial' changes I had already made. After engaging him in a dialogue, he stated that there were inherent rules that women avatars needed to follow in order to 'fit in' with other avatars. He reported that I needed to change my height as male avatars do not prefer 'shorter' women. He stated that it would require some advanced avatar manipulation, which he offered to walk me through. Along with my avatar stature, he stated that I needed to reduce my shoe size to '0'. He reported that most women shoe stores only make shoes for sized '0' feet. This conversation initiated some concerns I had about body image issues being translated into avatar representations. This concern was further amplified by this resident stating that no female avatar truly represents themselves in avatar form. After questioning him on this statement, he said that most women choose to represent their actual selves in avatar format, but mostly chose to do so with women who are 'classic hourglass' figures. He stated that hardly anyone goes against this 'tradition'.

My initial few months within *SL* provided me with much enjoyment, however it also inspired many questions about the psychology of VWs. In particular, understanding the relationship between the avatar, in-world experiences, and their relationships to the actual world appear much less straightforward than I initially thought. A sincere appreciation for concepts such as Mann's theory of identity, Castranova's 'bubble' experience and the theory of the mind transpired through this experiential learning experience.

During several years of living as a resident in *SL*, I (PJ) noticed several turning points in my use of an avatar. I started with a stock avatar that did not match my off-line appearance. His chosen name (Dirk) was a play on a science fiction hero with the odd side effect of people thinking I was Dutch in real life. Over time, I found myself spending time and money on 'his' look, from shape and skin, to clothing. For a period, I wore only black tuxedos. Roughly one year in, I stumbled (virtually) across an island that had a system that would allow me to upload a photograph headshot that was converted into a skin for my avatar. Once applied, my avatar actually looked like my offline self. Because of the constraints on the process, I was forced to settle on one body shape and size, otherwise the skin didn't 'fit' properly. This marks the point where my avatar became static. Since then, he has not changed shape or height. (As an aside, avatars in *SL* often seem to take on slightly oversized proportions. Dirk would be 7 foot 2 inches / 218 cm tall. Many avatars in *SL* are oversized and if Dirk was the same 6 foot 1 inch / 185 cm as I am, he would appear shorter than average. My own personal experience in my life is of being taller than average. It is rare that I look up to someone. I found that I was unable to 'use' Dirk to interact in *SL* until I made him proportional to my own height experience in real life, looking down on most others.)

The second turning point occurred when I joined a role play (RP) community. Many such communities exist in *SL* and because of my offline rural, western existence, I joined a 'wild west' RP sim. After an acculturation period, including demonstrating my abilities to RP and to properly use a virtual gun and healing meter system, I was offered a role in the community, playing as one of the town doctors. Given the number of gunfights, this made for some busy RP opportunities but it also added a layer of identity to my avatar. In that context, he is always referred to as 'Doc', even when he has been absent for long periods and even when other RP doctors are present. With this shift came a second cementing of avatar identity, mainly through clothing choices. Even after leaving the RP community, Dirk retained the title of Doc in his group tags (identity tags that 'hover' over an avatar's head) and still goes by that title today. The title bridges the gap between *SL* and offline, given that the author is often addressed as 'Doc' in his social life by friends. Some ten months after ending his participation in the RP community, Dirk finally bought non-western themed clothing to wear while exploring *SL*.

The most recent shift came with this increased public visibility and interaction in the RP community. Not satisfied with the photo head and mismatched body skin colour, I found new skin (more bronze and less ruddy than my own) and longer hair (same colour.) Dirk has maintained this look for nearly a year, and I resist participating in events that ask me to change the colour, shape or size of my avatar because then it 'wouldn't be Dirk.'

On reflection, I have posed the question 'who is Dirk?' many times. In some sense, he is an extension of me, clearly idealized but based in my own physical reality.[33] He began as a blank slate, a means to navigate a VW. He has become someone, an extension of me. Recently, during a presentation to my faculty on the use of *SL* as a location for complex health simulations, audience members (many of whom had never seen *SL* or virtual worlds before) commented that I continually slipped between referring to Dirk as Dirk, and referring to Dirk as 'myself' and 'me'. I had not noticed. Dirk's evolving 'personality' has influence from *SL* to the offline world as well. Not unlike the transfer of experience as noted by some researchers who use *SL* to help with socialization skills.[34] I found that in some offline social situations that I had successfully interacted in while in *SL*, I was more open and outgoing than I might otherwise have been. Some of Dirk's directness had rubbed off. Returning to Mann's theory of the self, there is some sense that Dirk's virtual embodiment has evolved to a kind of parity with my own offline sense of embodiment.

9. Implications for Educators

It appears that when an individual spends time with his or her avatar, it becomes an extension of the self.[35] An avatar may meet the domains Mann's theory of the self. It is a virtual embodiment of an individual's self-image, whether idealized or not. Certainly not all avatars are obvious representations of their RW users. However, we behave as if the avatar body is real in the VW.[36] Some authors have argued, from the perspective of medical ethics, that an avatar meets the criteria to be considered to have the extended legal rights of a body, not unlike a prosthesis.[37] Even if the bodily representation of the avatar is not a duplicate of the off-line body, its presence appears to become something of the predictable, echoing the and suggesting the user's application of a TOM to the avatar: 'If my avatar exists as a resident of a VW, or as a character in a RP community, where I am both me and not me, what would I (my avatar) do next in a given situation?' We project a TOM about a virtual representation. The avatar persists in time. Again, with this consistency, we develop a kind of personality that is predictable and characteristic of the self. We return to the avatar after an absence and we resume the consistency of its/our/my interactions.

'Immersion' in a VW requires time and experience. In virtual spaces where it is necessary to navigate using an avatar, there comes a point when many individuals spend time, even to the exclusion of on-going events in the VW, modifying, clothing, upgrading, and equipping their avatars. It may be important for an educator who is considering using an avatar mediated VW to consider the potential difference between students who have experience with such self representations and those who do not. It may also be worth (re-)considering the question of 'who learns?' in an avatar mediated environment, and more – does the experienced individual with their own long-term avatar experience virtual world learning differently than the new student who is handed a stock 'for-classroom-use' avatar? In other words, is the engagement with the medium an issue of psychological closeness or identification with the avatar as self-representation, and less an issue of the 'immersiveness' of the environment or the ease of use of the browser that gives access to the VW?

Educators will also need to be aware that along with learning the technology of the VW and equipping their avatars, students using a space like *SL* will also need to learn about the culture, the notion of the bubble (Castranova's 'magic circle'), the applicability of immersion in the medium versus the right to break the fourth wall, and the impact of how these phenomena will influence their learning experience. In fact, it may be necessary for the teacher/professor/facilitator to actively consider these dynamics in the design of the learning experiences prior to moving the classroom wholesale into the VW. Is *Second Life* really the best medium for a lecture with slides? Likely not, but it is the best medium for an activity that requires an embodied interaction (such as environmental/architectural design – the size of rooms and hallways vis-a-vis the number of bodies in the space.)

Finally, when new participants choose to enter VWs, they should be cognizant of the inherent challenges that come with learning a new culture. Knowing that the experience is likely to challenge them in the normally unconscious domains of embodiment, time and reflexivity, in addition to whatever the educational tasks might be, may serve to enhance the usefulness of these exciting virtual spaces.

Notes

[1] 'Virtual Worlds: Industry and User Data' last modified 30 September 2010, Viewed 20 January 2012, http://www.slideshare.net/nicmitham/kzero-universe-chart-q3-2010.
[2] Mark Bell, 'Toward a Definition of "Virtual Worlds",' *Journal of Virtual Worlds Research* 1 (2008): 1-5.
[3] Philip Rosedale, *Second Life*, Linden Research, Inc., San Francisco, CA.
[4] 'New World Notes: Top 50 Most Popular *Second Life* Sims for December 2011,' last modified 5 January 2012, Viewed 5 January 2012, http://nwn.blogs.com/nwn/2012/01/top-second-life-sims-december-2011.html.
[5] James Doodson, 'The Relationship and Differences between Physical- and Virtual-World Personality,' (BA diss., University of Bath, 2009).
[6] 'CEO Rodvik Humble Shares What's New in *Second Life*,' last modified 4 October 2011, Viewed 10 January 2012, http://community.secondlife.com/t5/blogs/blogarticleprintpage/blog-id/blog_feature_news/article-id/7198.
[7] 'Market Data Demographic Studies,' last modified 12 May 2011, Viewed 27 December 2011, http://wiki.secondlife.com/wiki/Market_Data_Demographic_Studies.
[8] Anna Peachey and Mark Childs, *Reinventing Ourselves: Contemporary Concepts of Identity in Virtual Worlds* (London: Springer-Verlag, 2011), 129-151.
[9] David Mann, *A Simple Theory of the Self* (New York: Norton, 1994), 31-32.
[10] Ibid., 36-37.

[11] Paul Jerry, 'The Courtship Hypothesis and *Second Life*: Explaining Sexual Behaviour in a Virtual World,' *Experiential Learning in Virtual Worlds: Opening an Undiscovered World*, eds. Paul Jerry and Linda Lindsey (Oxfordshire: Inter-Disciplinary Press, 2011), 57-67.

[12] Nick Yee et al., 'The Unbearable Likeness of Being Digital: The Persistence of Nonverbal Social Norms in Online Virtual Environments', *CyberPsychology* and *Behavior* 10 (2007): 115-121.

[13] David Mann, *A Simple Theory of the Self* (New York: Norton, 1994), 37.

[14] Cathy Goerz, http://www.prweb.com/releases/2007/04/prweb520979.htm.

[15] Edward Castranova, *Synthetic Worlds: The Business and Culture of Online Games* (Chicago: University of Chicago Press, 2006).

[16] Ibid., 148.

[17] Paul Jerry, 'The Courtship Hypothesis,' 57-67.

[18] http://en.wikipedia.org/wiki/Fourth_wall.

[19] John Hughes, *Ferris Bueller's Day Off*, dir. John Hughes, Los Angeles: Paramount Pictures, 1986, DVD.

[20] http://en.wikipedia.org/wiki/Red_vs._Blue#Impact_on_machinima.

[21] Ted Honderich, ed., *The Oxford Companion to Philosophy* (Oxford: Oxford University Press: 1995), 189-190.

[22] Nick Yee and Jeremy Bailenson, 'The Proteus Effect: Implications of Transformed Digital Self-Representation on Online and Offline Behavior', *Communication Research* 36 (2009): 285-312.

[23] Andre Weitzenhoffer and Ernest Hilgard, *Stanford Hypnotic Susceptibility Scale, Form C.* (Stanford, CA: Stanford University, 1962); Herbert Spiegel, 'An Eye-Roll Test for Hypnotizability', *The American Journal of Clinical Hypnosis* 16 (1972): 25-28.

[24] H. Wimmer and J. Penner, 'Beliefs about Beliefs: Representation and Constraining Function of Wrong Beliefs in Young Children's Understanding of Deception', *Cognition* 13(1), 103-128.

[25] Mark Korkman, Ursula Kirk and Sally Kemp, *NEPSY: Second Edition*, Pearson Assessment, 2007.

[26] Paula Sauuko, *Doing Research in Cultural Studies* (London: Sage, 2003), 55.

[27] Ibid., 56.

[28] Matthew Miles and Michael Huberman, *Qualitative Data Analysis* (London: Sage, 1994).

[29] Abbas Tashakkori and Charles Teddlie, *Combining Qualitative and Quantitative Approaches* (Thousand Oaks, CA: Sage, 1998).

[30] Paul Jerry, 'Methods of Transpersonal Research,' *The Journey of the Everyday Mystic* (Saarbruken: VDM Verlag: 2010), 80-103.

[31] The shift to first-person voice reflects the nature of the data.

[32] Tom Boellstorff, *Coming of Age in* SL (Princeton: Princeton University Press, 2008), 89-117.
[33] 'New World Notes: *Second Life* Undermines Post-Modernism, Sociologist Argues,' last modified 10 December 2010, Viewed 13 December 2012, http://nwn.blogs.com/nwn/2010/12/second-life-undermines-post-modernism.html.
[34] Michelle Kandalaft, Nyaz Didehbani, Daniel Krawczyk, Tandra Allen and Sandra Chapman, 'Virtual Reality Social Cognition Training for Young Adults With High Functioning Autism', *Journal of Autism and Developmental Disorders, Online First*, 9 May 2012.
[35] Mark Meadows, *I, Avatar: The Culture and Consequences of Having a Second Life* (Berkeley: New Riders Press, 2008), 48.
[36] Yee and Bailenson, 'Proteus Effect', 115-121.
[37] Mark Alan Graber and Abraham David Graber, 'Get Your Paws off of My Pixels: Personal Identity and Avatars as Self', *Journal of Medical Internet Research* 12(3): e28, Viewed 10 January 2012, http://www.jmir.org/2010/3/e28/.

Bibliography

Au, Wagner James. 'New World Notes: Top 50 Most Popular *Second Life* Sims for December 2011'. Last modified January 5, 2012. http://nwn.blogs.com/nwn/2012/01/top-second-life-sims-december-2011.html.

———. 'New World Notes: *Second Life* Undermines Post-Modernism, Socialist Argues'. Accessed January 24, 2012. http://nwn.blogs.com/nwn/2010/12/second-life-undermines-post-modernism.html.

Bell, Mark. 'Toward a Definition of 'Virtual Worlds'. *Journal of Virtual Worlds Research* 1 (2008): 1-5.

Boellstorff, Tom. *Coming of Age in Second Life*. Princeton: Princeton University Press, 2008.

Castronova, Edward. *Synthetic Worlds: The Business and Culture of Online Games*. Chicago: University of Chicago Press, 2006.

Doodson, James. 'The Relationship and Differences between Physical- and Virtual-World Personality'. BA diss., University of Bath, 2009.

Ferris Bueller's Day Off. Directed by John Hughes. Los Angeles, CA: Paramount Pictures, 1986. DVD.

Goerz, Cathy. 'Latest GMI Poll Reveals *Second Life*'s Potential for Virtual Consumer Marketing and Branding'. Last modified April 24, 2007. http://www.prweb.com/releases/2007/04/prweb520979.htm.

Graber, Mark Alan and Abraham David Graber. 'Get Your Paws off of My Pixels: Personal Identity and Avatars as Self'. *Journal of Medical Internet Research* 12(3) (2010): e28.

Honderich, Ted, ed. *The Oxford Companion to Philosophy*. Oxford: Oxford University Press, 1995.

Jerry, Paul. 'Methods in Transpersonal Research'. *The Journey of the Everyday Mystic*, 80-103. Saarbruken: VDM Verlag: 2010.

Jerry, Paul. 'The Courtship Hypothesis and *Second Life*: Explaining Sexual Behaviour in a Virtual World'. In *Experiential Learning in Virtual Worlds: Opening an Undiscovered World*, edited by Paul Jerry and Linda Lindsey, 57-67. Oxfordshire: Inter-Disciplinary Press, 2011.

KZero Worldwide. 'Virtual Worlds: Industry and User Data'. Last modified September 30, 2010. http://www.slideshare.net/nicmitham/kzero-universe-chart-q3-2010.

Lehdonvirta, Mika, Vili Lehdonvirta, and Akira Baba. 'Collecting conversations: Three Approaches to Obtaining User-to-User Communications Data from Virtual Environments'. *Journal of Virtual Worlds Research* 3 (2011): 7-8.

Linden, Rodvik. 'CEO Rodvik Humble Shares What's New in *Second Life*'. Last modified October 4, 2011. http://community.secondlife.com/t5/blogs/blogarticleprintpage/blog-id/blog_feature_news/article-id/7198.

Mann, David. *A Simple Theory of the Self*. New York: Norton, 1994.

Meadows, Mark. *I, Avatar: The Culture and Consequences of Having a Second Life*. Berkeley: New Riders Press, 2008.

Miles, Matthew and Michael Huberman, *Qualitative Data Analysis*. London: Sage, 1994.

Peachey, Anna and Mark Childs. *Reinventing Ourselves: Contemporary Concepts of Identity in Virtual Worlds*. London: Springer-Verlag, 2011.

Rosedale, Philip. 'Market Data Demographic Studies'. Last modified May 12, 2011. http://wiki.secondlife.com/wiki/Market_Data_Demographic_Studies.

Sauuko, Paula. *Doing Research in Cultural Studies*. London: Sage, 2003.

Spiegel, Herbert. 'An Eye-Roll Test for Hypnotizability'. *The American Journal of Clinical Hypnosis* 16 (1972): 25-28.

Tashakkori, Abbas and Charles Teddlie. *Combining Qualitative and Quantitative Approaches*. Thousand Oaks, CA: Sage, 1998.

Weitzenhoffer, Andre and Ernest Hilgard. *Stanford Hypnotic Susceptibility Scale, Form C*. Stanford, CA: Stanford University, 1962.

Wikipedia. 'Red vs. Blue: Impact on Machinima'. Last modified January 22, 2012. http://en.wikipedia.org/wiki/Red_vs._Blue#Impact_on_machinima.

Wikipedia. 'Fourth Wall'. Last modified January 25, 2012. http://en.wikipedia.org/wiki/Fourth_wall.

Yee, Nick and Jeremy Bailenson. 'The Proteus Effect: Implications of Transformed Digital Self-Representation on Online and Offline Behavior'. *Communication Research* 36 (2009): 285-312.

Yee, Nick, Jeremy N. Bailenson, Mark Urbanek, Francis Chang, and Dan Merget. 'The Unbearable Likeness of Being Digital: The Persistence of Nonverbal Social Norms in Online Virtual Environments'. *CyberPsychology* and *Behavior* 10 (2007): 115-121.

Paul Jerry is Associate Professor and Director of the Graduate Centre for Applied Psychology, Athabasca University. His research interests include clinical training from a psychoanalytic perspective, regulation of professional psychology, and the use of counselling skills to manage virtual education experiences. He is a Past President of the College of Alberta Psychologists and is a Registered Psychologist maintaining a clinical practice in rural Canada. He has been a resident of *Second Life* since 2010.

Nancy Tavares-Jones is in her final year of her Masters of Counselling Psychology degree program at Athabasca University. Her research interests include psychometric assessments and their applications, psychoanalytic theory, personality theory and understanding the concept of 'identity' in actual and virtual worlds. She has been a resident of *Second Life* since 2011.

Transformative Learning as a Framework for Designing Experiences in Virtual Worlds: Counsellor Education as a Pertinent Example

Thomas Edwards and Michael Walker

Abstract
Teaching seeks to deliver curriculum within a pedagogical context to guide student learning. Virtual worlds (VWs), such as *Second Life*, provide unique experiential teaching spaces whose benefits are being recognised by large and small institutions alike. However, the literature does not often articulate clear pedagogical approaches to the design of educational experiences within VWs. This is a concern. One pedagogy particularly well suited to a VW environment is Transformative Learning (TL). The intent of this pedagogy is to create in students more adaptive frames-of-reference when dealing with complex problems that often have a social component. The process of TL has three stages: (1) a disorientating dilemma; (2) critical-reflection; and (3) a persistent change in attitudes/values/ beliefs as opposed to simply a conditioned change in behaviour. However, experiences are not necessarily transformative, nor may they be transformative in a deep or positive way, nor in a manner appropriate to the educational context. To further develop TL Tabor Victoria has embarked on a research project whereby experiences within a VW environment have been constructed according to a TL pedagogy. Elements of narrative therapy designed to assist the transformation process were also included in the experiences. The unit Professional Ethics, within the BA(Counselling) degree, was chosen as an exemplar as this unit seeks to develop in students an ability to engage complex professional/social/legal problems adaptively, noting care of others and of self. The VW experiences are discussed with respect to both VW design challenges and other issues likely to underpin positive transformation. Taken together, experiential learning in VWs is likely to provide important opportunities for teachers and students alike in the coming years. TL provides a unique pedagogy well suited to students who must engage complex social problems. VW's provide unique environments which likely foster TL in a time-limited and cost effective manner.

Key Words: Transformative learning, virtual worlds, *Second Life*, pedagogy, counsellor education.

*****

1. Introduction

On-line learning is ubiquitous in higher education but current learning management systems are often used simply to replicate activities which have traditionally been done face-to-face. These include accessing educational content, assignment submission, undertaking quizzes and communicating with other students.[1] However, as the 'digital generation' now approaches university there exists creative opportunities for academics to engage with a variety of cost-effective technologies which can provide experiences beyond that of a traditional classroom. Foremost amongst these are the virtual worlds (VWs) of which *Second Life* is the best known. By 2009 over 100 cutting-edge universities owned or rented land in *Second Life* providing market exposure and a unique environment for the delivery of lectures, performances and class discussions.[2] Nevertheless VWs still represent a new style of educational engagement with academics creatively exploring there potential.

In 2011 Tabor Victoria commenced a research project into counsellor education using *Second Life*. Training in counselling provides specific challenges to both students and institutions alike. Imparting only academic knowledge is insufficient. Skills must be taught and practiced, an understanding of clients as social beings imparted and a degree of counsellor self-awareness developed. As such, non-traditional methods of education are likely to be of benefit. However, it is recognized then when designing for learning pedagogy must provide the context in which the learning is to take place. Moreover, given the complexity of counsellor education it is necessary to pay particular attention to the design of learning so that students graduate as more-or-less integrated practitioners. One pedagogy gaining prominence is that of transformative learning (TL) which may assist students in making more nuanced decisions within a complex professional environment.[3,4] Importantly, TL is well positioned to work alongside VW activities as it is based in a constructivist approach whereby learners are encouraged to be active participants making new meanings within a social context.

Taken together, it is the intent of this chapter to outline current pedagogical approaches to learning in VWs, discuss the benefits of TL specifically and report on project outcomes in light of TL theory. As such recommendations can be made to further enhance student learning within a VW environment.

2. Virtual World Activities: Pedagogy and Authenticity

The internet is now a ubiquitous feature of life in the developed world and has revolutionized the ways in which we communicate and interact. For education its genius lies in the adequate provision of access for students at distance to the institution. Such access may include viable means for asynchronous communication and the ability to utilize vast repositories of information allowing a depth of academic engagement not previously seen.[5] More specifically, online classes enable less outgoing students greater opportunity to contribute, allow students to review discussions or processes and to reflect on alternatives especially in light of problematic or unsuccessful outcomes.[6]

Beyond the broad category of on-line learning are specific virtual learning environments. These are identified by the following criteria:[7] (1) a space that is overtly educational; (2) a designed information space providing functional relationships in such a way that information is organised to optimise learning; (3) a social space where students become participants in their education and not simply consumers; (4) an educational space not simply designed to facilitate distance education but to enhance learning in its own right; (5) a degree of adaptation exists to permit the use of various educational resources and pedagogies; and (6) a degree of consistency exists with the real world so that virtual tools and equipment can be utilised and even field trips taken.

From the above criteria it is clear that VWs represent a unique learning environment with a level of sophistication in design and application beyond standard learning management systems.

VWs, most often *Second Life*, provide new and exciting opportunities for educationalists and students alike. For here is a way to create learning communities online,[8] provide skills training in a safe environment[9] and engage students in experiences not typical – or not possible – in the real world. Table 1 provides examples of VW experiences currently used in education beyond the provision of instruction in simple VW classrooms.[10] As such, these activities may be described as state-of-the-art.

Moving from educational activities in a VW to the design of learning it is unfortunate to note that many authors only engage pedagogy to the extent of recognizing a subset of VW features, or benefits. For example, within *Second Life* a number of authors note strong experiential, immersive and collaborative benefits.[11] Nevertheless, this provides an important guide as to what pedagogies may be best suited to VW activities.

Beyond such benefits are the ways in which students engage VWs. Interestingly, *Second Life* has been shown to have a strong influence on affect, empathy and motivation.[12] With perhaps the greatest impact being on the affective.[13] In addition, psychosocial aspects of learning become important in a VW environment so much so that '...the *Second Life* experience impacted on the relational aspects of the learning experience to a greater extent than the cognitive ones.'[14]

As to specific pedagogical approaches appropriate to teaching within a VW some argue for entirely new pedagogies given the shift to affective and relational learnings. However, what this new pedagogy may look like remains unclear.[15] Although this approach demonstrates the creativity and optimism in the VW educational community it may not be necessary to re-invent the wheel. For example, some authors already explicitly state their pedagogical approach in terms of experiential learning, action learning or problem-based learning.[16]

Table 1: Educational activities currently used in *Second Life*[17]

Development of personal skills	Development of professional skills	Development of professional reasoning	Development of research ability	Other
Educational games to foster task completion and competition.

Demonstrate conflict resolution skills.

Exercises in which anonymity is used to provoke honest discussions, risk taking and assertiveness by students.

Develop '…less tangible skills such as critical thinking, problem solving, team building and collaboration.' | Language and cultural immersion.

Role-plays demonstrating psychological principles amongst others.

Provide workplace or site experience such as in archaeology or nursing. | Teaching business case studies in an interactive manner.

Develop art criticism and practice through exhibitions

Provide simulations such as realistic paramedic scenarios to students.

Provide simulated excursions to ancient ruins or distant galleries. Provide social interactions designed to break convention. | Allow research into a 'micro society' through which students study economics and sociology. | Develop interactive libraries where students inform information content.

Treasure hunts and quests.

The recording of in-world educational experiences for later reflection.

Self-paced tutorials.

Create a hub for social contact. |

More recently, authors have implicitly,[18] and explicitly picked-up on the value of constructivist approaches to pedagogy given the dynamic,[19] experiential and social nature of VW activities. In brief, the constructivist model builds new meanings by having students internalise observations and experiences and process these in relation to their personal social and historical context. This approach therefore highlights the context of the learner's environment as well as the importance of personalised meaning.[20] Of great advantage in Higher Education is that the constructivist approach is learner-centred and so has the potential to produce thoughtful professionals able to engage society in nuanced ways.

Transcending specific pedagogies is the notion of an authentic VW activity. Authentic activities derive their power from a willingness by both teacher and student to engage in the activity in an open manner. For example, if the instructor assumes that students are already *au fait* with the technology – and they are not – the students may be easily overwhelmed if not disengaged. More subtlety, students may not deeply engage the learning offered nor see its contextual relevance.[21] As such, authentic activities promote the teacher as a facilitator who guides student learning and opens the possibility for rich discovery. As a consequence, students gain control over their own learning and become autonomous. More precisely Herrington identified several characteristics of authentic activities which include:[22] (1) real-world relevance; (2) a relevance beyond the immediate pragmatics of completing the activity; (3) a sense of collaboration; (4) active engagement by students in defining tasks and grappling with several possible solutions over a sustained period of time; (5) time for reflection; and (6) well integrated assessments.

Taken together, designing for learning requires more than a willingness to just engage VW technology. Designing VW activities within the context of a specific pedagogy and referencing the notion of authenticity is of great assistance to students. Given the ability of a VW environment to promote personalized meaning-making within an experiential, immersive and social context some pedagogies may be favoured over others. That VWs promote an affective and relational response by students also suggests particular pedagogical approaches. One pedagogy drawn from the constructivist tradition which specifically relies on affective and relational responses is Transformative Learning (TL). This pedagogy, although by no means the only one which can be applied to VW's, nevertheless appears particularly well suited.

3. Transformative Learning

Over the last decade and a half our understanding of how people transform from one set of meanings to another has significantly increased. Taylor has both demonstrated the importance of key elements of transformation as well as recognizing the role of context in meaning making.[23] In 2007, Taylor also demonstrated support for TL as a valid theory of change noting that interest in TL had grown substantially in recent years such that 35% of the research into TL now occurred outside the USA.[24] Research studies had also become more 'sophisticated through the use of longitudinal designs, action research, scales, surveys and content analysis…'[25] Importantly for the present discussion much research has focused on Higher Education and thus on early to middle adulthood.[26]

To begin with, it is generally wrong to think that knowledge acquisition alone will create transformation although in some instances it surely does.[27] TL is something that cannot be taught so much as needs to be experienced.[28] In a more classic conceptualization of TL theory, students come to identify narrow ways of understanding the world (frames-of-reference) gained through uncritical acceptance of family, social and cultural norms.[29] Such ways of engaging the world are often maladaptive in so far as they allow little freedom to explore alternative solutions to complex, if not ambiguous, situations. A broadening of these narrow frames-of-reference opens the student to a world of greater complexity – and alternatives – than they would otherwise be aware.[30] As such TL is designed to foster the autonomy of each learner.[31]

Key to the process of TL is to recognize narrow frames-of-reference through a disorientating experience thus problematising current attitudes, values and beliefs.[32] Through subsequent critical reflection there occurs a transformation whereby new, more adaptive, frames-of-references come into being.[33] Such adaptive frames-of-reference have the quality of being 'more inclusive, discriminating, open, emotionally capable of change and reflective…'[34] Therefore TL does not seek the accumulation of facts so much as the making of new meanings.[35]

At its core, TL sits on a tripod of: a humanist approach; constructivist epistemology; and the value of critical social theory. Humanist psychology posits individual growth towards self-actualisation and respects the inherent goodness in all people.[36] As such a person gleans a sense of clarity about themselves and the world. Constructivism also suggests an agentic approach to life but one which highlights the learner as a unique and dynamic meaning maker.[37] Finally, critical social theory is a useful lens through which transformation can take place as it highlights dominant ideologies which perpetuate inequalities.[38] TL seeks to question their validity.[39]

Dividing the TL process into parts, a disorientating dilemma represents the trigger by which learning can occur, but not the learning moment. Two types of disorientating dilemma exist. The first comes about through an interaction with value-laden content and may provoke a socially engaged reaction while the second occurs following an intense personal experience.[40] Following the disorientating dilemma critical reflection occurs and this represents the process of change. As such, there may well be no learning moment in TL so much as a process of making richer meanings over time.

In this process of critical reflection, there are two ways in which perspectives can undergo reframing: the objective; and the subjective. Objective reframing is the critical reflection of information that comes to the learner externally. For example, through reading a magazine article, watching the nightly news or listening to a lecture. Alternatively, subjective reframing occurs when one critically reflects on one's internal world including beliefs, ideas and assumptions.[41]

No matter whether the critical reflection is objective or subjective in its type two components interact to bring about transformation. The first is a rational, cognitive process that analytically explores and expresses the experience. The second is a subtle, but more interesting, intuitive process by which unconscious forces interact with conscious emotions. This interaction, albeit both nebulous and abstract, creates a rich awareness of self.[42] The learner now has both the voice to articulate their situation and a personal depth from which alternatives spring to assists the creation of new narratives of meaning.[43] Finally, as the theory has evolved the role of learners critically reflecting together in groups has also become important while Taylor now also discusses '…a holistic orientation, awareness of context and an authentic practice' as significant in the transformative process.[44]

4. *Second Life* and Transformative Learning: An Example Drawn from Counsellor Education

Counsellor education is undergoing considerable change within Australia. Educationalists have to design for courses from Certificate- to Masters-level.[45] Within a Bachelor's degree, graduates will have typically completed a major sequence in counselling including a supervised field placement. Within a major sequence it is not unreasonable to find four types of units: (1) units dealing with mental health facts; (2) units which teach counselling skills; (3) units considering the legal and personal parameters of professional practice; and (4) supervised practice units.[46] Reasonably no single technology or pedagogy will suit all units. However, that graduates must engage a diversity of client types who are seeking assistance for problems as diverse as relationship issues, homelessness, addiction, mental health, life satisfaction, faith and sexuality to name but a few suggests the importance of graduating integrated professionals who can take a nuanced view of the world. To this end TL theory provides an important means through which students can grapple with such complex issues in a safe environment before commencing professional practice.

In 2011, Tabor Victoria commenced a research project to investigate the potential of a curriculum which adhered to a TL pedagogy. The subject Professional Ethics, within the BA(Counselling) degree, was chosen as an exemplar as this unit seeks to develop in students an ability to engage complex professional/social/legal problems adaptively, noting care of others and of self. The project duration was two years. Year one used a TL pedagogy in a face-to-face setting. Year two has then adapted the TL pedagogy to a VW environment.

In both years the first half of the unit, on ethics and the law, would not specifically adhere to transformative principles and so act as a comparison. The curriculum used in the second half of the unit, on counsellor self-care, would conform to TL theory. In each year the same student cohort were exposed to both curriculums. Two experienced teachers were used in this unit, one for each half, both were trained counsellors and both taught across the two years of the project's duration.

In both years recruitment and data collection were conducted by an independent research assistant using focus group and/or semi-structured interviews. Participants were students who volunteered and were selected based on their well-developed reflective ability as demonstrated using the *Groningen Reflection Ability Scale* (GRAS).[47] These students, male and female, were mature entry students who had completed approximately two thirds of their degree. Both teachers consented to a semi-structured interview.

Six topics areas were dealt with in the TL counsellor self-care component: (1) the self understood through managing conflict; (2) burn-out; (3) self-renewal; (4) failure; (5) the counsellor in body; and (6) self and others understood through transference/counter-transference. Class activities were diverse including managed confrontation, writing (including a personal epitaph), undertaking a positive novel experience and representing concepts through object manipulation. Assessments included meeting with an experienced counsellor and journaling. In all activities personal and/or group reflection was utilized. As to procedure, each week a new topic would be introduced with the teacher providing a disorientating experience. Opportunities were then afforded students to critically reflect on their way of being.

That TL is based in Humanistic principles allowed self-care to be taught in a deliberately inclusive and welcoming environment where the Rogerian ideals of empathy, unconditional positive regard and authenticity were practiced by both teacher and students.[48] As humans typically communicate in meaningful narratives – and the process of transformation is about new meaning making – narrative therapy skills were used in each class included externalizing, thickening the alternative story, exploring the absent yet implicit in the story and providing opportunities for an outsider witness stance.[49] In this way it was hoped that the transformative effect would be maximised.

A summary of the Year 1 findings are presented in Table 2.

From the below findings, several conclusions can be drawn: (1) transformation may occur due to contextual or personal aspects even when the pedagogy is designed to not be transformational; (2) one may speculate that stress engenders negative transformation causing the creation of narrower frames-of-reference; (3) that the use of TL in counsellor self-care led to positive transformation; (4) for positive transformation to occur the context in which the experience is placed must be welcoming; (5) intellectualism was not key to transformation; (6) the disorientating experiences work best when they have a personal element; (7) transformation is a social activity whereby small groups construct new knowledges through critical reflection; and (8) that care must be given to small group construction, management and duration to promote a positive environment for self-disclosure. The specificity of these recommendations extend the literature but remain broadly consistent with it.[50]

Table 2: Year 1 findings

Topic	Findings
Counselling and the law	That ethics and the law was intended to represent a non-transformative curriculum was confirmed by the teacher's intention to '...[make] them think...' for students to be able to make '...a decision...' and the wish to form '... cautious...' practitioners.
	It is likely that some *ad hoc* transformation took place given student responses such as '...I considered ethics to be probably something external and I would now consider ethics to be something that is very much integrated into your (sic) life and thinking, your personal life as well as your professional life...'.
	The course material engendered a degree of 'Fear.' in multiple students with one discussing their experience as a '...baptism of fire...'. Two students reflected on the importance of now taking a legalistic stance when encountering ethical problems. Another also commented that 'The consequences of not being ethical are huge...'.
Counsellor self-care	Transformation is suggested by one student who commented '...it began to give me the courage to be willing to tune into others' reality and not [be] afraid to risk and change in the experience...'. Although another student referred to both components of the unit as '...equally transformational...' two other students plainly stated that self-care was, for them, more transformative.
	A student commented about the importance of a '...non-judgmental attitude towards self, and...positive regard...'. With specific reference to the disorientating experiences, that they were '...personally challenging...' and that '...transformation was most apparent...' when students discovered aspects about themselves.
	All participants noted the value of critical reflection as occurred in small group discussions following a disorientating experience. As to what made such groups so successful one student commented, with another agreeing, on the value of groups being '...intimate...' and '...[a] very encouraging supportive environment...'.
	The narrative therapy tools considered to hold the greatest transformative potential were externalization and identifying the absent but implicit within student narratives.

Based on these findings Year 2 of the project has seen Tabor Victoria create an island within *Second Life* the design and use of which is consistent with TL principles. Structurally, TL may be potentiated through specific environmental design elements acting as disorientating dilemmas or which permitting critical reflection. For example, in the spirit of TL, building design has purposely shunned virtual representations of lecture theatres. Disorientating dilemmas may be potentiated by these unique learning environments which include levitating rocky outcrops, a worship space, creative space and a graveyard. To assist with critical reflection building design has reflected intimate learning spaces in which small groups of students can meet regularly. Interior design has become an important element with the use of bright colours, large windows, water and the arrangement of furniture. Specifically, spaces for critical reflection represent welcoming social environments such as lounges and a café.

Beyond static design elements which may potentiate TL six set-piece activities, consistent with TL, have also been created and are facilitated by the teacher who is a narrative therapist. As TL attempts to make new meanings, and as narratives are the building blocks of meaning, a narrative therapist is particularly useful. Each activity begins with a disorientating dilemma and follows with critical reflection. During periods of critical reflection the teacher is particularly interested for students to: (1) notice the *what*; (2) discern what their reaction is *about*, and (3) reflect on the *why*. Narrative techniques of externalizing, thickening an alternative story, exploring the absent yet implicit and outsider witness practices are used to achieve this.[51]

Prior to the first activity students meet in the real world for training on how to use *Second Life*. The importance of this is indicated by past research, is intended to limit a stress responses and thus decrease the chance of negative transformation.[52] Moreover, cyber-safety can be discussed.[53]

Moving into *Second Life*, the first activity is avatar creation. Avatar creation represents an immediately personal and reflective experience. Who am I now and who will I be in this new world? At a broad level, students may reasonably reflect on notions of self especially if wishing to have an avatar that is discrepant to their species, age, or gender. The wish to enhance physical appearance is also a pertinent topic for reflection about self and self-in-community.[54] The reflection can then be broadened to encompass a counselling context where self is unpacked with respect to issues of transference and counter-transference.[55] As such, one's narratives of power and sexuality, amongst others, may be exposed to critical reflection.

The second set-piece activity is to provide students with a safe experience of stress, if not burn-out. *Second Life* provides ample opportunities to create stress in the novice user as they learn to walk, fly, view, talk and interact in this new environment. Using the disorientating experience of having to follow instructions from a competent *Second Life* user in a timely manner students journal their reactions as a basis for subsequent reflection. Critical reflection then followed in small groups which also consider professional issues such as compliance, choice, prioritizing and self-awareness. Students adopt an outsider witness stance as they listen to one another's accounts.

The next activity represents a technologically interesting, if not challenging, exercise for both the teacher and students. It also makes use of the narrative tools of externalization and outsider witness. The topic is about failure and within *Second Life* students view a movie clip of their teacher discussing an experience of professional failure. Meanwhile, students use their webcams to video themselves watching their teacher. Finally, students watch both video clips together providing the perspective of an outsider witness as they note their own reactions to failure and reflect on their meanings.

The fourth activity represents a classic use of *Second Life*, but within the context of counsellor self-renewal. Students leave the Tabor Victoria Island for the first time to explore *Second Life*. They are to use *Second Life* to have a set of positive experiences such as attend an art gallery, go to a beach or undertake a worship service. They will also meet other users. Meeting people of diverse backgrounds is often transformative and a mainstay of both counselling and *Second Life*.[56]

Next comes a role-play. VWs are excellent forums for role play.[57] Although counselling micro-skills may not yet be possible to practice in VWs, due to the subtlety of human communication, it is nevertheless possible for students to engage meaningfully with teacher-controlled client avatars. Ideally this would be done in the context of a VW counselling centre and a variety of client avatars used to represent oppositional, disorganized and depressed clients amongst others. However, given time restrictions students engage a single teacher-controlled avatar which is designed to appear mildly menacing. This is invoked by inappropriate dress and demeanour. Students engage this avatar while monitoring their own cognitive and emotional changes. To assist in professional development, students will then be encouraged to utilize a limited number of strategies to regulate their sympathetic nervous system response to stress and then engage the avatar for a second time.[58] Opportunities for reflection follow.

The final activity is primarily to have students reflect on their finite lives, their expectations, hopes and dreams and to motivate them towards wellbeing. It will occur in two parts but most interestingly utilize a graveyard within the Tabor Victoria island and ask students to write their epitaph to be engraved on a headstone. The key narrative tool is for students to find the absent yet implicit in their stories. Given the potential for distress student safety is an important consideration in this exercise. To this end the exercise is completed in the real world as a debriefing.

In sum, Tabor Victoria has developed a *Second Life* island which in its structure and function takes note of TL principles. The extent of transformation is also expected to be enhanced by imbuing times of critical reflection with narrative therapy techniques.

5. Cautions

Although very rich exercises can be undertaken in VWs some limitations, if not cautions, need to be stated. First, not all units of study need to be purposefully, or largely, transformative. For example, when teaching research design and statistics as part of the BA(Counselling) degree students are expected to learn methods of problem solving and evaluation. Whilst it is true that competency in these areas may engender confidence and thus the transformation of their personal narrative this is not a deliberate intention of the teacher nor a key learning outcome. Therefore pedagogy must be targeted to the type of learning expected of students. As such, TL is particularly well suited to units in which students must learn to make nuanced, if not wise, judgments. Such units typically engage elements of society and/or ethical practice but may not necessarily be limited to them.

Second, units of study which draw on the personal are more likely to be transformative. However, students exist in the real world where negative personal experiences happen from time-to-time. A teacher wanting to engage in activities which call upon the personal and existential may wish to seek informed consent from students, provide alternate safe exercises and make debriefing, if not independent counselling, available.[59]

As to the type of student best suited to manage the personal elements of TL one would hope to see a degree of self-insight, well developed autonomy and an ability to hold themselves comfortably in the midst of any angst which may be experienced. As such, TL may be better suited to either older students returning to study and/or students well advanced in their degree. Moreover, class size should be limited so that the teacher can adequately monitor students.

6. Emerging Questions

The use of TL in VWs presents several interesting and emerging questions. These can be divided into theoretical, technological or pedagogical. Theoretically, Year 1 of the project (see Table 2 for outcomes) noted that some students retreated into more secure and limited frames-of-reference when experiencing stress. As such the level of arousal produced by a disorientating dilemma appears to be an important consideration in determining whether the resultant transformation will be positive or negative. That is, will it lead to broader and more adaptive frames-of-reference, or to narrower fames-of-reference. One may even speculate that the degree of positive transformation, as a function of arousal, follows an inverted U-shaped curve whereby little arousal produces little positive transformation, a degree of arousal produces substantial positive transformation, but that a high degree of arousal produces little positive transformation or even negative transformation. This sort of inverted U-shaped function is common in the stress literature and is most easily conceptualized as the Yerkes-Dodson law. Taken further, if a disorientating dilemma can be considered a stressor requiring cognitive appraisal then TL can be conceptualized in terms of stress and a new set of investigative tools become available.[60]

A second emergent question relates to the value of negative transformation. This is not clearly discussed in the literature and is an anathema to the liberationist spirit behind TL. Nevertheless, one may speculate that at times negative transformation may be as important as positive transformation. For example, when issues of safety, procedure or compliance need to be taught it is often important to have students constrict their frames-of-reference and thus understand clearly the difference between acceptable and unacceptable practice. This being so, it is also important to understand how negative transformation may be brought about without undue stress. Similarly, how one may limit negative transformation to only specific situations while potentiating worker autonomy or creativity in other areas remains an interesting question.

Several emergent technological questions also present themselves. First, given that the degree of arousal appears to be an important consideration in producing positive transformation its measurement and control become important. Measurements of heart rate and/or galvanic skin response represent potentially simple ways to observe,[61] in real time, student arousal levels while in a VW environment. For students to have this information available alongside their avatar would allow new levels of self-awareness and immersion. Students would then be able to use common relaxation techniques to manage arousal levels and thus remain within the zone which permits positive transformation. Using bio-sensor technology in conjunction with a VW environment is currently being used in the treatment of post-traumatic stress disorder but is yet to be used in educational settings.[62]

For those interested in human mimicry the second emergent technological question relates to the avatar's ability to demonstrate subtle human gestures and affect. Current off-the-shelf avatars lack sufficient subtly that limits their use in many aspects of counsellor training and in e-health more generally. Moreover, methods must be developed which allow greater ease of avatar control so that the user concentrates less on their manipulation of the avatar and more on the interaction between avatars.

The key emergent pedagogical issue is the need to evaluate a range of pedagogies to determine which are appropriate for use with VWs and in what circumstances. In section 2.0 other pedagogies used within VWs were noted. They were experiential learning,[63] action learning,[64] and problem-based learning.[65] However, the appropriateness of their use requires critical analysis at both the axiomatic level and at the level of application.

For example, experiential learning may be defined as '...the process whereby knowledge is created through the transformation of experience.'[66] Therefore experiential learning has at its heart the direct experience of something. Except for students engaged in the experience of designing VWs one may very well ask the question then whether experiential learning – as a pedagogy – is even possible in a VW where all interactions are mediated through an avatar? This does not deny the experiential nature of VWs nor the usefulness of immersive activities within them, but does question the appropriateness of this specific pedagogy. For experiential learning will only be to the extent that the VW mimics all real world elements of the task including sensory elements such as smell, force and touch.

Action learning is more likely of benefit to those wishing to use VW technologies to instruct students. In this pedagogy learning is a function of expert knowledge and group-based questioning designed to provoke insight. More recent adaptations of this model have included reflection as a third factor or even actions *per-se*.[67] What is particularly useful about this style of learning is that some problem can be effectively presented in a VW environment, usually as a simulation, alongside expert knowledge and the provision of room for social discourse. This fits comfortably within the classic uses of *Second Life*. Within the context of counsellor education action learning is an appropriate tool to explore case conceptualization especially when the individual's problems are atypical and thus beyond the simple application of expert knowledge.

Finally, problem-based learning is similar to action learning but may be distinguished by its emphasis on problem solving strategies through taking an ecological approach to the situation presented. This style of learning is commonly seen in medical schools whereby small groups of students meet to investigate a problem in a multi-factorial way. Within the context of counsellor education one could also apply this pedagogy to case conceptualizations but more potently to areas such as community psychology. On a grand scale one could envisage a simulated community struggling with social disadvantage and a variety of related health issues. This adequately adapts the medical example of a person as an ecology of organs to a community as an ecology of people. Thus multi-faceted problem solving can be applied and adjustments made to the simulated community as a result.

7. Conclusion

Experiential learning in VWs holds exciting prospects across the educational spectrum. This chapter has sought to highlight the need for intentional learning design beyond the adaptation of face-to-face exercises to a VW platform. Indeed by understanding pedagogy we provide an educational context for student learning and hopefully maximize the intended learning outcomes.

One pedagogy that is unique for focusing on attitudes, values and beliefs is TL. Although not appropriate to all educational contexts it provides an important way to understand how to structure classes when wishing to develop in students more nuanced thinking about the world, social problems and ethics. Moreover, that TL relies on disorientating experiences and critical reflection suggests that it is ideally suited to VW environments where students can have a variety of unique/challenging experiences and can meet to discuss these in a time/cost limited manner. Moreover, that a transformative curriculum can be developed, shown to be effective and adapted to *Second Life* provides useful understandings for future curriculum developers.

However, tasks remain. It is not yet clear how to control the extent and type of transformation (i.e. positive or negative). Nor are off-the-shelf avatars sufficiently subtle to facilitate complex human communication, nor in a manner that is intuitive for the user. These remain as the immediate barriers to the further development of TL within VWs.

Taken together, VWs provide an exciting vista for Higher Education by bringing together students from distant locations in a meaningful way, presenting them with challenging multi-faceted tasks and providing them with the means and time to reflect deeply on their experience. It will be interesting to observe the qualities such graduates bring to their employment and to society in the years to come.

Acknowledgements
Ms Bernadette Milsted, Mr Scott Morgan and members of the project team.

Funding
Support for this publication/activity has been provided by the Australian Government Office for Learning and Teaching (grant: PP10-1786). The views expressed in this publication/activity do not necessarily reflect the views of the Australian Government Office for Learning and Teaching.

Notes

[1] Paul Chin, *Virtual Learning Environments* (LTSN Physical Sciences Centre, 2003), 1 and 9.
[2] Suzanne C. Baker, Ryan K. Wentz, and Madison M. Woods. 'Using Virtual Worlds in Education: *Second Life* as an Educational Tool', *Teaching of Psychology* 36.1 (2009): 60.
[3] Uschi Bay and Selma Macfarlane, 'Teaching Critical Reflection: A Tool for Transformative Learning in Social Work?' *Social Work Education* 30.7 (2011): 745-758.
[4] Lisa Tsoi-Hoshmand, 'The Transformative Potential of Counseling Education', *Journal and Humanistic Counselling, Education and Development* 43.1 (2004): 82-90.

[5] Baker, 'Virtual Worlds in Education', 60; Hsiu-Mei Huang, 'Towards Constructivism for Adult Learners in Online Learning Environments', *British Journal of Educational Technology* 33, no. 1 (2002): 28.

[6] Baker, 'Virtual Worlds in Education', 60.

[7] Pierre Dillenbourg, Daniel K. Schnieder and Paraskevi Synteta, 'Virtual Learning Environments', in *Proceedings of the 3rd Hellenic Conference Information* and *Communication Technologies in Education*, ed. A. Dimitracopoulou. Greece: Kastaniotis Editions, 2002, 3-9.

[8] *Lynn Eaton, Mario Guerra, Stephanie Corliss* and *Leslie Jarmon*, 'A Statewide University System (16 Campuses) Creates Collaborative Learning *Communities* in *Second Life'*, *Educational Media International* 48, no. 1 (2011): 43.

[9] Diane J. Skiba, 'Nursing Education 2.0: *Second Life'*, *Nursing Education Perspectives* 28, no. 3 (2007): 156-157.

[9] Michelle Ryan, '16 Ways to Use Virtual Worlds in Your Classroom: Pedagogical Applications of *Second Life'*, in *ReLIVE '08: Proceedings of Researching Learning in Virtual Environments International Conference*, ed. Anna Peachey, 269. Milton Keynes, UK: The Open University, 2008

[10] Ryan, 'Pedagogical Applications', 269.

[11] Lu, 'Virtual Age: Art Café', 20; Steven Warburton, '*Second Life* in Higher Education: Assessing the Potential for and the Barriers to Deploying Virtual Worlds in Learning and Teaching', *British Journal of Educational Technology* 40, no. 3 (2009): 419 and 421; Gilly Salmon, 'The Future for (Second) Life and Learning', *British Journal of Educational Technology* 40, no. 3 (2009): 529.

[12] Warburton, '*Second Life'*, 419and421.

[13] Walker, '3d Virtual Learning', 10.

[14] Walker, '3d Virtual Learning', 10.

[15] Jarmon, 'Understanding Project-Based Learning', 2.

[16] Ryan, 'Pedagogical Applications', 269; Salmon, 'Future for *Second Life'*, 529; Warburton, '*Second Life'*, 415; Elaine Brown, Marie Gordon and Mike Hobbs, '*Second Life* as a Holistic Learning Environment for Problem-Based Learning and Transferable Skills', *Paper presented at Researching Learning in Virtual Environments International Conference* (Milton Keynes, United Kingdom: The Open University, 2008), 39-48.

[17] Constance Steinkuehler, 'Massive Multiplayer Online Games as Educational Technology: An Outline for Research', *Journal of Educational Technology* 48, no. 1 (2008): 10-21; Dena A. Evans and Anthony R. Curtis, 'Animosity, Antagonism, and Avatars: Teaching Conflict Management in *Second Life'*, *Journal of Nursing Education* 50, no. 11 (2011): 653-655; Ryan, 'Pedagogical Applications', 269.

[18] Lu, 'Virtual Age: Art Café', 20.

[19] Carina Girvan and Timothy Savage, 'Identifying an Appropriate Pedagogy for Virtual Worlds: A Communal Constructivism Case Study' *Computers and Education* 55, no. 1 (2010): 342-349.
[20] Terry Andersen, Ed., *The Theory and Practice of Online Learning* (Athabasca, Canada: AU Press 2008), 19-20.
[21] Cher Ping Lim, 'Engaging Learners in Online Learning Environments', *Techtrends* 48, no. 4 (2004): 16-17.
[22] Jan Herrington, Ron Oliver and Thomas C. Reeves, 'Patterns of Engagement in Authentic Online Learning Environments', *Australian Journal of Educational Technology* 19, no. 1 (2002): 2-3.
[23] Edward W. Taylor, *The Theory and Practice of Transformative Learning: A Critical Review* (Columbus, OH: Ohio State University, 1998), 25-26.
[24] Edward W. Taylor, 'An Update on Transformative Learning Theory: A Critical Review of the Empirical Research (1999-2005)'. *International Journal of Lifelong Education* 26, no. 2 (2007): 173-191.
[25] Taylor, 'Update on Transformative Learning', 176.
[26] Edward W Taylor and Patricia Cranton. *The Handbook of Transformative Learning: Theory, Research, and Practice* (San Francisco: Jossey-Bass, 2012), 40.
[27] Jack Mezirow, 'Transformative Learning: Theory to Practice', *New Directions for Adult and Continuing Education* 47, no. 2 (1997): 9.
[28] Valerie Grabove, 'The Many Facets of Transformative Learning Theory and Practice', *New Directions for Adult and Continuing Education* 74 (1997): 90.
[29] Mezirow, 'Transformative Learning', 8-9.
[30] Taylor, 'Update on Transformative Learning', 5.
[31] Mezirow, 'Transformative Learning', 8-9.
[32] Jack Mezirow, 'A Critical Theory of Adult Learning and Education', *Adult Education Quarterly* 32 (1981): 3-24.
[33] Joyce A. Mercer, 'Transformational Adult Learning in Congregations', *The Journal of Adult Theological Education* 3, no. 2 (2006): 163-178; Jack Mezirow, *Transformative Dimensions of Adult Learning* (USA: Jossey-Bass, 1991).
[34] Leona M. English and Marie A. Gillen, 'A Postmodern Approach to Adult Religious Education', *Handbook of Adult and Continuing Education*, eds. Wilson and Hayes (USA: Jossey-Bass, 2000).
[35] Mercer, 'Congregations', 163-178.
[36] Jack C. Willers, 'Humanistic Education: Concepts, Criteria and Criticism', *Peabody Journal of Education* 53, no. 1 (1975): 40.
[37] Jack Martin, 'Self-Regulated Learning, Social Cognitive Theory, and Agency' *Educational Psychologist* 39, no. 2 (2004): 136.
[38] Zeus Leonardo, 'Critical Social Theory and Transformative Knowledge: The Functions of Criticism in Quality Education', *Educational Researcher* 33, no. 6 (2009): 11.

[39] Taylor, *Handbook*, 5-7.

[40] Megan A. Taylor, Jerome M. Fischer and Linda Taylor. 'Factors Relevant for the Affective Content in Literature Survey: Implications for Designing an Adult Transformational Learning Curriculum', *Journal of Adult Education* 38, no. 2 (2009): 21; Lisa M. Baumgartner, 'An Update on Transformational Learning', *New Directions for Adult and Continuing Education* 89 (2001): 21.

[41] Mezirow, 'Transformative Learning', 7.

[42] John M. Dirkx, 'Images, Transformative Learning and the Work of the Soul', *Adult Learning* 12, no. 3 (2001): 15-16.

[43] Grabove, 'Many Facets', 90-95.

[43] Jack Mezirow, 'Transformative Learning as Discourse', *Journal of Transformative Education* 1, no. 1 (2003): 61.

[44] Mezirow, 'Transformative Learning', 10; Jack Mezirow and Edward W. Taylor, *Transformative Learning in Practice: Insights from Community, Workplace and Higher Education* (San Francisco: Jossey-Bass, 2009), 4.

[45] Australian Counselling Association Inc., viewed on 22nd January, 2012, http://www.theaca.net.au/approved_courses.php.

[46] *Psychotherapy and Counselling Federation of Australia* Inc., 'Training Standards', viewed on 22nd January, 2012, http://pacfa.ivt.com.au/sitebuilder/resources/knowledge/asset/files/2/ts2012finalfor webpage2012.pdf.

[47] Leo Aukes, Jelle Geertsma, Janke Cohen-Schotanus, Rein Zwierstra and Joris. Slaets, 'The Effect of Enhanced Experiential Learning on the Personal Reflection of Undergraduate Medical Students', *Medical Education Online* 13 (2008): 15.

[48] Carl Rogers, 'The Necessary and Sufficient Conditions of Therapeutic Personality Change', *Journal of Consulting Psychology* 21, no. 2 (1957): 95-103.

[49] Judy Apte, 'Facilitating Transformative Learning: A Framework for Practice', *Australian Journal of Adult Learning* 49, no. 1 (2009): 169-189; Jill Freedman and Gene Combs, *Narrative Therapy: The Social Construction of Preferred Realities* (NY: Norton, 1996); Alice Morgan, *What is Narrative Therapy?* (Adelaide: Dulwich Centre Publications, 2000); Michael White, *Maps of Narrative Practice* (NY: Norton, 2007).

[50] Ellen L. Marmon, 'Cross-Cultural Field Education: A Transformative Learning Experience', *Christian Education Journal* 7, no. 1 (2010): 70-84; Margret McAllister, Marion Tower and Rachel Walker, 'Gentle Interruptions: Transformative Approaches to Clinical Teaching', *Journal of Nursing Education* 46, no. 7 (2007): 304-312; Brian C. Parker and Florence Myrick, 'Transformative Learning as a Context for Human Patient Simulation', *Journal of Nursing Education* 49, no. 6 (2010): 326-332.

[51] Freedman and Combs, *Narrative Therapy*; Morgan, *What is Narrative Therapy?*; White, *Maps of Narrative Practice*.

[52] Lu, 'Virtual Age: Art Café', 22.

[53] Andersen, *Theory and Practice*, 350.

[54] Amy L. Baylor, 'The Design of Motivational Agents and Avatars', *Educational Technology Research and Development* 59, no. 2 (2011): 291-300.

[55] Gerald Corey, *Theory and Practice of Counseling and Psychotherapy (8th Ed.)*, (Thomson Brooks/Cole, 2009), 71-73.

[56] Marmon, 'Cross-cultural field education', 70-84.

[57] Gao, Noh and Koehler, 'Comparing Role-Playing Activities', 423-443.

[58] Tobias Esch, Gregory L. Fricchione, and George B. Stefano, 'The Therapeutic Use of the Relaxation Response in Stress-Related Diseases', *Medical Science Monitor* 9, no. 2 (2003): 23.

[59] Society of Counselling and Psychotherapy Educators, 'Ethical Guidelines', viewed 22nd January 2012, http://www.scape.org.au/adobe/SCAPE_Code_of_Ethics.pdf.

[60] Richard S. Lazarus and Susan Folkman, *Stress Appraisal and Coping* (New York: Springer Publishing Company Inc, 1984).

[61] *Rafal Ohme, Et al., 'Anaylsis of Neurophysiological Reactions to Advertising Stimuli by Means of EEG and Galvanic Skin Response Measures', Journal of Neuroscience, Psychology and Economics 2, no. 1 (2009): 21.*

[62] Claudia Repetto, and Giuseppe Riva, 'From Virtual Reality to Interreality in the Treatment of Anxiety Disorders', *Neuropsychiatry* 1, no. 1 (2011): 36.

[63] Ryan, 'Pedagogical Applications', 269.

[64] Ryan, 'Pedagogical Applications', 269-278.

[65] Brown, Gordon and Hobbs, 'Holistic Learning', 39-48.

[66] David A. Kolb, Richard E. Boyatzis and Charalampos Mainemelis. 'Experiential Learning Theory: Previous Research and New Directions,' *Perspectives on Cognitive, Learning, and Thinking Styles*, ed. Robert J. Sternberg and Li-Fang Zhang, (NJ: Lawrence Erlbaum, 2000), 227-247.

[67] University of Tasmania. 'Action Learning', viewed on 9th September, 2012. http://www.educ.utas.edu.au/users/ilwebb/Research/action_learning.htm; Victoria J. Marsick, and Judy O'Neil, 'The Many Faces of Action Learning', *Management Learning* 30, no. 2 (1999): 159-176.

Bibliography

Andersen, Terry, Ed. *The Theory and Practice of Online Learning*. Athabasca, Canada: AU Press 2008.

Apte, Judy. 'Facilitating Transformative Learning: A Framework for Practice'. *Australian Journal of Adult Learning* 49, no. 1 (2009): 169-189.

Aukes, Leo, Jelle Geertsma, Janke Cohen-Schotanus, Rein Zwierstra and Joris. Slaets. 'The Effect of Enhanced Experiential Learning on the Personal Reflection of Undergraduate Medical Students'. *Medical Education Online* 13 (2008): 15.

Australian Counselling Association Inc., Accessed January 22, 2012. http://www.theaca.net.au/approved_courses.php.

Baker, Suzanne C., Ryan K. Wentz, and Madison M. Woods. 'Using Virtual Worlds in Education: *Second Life* as an Educational Tool'. *Teaching of Psychology* 36, no. 1 (2009): 59-64.

Baumgartner, Lisa M. 'An Update on Transformational Learning'. *New Directions for Adult and Continuing Education* 89 (2001): 15-24.

Bay, Uschi and Selma Macfarlane. 'Teaching Critical Reflection: A Tool for Transformative Learning in Social Work?' *Social Work Education* 30, no. 7 (2011): 745-758.

Baylor, Amy L. 'The Design of Motivational Agents and Avatars'. *Educational Technology Research and Development* 59, no. 2 (2011): 291-300.

Bransford, John D., Robert D. Sherwood, Ted S. Hasselbring, Charles K. Kinzer and Susan M. Williams. 'Anchored Instruction: Why We Need It and How Technology Can Help'. *Cognition, Education and Multimedia*, edited by Don Nix and Rand Sprio. Hillsdale, N.J.: Erlbaum Associates, 1990.

Brown, Elaine, Marie Gordon and Mike Hobbs. '*Second Life* as a Holistic Learning Environment for Problem-Based Learning and Transferable Skills'. *Paper presented at Researching Learning in Virtual Environments International Conference.* Milton Keynes, United Kingdom: The Open University, 2008.

Chin, Paul. *Virtual Learning Environments.* LTSN Physical Sciences Centre, 2003.

Conradi, Emily, Sheetal Kavia, David Burden, Alan Rice, Luke Woodham, Chris Beaumont, Maggie Savin-Baden and Terry Poulton. 'Virtual Patients in a Virtual World: Training Paramedic Students for Practice'. *Medical Teacher* 31, no. 8 (2009): 713-720.

Corey, Gerald. *Theory and Practice of Counseling and Psychotherapy (8th Ed.).* Thomson Brooks/Cole, 2009.

Dillenbourg, Pierre, Daniel K. Schnieder and Paraskevi Synteta. 'Virtual Learning Environments'. *Proceedings of the 3rd Hellenic Conference Information* and *Communication Technologies in Education*, edited by A. Dimitracopoulou, 3-18. Greece: Kastaniotis Editions, 2002.

Dirkx, John M. 'Images, Transformative Learning and the Work of the Soul'. *Adult Learning* 12, no. 3 (2001): 15-16.

Eaton, Lynn, Mario Guerra, Stephanie Corliss and Leslie Jarmon. 'A Statewide University System (16 campuses) Creates Collaborative Learning *Communities* in *Second Life'. Educational Media International* 48, no. 1 (2011): 43.

English, Leona M. and Marie A. Gillen. 'A Postmodern Approach to Adult Religious Education'. *Handbook of Adult and Continuing Education*, edited by Wilson and Hayes. USA: Jossey-Bass, 2000.

Esch, Tobias, Gregory L. Fricchione, and George B. Stefano. 'The Therapeutic Use of the Relaxation Response in Stress-Related Diseases'. *Medical Science Monitor* 9, no. 2 (2003): 23 -34.

Evans, Dena A. and Anthony R. Curtis. 'Animosity, Antagonism, and Avatars: Teaching Conflict Management in *Second Life'. Journal of Nursing Education* 50, no. 11 (2011): 653-655.

Freedman, Jill, and Gene Combs. *Narrative Therapy: The Social Construction of Preferred Realities*. NY: Norton, 1996.

Gao, Fei, Jeong Min Noh and Matthew J. Koehler. 'Comparing Role-Playing Activities in *Second Life* and Face-to-Face Environments'. *Journal of Interactive Learning Research* 20, no. 4 (2009): 423-443.

Girvan, Carina and Timothy Savage. 'Identifying an Appropriate Pedagogy for Virtual Worlds: A Communal Constructivism Case Study'. *Computers and Education* 55, no. 1 (2010): 342-349.

Grabove, Valerie. 'The Many Facets of Transformative Learning Theory and Practice'. *New Directions for Adult and Continuing Education* 74 (1997): 89-96.

Halvorson, Wade, Victoria L. Crittenden and Leyland Pitt. 'Teaching Cases in a Virtual Environment: When the Traditional Case Classroom is Problematic'. *Decision Sciences Journal of Innovative Education* 9, no. 3 (2011): 485-492.

Herrington, Jan, Ron Oliver and Thomas C. Reeves. 'Patterns of Engagement in Authentic Online Learning Environments'. *Australian Journal of Educational Technology* 19, no. 1 (2002): 59-71.

Huang, Hsiu-Mei. 'Towards Constructivism for Adult Learners in Online Learning Environments'. *British Journal of Educational Technology* 33, no. 1 (2002): 27-37.

Inman, Chris, Vivian H. Wright and Julia A. Hartman. 'Use of *Second Life* in K-12 and Higher Education: A Review of the Research'. *Journal of Interactive Online Learning* 9, no. 1 (2010): 44-63.

Jarmon, Leslie. 'Pedagogy and Learning in the Virtual World of *Second Life*'. *Encyclopaedia of Distance and Online Learning (2nd Ed.)*, edited by Patricia Rogers, Gary Berg, Judith Boettcher, Carole Howard, Lorraine Justice and Karen Schenk. Information Science Reference, 2008.

Jarmon, Leslie, Tomoko Traphagan and Michael Mayrath. 'Understanding Project-based Learning in *Second Life* with a Pedagogy, Training and Assessment Trio'. *Education Media International* 45, no. 3 (2008): 157-176.

Johnson, Scott. D., Steven R. Aragon, Nagmuddin Sheik, and Nilda Palma-Rivas. 'Comparative Analysis of Learner Satisfaction and Learning Outcomes in Online and Face-to-Face Learning Environments'. *Journal of Interactive Learning Research* 11, no. 1 (2000): 29-49.

Kay, J and S. FitzGerald. *Educational uses of Second Life.* Retrieved 12th December 2008, http://sleducation.wikispaces.com/educationaluses.

Kapp, Karl and Ben Hamilton. 'Designing Instruction to Teach Principles (Softskills)'. White paper. Department of Instructional Technology and Institute for Interactive Technologies, 2006.

Kolb, David A., Richard E. Boyatzis and Charalampos Mainemelis. 'Experiential Learning Theory: Previous Research and New Directions'. *Perspectives on Cognitive, Learning, and Thinking Styles*, edited by Robert J. Sternberg and Li-Fang Zhang, 227-247. NJ: Lawrence Erlbaum, 2000.

Kriz, Willy, C. 'Creating Effective Learning Environments and Learning Organisations through Gaming and Simulation Design'. *Simulation and Gaming* 34, no. 4 (2003): 495-511.

Lazarus, Richard S. and Susan Folkman. *Stress Appraisal and Coping*. New York: Springer Publishing Company Inc, 1984.

Leonardo, Zeus. 'Critical Social Theory and Transformative Knowledge: The Functions of Criticism in Quality Education'. *Educational Researcher* 33, no. 6 (2009): 11-18.

Lim, Cher Ping. 'Engaging Learners in Online Learning Environments'. *Techtrends* 48, no. 4 (2004): 16-23.

Lu, Lilly. 'Teaching 21st-Century Art Education in a Virtual Age: Art Café @ Second Life'. *Art Education* 63, no. 6 (2010): 19-24.

Marmon, Ellen L. 'Cross-Cultural Field Education: A Transformative Learning Experience'. *Christian Education Journal* 7, no. 1 (2010): 70-84.

Marsick, Victoria J. and Judy O'neil. 'The Many Faces of Action Learning'. *Management Learning* 30, no. 2 (1999): 159-176.

Martin, Jack. 'Self-Regulated Learning, Social Cognitive Theory, and Agency'. *Educational Psychologist* 39, no. 2 (2004): 135-145.

McAllister, Margret, Marion Tower and Rachel Walker. 'Gentle Interruptions: Transformative Approaches to Clinical Teaching'. *Journal of Nursing Education* 46, no. 7 (2007): 304-312.

Mercer, Joyce A. 'Transformational Adult Learning in Congregations'. *The Journal of Adult Theological Education* 3, no. 2 (2006): 163-178.

Mezirow, Jack. 'A Critical Theory of Adult Learning and Education', *Adult Education Quarterly* 32 (1981): 3-24.

———. *Transformative Dimensions of Adult Learning*. USA: Jossey-Bass, 1991.

———. 'Transformative Learning: Theory to Practice'. *New Directions for Adult and Continuing Education* 47, no. 2 (1997): 5-12.

———. 'Transformative Learning as Discourse'. *Journal of Transformative Education* 1, no. 1 (2003): 58-63.

Mezirow, Jack and Edward W. Taylor. *Transformative Learning in Practice: Insights from Community, Workplace and Higher Education*. San Francisco: Jossey-Bass 2009.

Morgan, Alice. *What is Narrative Therapy?* Adelaide: Dulwich Centre Publications, 2000.

Ohme, Rafal, Dorota Reykowska, Dawid Wiener and Anna Choromanska. 'Anaylsis of Neurophysiological Reactions to Advertising Stimuli by Means of EEG and Galvanic Skin Response Measures'. *Journal of Neuroscience, Psychology and Economics* 2, no. 1 (2009): 21-31.

Parker, Brian C., and Florence Myrick. 'Transformative Learning as a Context for Human Patient Simulation'. *Journal of Nursing Education* 49, no. 6 (2010): 326-332.

Psychotherapy and Counselling Federation of Australia Inc., 'Training Standards'. Accessed January 22, 2012. http://pacfa.ivt.com.au/sitebuilder/resources/knowledge/asset/files/2/ts2012finalfor webpage2012.pdf.

Repetto, Claudia, and Giuseppe Riva. 'From Virtual Reality to Interreality in the Treatment of Anxiety Disorders'. *Neuropsychiatry* 1, no. 1 (2011): 31-43.

Riggs, Larry, and Sandra Hellyer-Riggs. 'Beyond Information, Through Participation, to New Learning for Personal and Cognitive Growth in Higher Education: Focusing on the Process'. *The International Journal of Learning* 16, no. 5 (2009): 399-408.

Rogers, Carl. 'The Necessary and Sufficient Conditions of Therapeutic Personality Change'. *Journal of Consulting Psychology* 21, no. 2 (1957): 95-103.

Rogers, Luke. 'Developing Simulations in Multi-User Virtual Environments to Enhance Healthcare Education'. *British Journal of Educational Technology* 42, no. 4 (2011): 608.

Ryan, Michelle. '16 Ways to Use Virtual Worlds in Your Classroom: Pedagogical Applications of *Second Life*'. In *ReLIVE '08: Proceedings of Researching Learning in Virtual Environments International Conference*, edited by Anna Peachey, 269-278. Milton Keynes, UK: The Open University, 2008.

Ryman, Sall'ee, Lisa Burrell, Gregory Hardham, Bruce Richardson and Jane Ross. 'Creating and Sustaining Online Learning Communities: Designing for Transformative Learning'. *International Journal of Pedagogies and Learning* 5, no. 3 (2009): 32-45.

Salmon, Gilly. 'The Future for (Second) Life and Learning'. *British Journal of Educational Technology* 40, no. 3 (2009): 526-538.

Skiba, Diane J. 'Nursing Education 2.0: *Second Life*'. *Nursing Education Perspectives* 28, no. 3 (2007): 156-157.

Society of Counselling and Psychotherapy Educators, 'Ethical guidelines', http://www.scape.org.au/adobe/SCAPE_Code_of_Ethics.pdf. Accessed January 22, 2012.

Steinkuehler, Constance. 'Massive Multiplayer Online Games as Educational Technology: An Outline for Research'. *Journal of Educational Technology* 48, no. 1 (2008): 10-21.

Taylor, Edward W. *The Theory and Practice of Transformative Learning: A Critical Review*. ERIC Clearing House on Adult, Career, and Vocational Education. Columbus, OH: Ohio State University, 1998.

———. 'An Update on Transformative Learning Theory: A Critical Review of the Empirical Research (1999-2005)'. *International Journal of Lifelong Education* 26, no. 2 (2007): 173-191.

———. 'Transformative Learning Theory'. *New Directions for Adult and Continuing Education* 119 (2008): 5-15.

Taylor, Edward W. and Patricia Cranton. *The Handbook of Transformative Learning: Theory, Research, and Practice*. San Francisco: Jossey-Bass, 2012.

Taylor, Megan A., Jerome M. Fischer and Linda Taylor. 'Factors Relevant for the Affective Content in Literature Survey: Implications for Designing an Adult Transformational Learning Curriculum'. *Journal of Adult Education* 38, no. 2 (2009): 19-31.

Tsoi-Hoshmand, Lisa. 'The Transformative Potential of Counseling Education'. *Journal and Humanistic Counselling, Education and Development* 43, no. 1 (2004): 82-90.

University of Tasmania. 'Action Learning'. Accessed September 9th, 2012. http://www.educ.utas.edu.au/users/ilwebb/Research/action_learning.htm.

Walker, Victoria. '3D Virtual Learning in Counsellor Education: Using *Second Life* in Counsellor Skill Development'. *Journal of Virtual Worlds Research* 2, no. 1 (2009): 3-14.

Warburton, Steven. '*Second Life* in Higher Education: Assessing the Potential for and the Barriers to Deploying Virtual Worlds in Learning and Teaching'. *British Journal of Educational Technology* 40, no. 3 (2009): 414-426.

White, Michael. *Maps of Narrative Practice*. NY: Norton, 2007.

Willers, Jack C. 'Humanistic Education: Concepts, Criteria and Criticism'. *Peabody Journal of Education* 53, no. 1 (1975): 39-44.

Wood, Anya and Carolyn McPhee. 'Establishing a Virtual Learning Environment: A Nursing Experience'. *The Journal of Continuing Education in Nursing* 42, no. 11 (2011): 510-515.

Zeskind, Philip S. 'Adult Heart Rate Responses to Infant Cry Sounds'. *British Journal of Developmental Psychology* 5, no. 1 (1987): 73-79.

Tom Edwards and Michael Walker, School of Arts, Social Science and Education, Tabor Victoria, Australia. tedwards@tabor.vic.edu.au.

Wild and Crazy: Confucian and Contemporary Selves and Their Attitudes towards Virtual Sexual Experience

C. A. DeCoursey

Abstract
Asian youth are well-known to be engaged and familiar with online gaming and role-play contexts. The use of avatars to represent self and their interactions in contexts such as MMORPGs are urban norms in cities such as Hong Kong. As virtual worlds and interactions are still relatively new, researchers can ask, are there cultural elements involved in the way Asians learn, play and interact in virtual worlds? How do Chinese students understand exceptional encounters such as sexual interactions, in the virtual world? In what ways do exceptional events involving virtual persona impact the here-and-now self? This chapter explores data from 82 blogs written by Hong Kong students who were engaged in English language learning activities in *Second Life*, as part of an undergraduate course. CorpusTool tagging of Appraisal analysis system networks are used to evaluate lexicogrammar related to feelings, judgments and appreciations, as realised in blogs which included spontaneous confessions and descriptions of sexual behaviours and encounters. In particular, Higgins' theory of multiple selves is used to interpret the relationship between the here-and-now student and the avatar. Students' descriptions of self are considered for what they show about varieties of the self and conceptions of how the avatar relates to and expresses self. Particular attention is paid to Confucian values including social solidarity, education, and family obligations.

Key Words: English language teaching, new media, self, Confucian values, appraisal analysis.

*****

1. Introduction

Asian youth routinely use avatars in virtual environments. Online experience with avatars has become a major element of Asian youth's means of exploring themselves, and encountering other people. Hong Kong youth reside in a city which is wirelessly and electronically highly connected. They are members of a society in which online gaming experience is ubiquitous. Hong Kong Chinese tertiary students now have many of their social, intellectual and adult experiences online. At the same time, Confucianism remains an important influence shaping Hong Kong social values, such that many Hong Kong youth have relatively little experience exploring and defining their sexuality, a key aspect of identity. This study used Higgins' theory of multiple selves to articulate how Chinese students manage versions of themselves in virtual sexual interactions. Appraisal analysis was applied to 82 blogs written by Hong Kong students, to investigate attitudinal lexicogrammar associated with their feelings, judgments and appreciations about these virtual sexual experiences. *Second Life* (*SL*) emerged as a powerful venue and tool in assisting students to explore sexual identities and desires, within the requirements of a traditional Confucian society.

2. Literature Review

Gaming has been part of Asian and Hong Kong cultures for two decades. Virtual environments are widely used in Hong Kong education, especially in English second language (2L) classrooms, as well as socially in gaming. In both situations, computer-mediated communication (CMC) is enhanced by the sense of personal connection to avatars. Multi-User Virtual Environments (MUVEs) with advanced affordances, such as *SL*, support the detailed representation of self crucial to creating and sustaining the sense of avatar subjectivity.[1] Users 'feel as if their avatar on the screen were their real self',[2] which 'greatly influences the perceived sensation of presence'.[3] This engages users' emotions. Avatars, like physical selves, are understood as multiple. In virtual environments, this can be seen in players' use of affordances to edit their appearance and change their actions in order to represent various aspects of the self in various virtual contexts, as well as the practice of having multiple avatars for use in expressing, exploring and performing different identities with different communities. Avatars, as virtual selves, are 'not stable and unitary, but dynamic and multiple'.[4] Virtual affordances 'allow new configurations of self that fulfill wishes and fantasies'.[5]

This chapter analyses linguistic data in order to explore the avatar as virtual self, and its relation to other versions of the self, in negotiating virtual sexual experiences. A model of the multiple self in widespread use in both psychological and linguistic research is Higgins' self-discrepancy model. This long-standing research paradigm has been validated in both fields.[6] Higgins' model is based in a theory of self as multiple and dynamic. People imagine several selves. These include the here-and-now, ought, desired and possible selves. The here-and-now self is what people refer to as their 'real' selves. This references the physical self, for example the self sitting at the keyboard and managing computer input, as well as the operational self which manages currently relevant daily details, makes plans, and so on. People are little aware of the fact that the here-and-now self is constantly changing. The ought self reflects and attempts to enact views and voices coming from authority figures, such as parents and teachers, which have been accepted regarding what the here-and-now self should be like. For 2L students, this includes ideas about language proficiency such as 'I should be a good English speaker' or 'I should learn English very well'. The ideal self is aspirational, composed of a person's dreams and desires for themselves. People often have several different aspirational selves reflecting favorite film and popular culture role models, idealised employment futures, romantic aspirations and so on.

When a desired self is unaligned with the ought and the here-and-now selves, people feel a sense of discrepancy. As this is uncomfortable, they are motivated to change this situation. In order to mitigate the discomfort, they imagine desired selves in which all these versions of the self exist in harmony, and fit together in a comfortably coherent manner. In some cases, these desired selves are quite unrealistic, and so they are unlikely to assist a person in taking concrete actions that move the here-and-now self towards the ought and / or desired selves. But in some cases, desired selves are effective in moving people towards realising a new version of the here-and-now self. This new version is one which has achieved some of its ought and desired goals. Desired selves which can function to change the here-and-now self are called possible selves, or self-guides. Possible selves can function to guide people to take action and make decisions to diminish the sense of discrepancy, and move the current here-and-now self towards the desired or ought self, if they fulfill three conditions. First, the imagined self must feel positive to here-and-now self. Second, it must be accompanied by processes of visually-rich and sensorily-detailed imaginations. Second, the tasks required to be accomplished by the here-and-now self as it moves towards the possible self must be realistic and practicable.

Higgins' theory has been used to describe the sustained effort required to learn a second language. For 2L learners, relations between their here-and-now, desired and ought selves is a dynamic, ongoing process of revision and reconstruction of imagined selves. Motivation research shows that 2L learners are particularly practiced at imagining and coordinating multiple desired selves. This is because language learning tasks and activities require them to spend time imagining identities associated with other languages, cultures and communicative situations. This realistic use of imagination is routinely required for 2L classroom interactions, role-plays, exercises, essays and so on. So, when 2L learning arouses a sense of discrepancy, proficient 2L learners find it relatively easy to imagine a self-guide to assist them in reducing this discomfort. Their years of practice imagining self-guides assists them in moving forward in the time-consuming effort of learning another language. Over time, desired possible 2L selves which effectively reduce discomfort become part of the more linguistically-proficient here-and-now self.[7] We can anticipate that 2L learners would take their imaginative practices into other areas of their experience, including online activities and sexuality. Studies of avatar self-presence are now also using Higgins' model to investigate virtual subjectivity.[8]

Confucian Heritage Cultures (CHC) have been extensively researched, as have Confucian values, both in Chinese nations and cultures, and in the diaspora.[9] Confucian values include the obligation of children to study diligently, as a duty and part of family solidarity.[10] Studying diligently is an aspect of maintaining social and family stability through the fulfilment of obligations. Confucian values for the student as for others, emphasise enacting cooperation rather than individuality, and collectivity rather than independence.[11] Within the family, children primarily fulfil a responsibility to study diligently. They must reflect deeply to develop their character, and study persistently to ensure success in employment, thus becoming able to gain a good job, and fulfil their obligation to support the extended family.[12] These obligations extend to adult children and university students. Studying English is connected to job success through persistence.[13] Long-term orientation and harmony are the terms used to explain the integration of all these values within the processes of self- and social regulation.[14] The personal exploration of one's sexuality is not a part of the Confucian model of the good student or good family member.

This chapter will explore Hong Kong students' blogs about their sexual experience in *SL*. Research questions include: how does Higgins' self-discrepancy model help us understand Chinese students' management of sexuality and self? How well does this model apply to the functioning of multiple selves in virtual environments? How do Hong Kong students reconcile what is possible in virtual worlds with what is mandated by their Confucian values and heritage? Lexicogrammar expressing attitude is analysed using Appraisal analysis. Examples illuminate how this realises Confucian values and versions of the self. Some longer examples are explored.

3. Method

In this study, attitudes realised in short written blogs about students' virtual selves were aggregated and analysed, in order to understand Chinese students' virtual sexual identities.

Participants in this study were 82 Cantonese- and Putonghua-speakers enrolled in an English-medium university course. Two (2.44%) reported prior *SL* experience, most (72 = 87.80%) reported prior experience of MUVEs. Participants received one hour of *SL* instruction and one hour of assisted lab practice. Thereafter, they spent weekly unsupervised time on virtual tasks related to course content, and wrote weekly blogs. Blogging and CMC elicit more expression of subjectivity and culture than academic essays.[15] In the final week, students were invited to 'Do something wild and crazy of your own choice'. Although it was unanticipated, 68 of 82 students (82.93%) wrote about virtual sexual experiences. Of the 14 (17.07%) blogs which did not deal with sexuality, 9 (10.98%) focused on vampires, breaking the Confucian cultural taboo on referencing death ('It's so horrible but exciting! Like something in the Chinese tradition, it will be followed by bad luck if you encounter anything related to death, like coffin or grave in real life.') A few recounted extreme sports, becoming monsters, and karaoke.[16]

Sentiment analysis is a well-established research tool in both linguistics and psychology. Schematic representations of attitudinal areas and their linguistic breaks-downs are converging, in these two fields. Appraisal analysis is based in the understanding that, when expressing opinions, people make choices and select words from among a wide array of possible expressions. These choices and selection can be interpreted.[17] Appraisal analysis maps how individuals realise their personal opinions, selecting from a large body of potential English lexicogrammar. Attitude is divided into three areas – emotion, judgment, and appreciation – and then further articulated into subnetworks,[18] as in Figure 1.

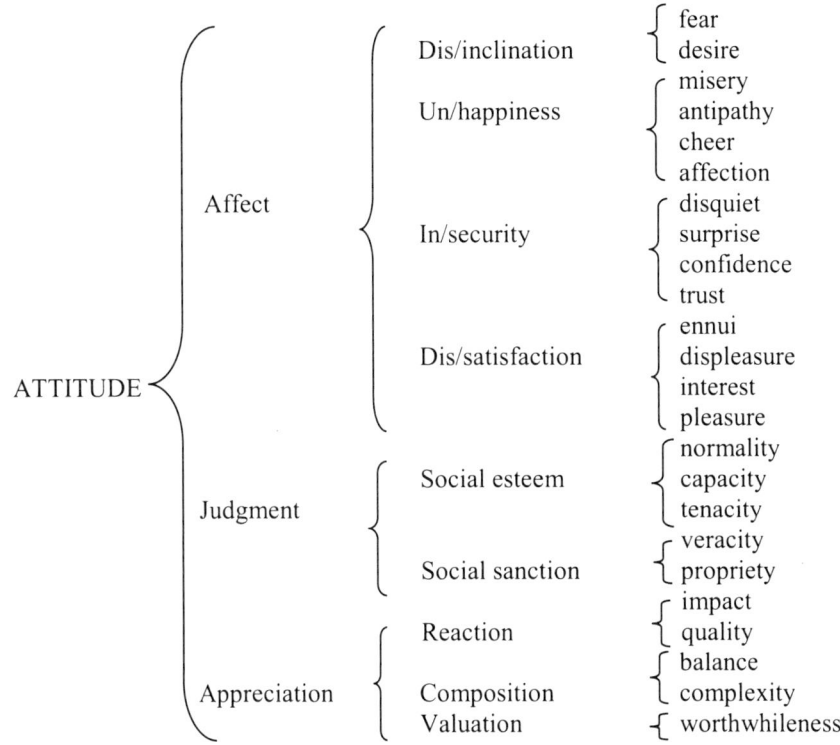

Figure 1: The Attitude System

Software tools like CorpusTool (CT)[19] are conventionally used in computational linguistics. Automatic and human text-tagging remain imperfect due to the intricacies of language and variance in attributions. Still, this method is viewed as robust.[20] The increasing convergence of linguistics and psychology classifications supports its validity.[21]

4. Data

Blogs were concordanced and attitude attributions were made by two human taggers trained in Appraisal and CT. The Cohen's κ value for inter-rater reliability

Wild and Crazy

was .721, greater than we would attribute to chance. The mini-corpus comprised 82 blogs (70,556 words). Within this corpus, attitude was infrequently realised for the ought self. The here-and-now and the desired selves were frequently evoked, using about three times as many positive as negative realisations, as in Table 1.

Table 1: Realisations of attitude towards here-and-now and desired selves

	ATTITUDE							
	here-and-now self (n=513)				desired self (n=811)			
	positive (372=72.51%)		negative (141=27.49%)		positive (616=75.96%)		negative (195=24.04%)	
	n	%	n	%	n	%	n	%
AFFECT	(301=58.67%)				(483=59.56%)			
dis/inclination *fear*	-	-	-	-	2	0.25	24	**2.96**
desire	21	4.09	3	0.58	21	2.59	5	**6.17**
un/happiness *misery*	-	-	5	0.97	6	0.74	13	**1.60**
antipathy	-	-	8	1.56	13	1.60	-	**-**
cheer	5	0.97	7	1.36	49	6.04	16	**1.97**
affection	-	-	-	-	41	5.06	27	**3.33**
in/security *disquiet*	-	-	18	3.51	1	0.12	17	**2.10**
surprise	48	9.36	9	1.75	52	6.41	7	**0.86**
dis/satisfaction *ennui*		-	11	2.14	15	1.85	6	**0.74**
displeasure	-	-	-	-	2	0.25	-	**-**
interest	66	12.87	21	4.09	65	8.01	17	**2.10**
pleasure	73	14.23	6	1.17	77	9.49	8	**0.99**
JUDGMENT	(97=18.91%)				(173=21.33%)			
esteem *normality*	14	2.73	2	0.39	43	5.30	18	**2.22**
capacity	2	0.39	15	2.92	33	4.07	1	**0.12**
tenacity	20	3.90	13	2.53	46	5.67	3	**3.70**
sanction *veracity*	2	0.39	1	0.19	1	0.12	13	**1.60**
propriety	28	5.46	-	-	12	1.48	3	**0.37**
APPRECIATION	(115=22.42 %)				(155=19.11%)			
reaction *impact*	37	7.21	16	3.12	5	0.62	5	**0.62**
quality	44	8.58	4	0.78	9	1.11	9	**1.11**
composition *balance*	1	0.19	1	0.19	1	0.12	1	**0.12**
complexity	-	-	1	0.19	2	0.25	2	**0.25**
value	11	2.14	-	-	-	-	-	-

Both the here-and-now, and the desired selves evoked about 60% affect, 20% judgment and 20% appreciation. The desired self, evoked nearly twice as many realisations of attitude as the here-and-now self. Both elicited positive attitudes in affect-security, affect-satisfaction (pleasure, interest), and appreciation-reaction (impact, quality). The desired self also elicited positive attitudes in affect-happiness (cheer, affection), and social esteem (normality, capacity). Frequently-realised attitudes are ranked in Table 2.

Table 2: Frequent attitudes applied to here-and-now and desired selves
(n=268, n= 479)

rank	here and now self (n=268)		desired self (n=479)	
	evaluation	n	evaluation	n
1	satisfaction (pleasure)	73	satisfaction (pleasure)	77
2	satisfaction (interest)	66	satisfaction (interest)	65
3	security (surprise)	48	reaction (quality)	63
4	reaction (quality)	44	reaction (impact)	56
5	reaction (impact)	37	security (surprise)	52
6			happiness (cheer)	49
7			social esteem (normality)	43
8			happiness (affection)	41
9			social esteem (capacity)	33

All frequently-realised categories were positive, none were negative. Three of five realised for both the here-and-now and desired selves were positive emotions: pleasure, interest and surprise. Two positive appreciations realised for both the here-and-now and desired selves were appreciations of reaction, to the quality and impact of the virtual experience. But desired selves elicited four more categories – feelings of cheer and affection, and judgments of social esteem in normality and capacity. Positive realisations of social esteem-normality included words and phrases such as different, special, unusual, extraordinary, cool, unique, distinct, out of my experience. Positive realisations of social esteem-capability involved words and phrases such as I can, I am able to, I have the ability, I have the flair, I know how to, I am capable of, I have the capacity to, I am skilled at, I have the expertise to, I am proficient at, I am competent in, I have the aptitude to, and I've got the knack.

The frequency of reported sexual activities are ranked in Table 3. This data suggests that Chinese students' virtual sexual experiences, at least those that are reported, involve traditional forms of interaction which are not explicitly sexual, such as meeting, dating and flirting. Explicit sexual interactions mainly involved consensual nudity. Virtual sexual intercourse was unusual, reportedly occurring in about 7.32% of cases.

Students' comments about these virtual interactions can be analysed using appraisal analysis, to explore in greater detail how Chinese students manage Confucian values and desired selves in virtual sexual activities.

Table 3: Frequently- and less frequently-reported sexual activities in blogs

rank	reported sexual activities	n	%
1	meeting potential romantic others	63	76.83
2	nudity	56	68.29
3	dating	38	46.34
4	virtual cross-gender experiences	21	25.61
5	flirting	17	20.73
6	having sex	6	7.32
7	pole dancing	5	6.10
8	sex requests	5	6.10
9	same-sex marriage	4	4.88
10	sexy chat	3	3.66

5. Discussion

The frequently-realised categories for here-and-now and desired selves (Table 2) suggest the positive potential of avatars, virtual selves, in supporting the here-and-now self to generate desired selves which function as viable possible selves, or as self-guides. To be self-guides, desired selves must be experienced positively, as has been found in this data, in the areas of pleasure, interest, a positive quality and impact. To be self-guides, desired selves must be accompanied by a rich visual imagination of the possible self. Virtual worlds such as *SL*, with their detailed visual affordances, clearly support this condition. We can use examples from the blogs to begin to explore the third condition, that the associated tasks must be realistically achievable. Desired selves' frequent realisation of judgments of social esteem in the area of normality and capability provides initial support for the idea that participants did experience these tasks as viable and achievable. Overall, this data suggests the value of using MUVEs such as *SL* in 2L teaching in Asia, where Confucian values may stress studies useful to employment and family provision, and not facilitate much exploration within the self.

Most blogs included recounts of virtual interactions undertaken during the time spent in *SL*. Most combined more than one of the above sexual activities, for example this case of nudity used to meet romantic partners:

> 1. I pressed take-off my clothes. 2. He took off his clothes after me as he said this can attract more girls. 3. The other avatars saw this and they were all excited. 4. This made us form a social group and we were all excited to do this together. 5. We giggled

and laughed – all of us knew that this is a thing that we will do
only in Secondlife but not in reality.

In this case, 'I' in sentence 1 is the here-and-now self, seated at the computer, who takes off the avatar's clothes. '[M]e' in sentence 2, causing other avatars to do the same as recounted in sentences 2 and 3 is the avatar, and in this case a sexually active desired self. The distinction between the here-and-now selves ('us', 'we' in sentence 5) who never do this in 'reality' and the 'excited' and 'giggl[ing] and laugh[ing]' nude avatar indicates the discrepant distance felt between these selves. It seems, then, that relations between versions of the self in daily life are similar in virtual environments.

The most frequently-reported sexual activity was meeting others. Most cases of meeting romantic others (57, 69.51%) realised a discrepant here-and-now self, which was compared with a desired sexual self, with virtual selves understood to facilitate this desired self. For example:

> 1. In our real life, people are shy to making new friends. 2. It is difficult if a girl want to make friends with boys or even have dating with boys. 3. In contrast, we could do anything we want and like in SecondLife.

'[O]ur', 'people' and 'girl' in sentences 1-2 reflect the here-and-now self of the student writer. English offers more- and less-direct lexicogrammar (Halliday 1985). The expression 'I am shy' is congruent, directly expressing personal experience. By comparison, lexicalised realisations are indirect – 'people are shy to', 'it is difficult if a girl want to'. When a person chooses indirect realisations, they distance the experience recounted from the self somewhat, often to manage social demands. In sentence 2, the student writer distances the desire to meet a boy from herself, possibly to conform to Confucian social values. However, sentence 3 uses 'we' (x2) with the congruent 'want' and 'like', positively evaluating (affect inclination-desire, happiness-affection) the avatar as a desired, sexually active self 'In Secondlife'.

Many recounts of nudity appreciated the potential of avatars as self-guides in helping sexually inactive here-and-now selves generate sexually-active virtual desired selves, which functioned to assist in making decisions and taking actions which reduced the discomfort of discrepancy :

> 1. I ask him do you want to do something crazy, he answered me I am a crazy person and did something crazy all the time. 2. Well, I am lucky to find a person in same channel. 3. I suggested him dance in the middle of Hyde Park but with something more, dance in nude. 4. Personally I love to dance but I am not a good

dancer, that's why I seldom dance in reality, all because my self esteem. 5. And at that moment, I just want to do something more, so I add a criteria dance in nude. 6. First of all I took off my clothes and start to dance; [Av-Male B] laughed on me and not followed me from the beginning. 7. Finally he did not feel shy anymore, and two people take off their clothes and dance together. 8. And I keep on saying Thriller Thriler, I pretending Michael Jackson. 9. Not only crazy in Secondlife, I am crazy in reality during that moment too, I can't control myself I keep on laughed in front the computer and nonstop. 10. We get closer eventually and [Av-Male B] take off his pants as well. 11. At that crazy moment I followed him without any consideration. ... 12. This is a happy and remarkable experience for me, not only I do something crazy; it is because someone accompanied me to do something crazy. 13. In the future once I am under pressure I will release in Secondlife.

'I' in sentences 1 and 3 is the avatar, a desired self, but in sentence 2 reflects here-and-now self. In sentence 4, 'I' (x2) and 'my' reflect the here-and-now, self which feels discrepant about the fact that he 'seldom' dances. In sentences 5-7, 'I' is the virtual-desired self who 'want[s] to do something more', who is positively evaluated for his nudity, confidence and leadership. This 'I' adopts a second desired self – notable dancer, rule-breaker and popular dance-leader Michael Jackson, whose attributes the author takes on in order to support the decision-making process. Sentence 9 relates the effect on here-and-now self congruently ('I am crazy', 'I can't control myself', 'I keep on laughed'). In sentences 10-11 'we' and 'I' reverse roles. In sentences 12-13, here-and-now self positively evaluates this experience (affect, satisfaction-pleasure in 'happy', appreciation-valuation in 'remarkable'), concluding with an intention to continue these activities. We see virtual-desired self, functioning as self-guide in assisting decision-making that reduces discrepancy. Even if limited to times of pressure, this example shows how *SL* may support self-guides .

Many students specifically articulated decisions made to diminish discrepancy. Dating often involved discrepant here-and-now reflecting on sexually-active virtual desired selves:

1. A thought came to my mind was to date with movie stars. 2. It was always a dream that could ever happen in my real life. 3. So I go to LA rock club island. 4. But when I am in that lounge someone, as a stranger, teleported me to a secret corner immediately and wanted to have sex with my avatar. 5. Of course I ran away immediately. 6. Over the past weeks, I found that if

you want to get the greatest joys and the greatest satisfaction and recognition in *SL*, you need to get 100% involved in the life there. 7. But for me, since I need to accomplish the required tasks in *SL*, I have not been fully involved in the process. 8. Therefore, I used to be as normal as myself in real life that it gives me many constraints. 9. It is ashamed that I had not been so wild and crazy in the *SL* as I could hardly do the actions in my real life. 10. It is not acceptable. 11. After completed this blog, I will certainly get myself involved in the *SL* and experience the real fun there. 12. I am looking forward to it.

Despite unpleasant experiences, in sentences 6-8 'I', here-and-now self, critiques her distance from 'joys' and 'satisfactions' because ought self, sentence 7 'me' and 'I' 'need to accomplish the required tasks' in the Confucian manner, and avatar 'I' in sentence 8 followed ought self, meaning 'many constraints' for 'me', desired self. But in sentences 9-12, here-and-now student negatively evaluates these choices (two negative judgments of social sanction-propriety in 'ashamed', 'not acceptable'), resolving to enable her sexually-active virtual desired self , 'myself', now positively evaluated (judgment, social esteem-normality 'real', 'looking forward', and affect satisfaction-pleasure 'fun').

Cross-gender avatars often elicited the modality of possibility: 'Impossible can turn into possible in this world. I can change my gender', and positive evaluations: 'I felt crazy and miraculous to be the man. It can be an unforgettable experience if you become a man.' Cross-gender avatars were complex, as self-guides:

1. [Av-Male C] asked if I am good at flirting with girls. 2. I am just idiot. 3. First, I am a female. 4. Second, I do not have flirting experience. 5. I could only say flirting is no cost and harm to many male. ... 6. Secondlife is a place for us to escape from reality. 7. I think I could get up and be brave to reality as well.

In sentence 1, 'I' is the avatar. In sentences 2-3 'I' is the discrepant here-and-now self, revealing her true gender identity in sentence 3 as female, and in sentences 4-5 negatively evaluating her inexperience (two negative judgments of social sanction-capacity ('not experience[d]', 'could only'). In sentence 7, here-and-now self 'I' (x2) weakly states an intention to flirt in reality.

Cross-gender avatars offered complex potentials as self-guides. A female student who chose a male avatar wrote:

1. When I am trying to talk with someone with this topic, I always try to find the male to talk, this is because in my mind I always think that for those things male is easier to accept and

chat with you. 2. That mean I can easy to open the topic and keep on this topic. 3. Also I think female may get a bad feeling to evaluate me as a heterogenous.

'I' (x3) and 'you' in sentence 1 is the discrepant-feeling here-and-now self whose use of a male avatar probably reflects her gender-role beliefs about her own female here-and-now self as well as about men. The positive evaluation (judgment, social esteem-normality in 'easy', 'easier'), and concern about being negatively evaluated (two negative judgments of social sanction-normality in 'bad' and 'heterogeneous') suggests she accepts her gender, still her (socially-constructed) gender-role feels discrepant when compared to a desired self which could talk about dating and sex easily.

This suggests that cross-gender avatars might function as self-guides where people do not accept their gender. Just as for the student pretending to be Michael Jackson, 2L students appear adept at using virtual-desired selves selectively. However, cross-gender avatars could also disconcert here-and-now selves enacting here-and-now gender roles. For example, one student recounted how her here-and-now self, felt disconcerted about engaging in sexual activity due to other avatars' responses to her cross-gender virtual self.

> 1. I thought it was exciting and wild so I tried to take [Av-Male D]'s shirt off. 2. However, he didn't want me to do that because I looked like a man instead of a pretty lady. 3. My appearance was not attractive at that moment. 4. But [Av-Male C] invited me to dance with him under a rose tree. 5. It was so wild and incredible! 6. For two guys to dance under such a romantic environment! 7. It is the period that I felt the most amazed, free to talk and do what I want.'

Here, the first 'I' in sentence 1 is the here-and-now self, where the second 'I' is the avatar, a virtual desired self which is sexually active. Discrepancy was felt by the here-and-now self when the other avatar rejected her, because that sexually active desired self, appeared virtually as a male, which she restates in sentence 4 negatively as 'not attractive', the phrase 'my appearance' bringing together the here-and-now with the desired selves. After her second, more pleasurable encounter, the here-and-now self in sentence 7 realises the strong positive experiences which her here-and-now self, had in 'amazed' (positive affect-satisfaction, pleasure), and 'free' (positive judgment of social esteem-capability). The sexually-active, desired virtual self is identified as 'do[ing] what I want', indicating that it has functioned as an aid in decision-making, moving the here-and-now and desired selves closer to each other .

Having virtual sex was infrequently reported, as might be expected. Comments focused on the insufficiency of technical affordances.

> 1. Sex is one of the things which I will never do in my daily life. 2. Only in 2L, I can do whatever I want. 3. Except it cannot be compared with that of actual life and I look funny on the computer.

The 'I' and 'my' in sentence 1 is abstinent here-and-now self, contrasted with virtual desired self, the 'I' (x2) of sentence 2. Discrepancy is noted in sentence 3, in a case where virtual self cannot function as a self-guide and discrepancy validates here-and-now self.

Many students reported feeling discrepancy due to their Confucian social values:

> 1. I decided to go to a club since I have never been to a club in Hong Kong. 2. My parents are conservative; they would never allow me to go those places and always monitor me to act like a good girl. 3. Sometimes I would think if I could ever go crazy and be wild, or maybe at least let me try once. 4. I always dreamed that I could go pole dance, but in fact would never have the dare to do this in my life. 5. Therefore, I tried to do that in Secondlife. 6. Acting like someone else and do something that you would never try in your real life are fun.

The first 'I' in Sentence 1 is the sexually-active desired self, doing what the here-and-now self wants to but does not or cannot, due to the parental monitoring mentioned in sentence 2. Confucian family obligations constrain the here-and-now self to acting 'like a good girl' or ought self. Yet clearly, this student does not equate her Confucian self with either her real, here-and-now self, or her dreamed-of desired self. In sentence 3, the here-and-now self, the second 'I', imagines a desired 'I' (first instance) and 'me' who wants to try pole-dancing. While a pole-dancing self is a desired self, as related in sentence 4, here-and-now self does not dare to actually try it. In sentence 5 'I', the avatar or virtual self , enacts the desired sexual self, trying it out. The distance between here-and-now and desired selves is indicated in the description of the experience as being 'like someone else', and 'you' (x2) for what should really be 'me'. At the same time, the experience is positively evaluated (affect satisfaction-pleasure in 'fun').

At the same time, Confucian values were also expressed in the pursuit of sexual experience. Among students recounting pole-dancing was one writer notable for expressing the Confucian value on success through persistent effort:

> 1. This week, I turned myself into a shocking pink chimpanzee and did pole dancing in Secondlife. 2. I have to say, it's not easy to dance with that clumsy outfit. 3. I looked awkward by still managed to do all the poses. 4. This is not my first time doing pole dancing but my first time doing it with chimpanzee costume. 5. It is also the very first time of other avatars started the conversation with me.'

This paragraph is structured as a brief narrative recount of a past experience followed by evaluation of the past event. The here-and-now self ('I' sentence 1) recounts becoming a virtual animal pole-dancer. Then the here-and-now self, offers a series of positive judgments of social esteem-capacity on the virtual self's actions ('not easy ... but still managed' sentence 2), again in sentence 3 ('looked awkward ... still managed'), and again in sentences 4-5 ('not my first time ... but my first time' and 'very first time'). This writer seems unaware of the absurd nature of this virtual sexual activity. Instead, this 2L student specifies conversation, that is human interaction in terms of language use, rather than anything overtly sexual, as the outcome of her virtual sexual efforts, and positively evaluates this as a form of success in the area of capacity.

Infrequently-reported activities included requests for sex, same-sex marriage, and sexy chat. For example: 'I invited him to be my man in a naughty manner. Unfortunately he declined me politely. At that moment my heart was totally broken for sure', 'I got another wild idea in my mind! How about two men got married in Secondlife? It sounded interesting as well' and 'She told me that she would love to talk something dirty'.

The efficiency of *SL* in aiding visually-rich detailed imaginations of sexually-active desired selves, leading to decision-making can best be seen over the whole text of a blog. One example is the following:

> 1. I went to a beach where people like going nude, there I thought I could behave more naturally as everybody was nude! 2. I went there, and be naked! 3. At first, I was so shy to get into the beach even if I was in a virtual world only! 4. I tried to ignore other people and flied into the sea! I tried to swim as fast as I can as I wanted to swim to a far sea where fewer naked people were. 5. I tried to relax my intense temper and intended to swim back to the crowd. 6. However, I found it's really not an easy thing as whenever I did so, I felt bashful even if 'I' was a virtual character. 7. But at the same time, I felt a burst of excited feeling and a sense of relieve. 8. I gradually found myself be able to swim freely in a less crowded sea, but I still found if impossible to join the crowd. 9. I tried to talk with the only avatar nearby.

10. I asked him if it's the first time he swam nakedly. 11. His answer was yes. 12. I asked him if he felt shy. 13. He said yes even he's a man. 14. Next, I asked him if he felt good and would try it later. 15. His answer was similar to me. 16. He said it's quite a special feeling and an unforgettable experience, but he would probably not try it anymore as he considered such deed crazy and wild! 17. Half an hour later, I left the sea. 18. This experience really impacts the way I interact with others. 19. Once, I considered doing something crazy and wild in a virtual world didn't matter anything. 20. However, it's not true. 21. As the virtual world is created to be similar to the reality, so it's likely for me to have some real feeling. 22. For example, when I went naked in virtual world, I would feel shy in reality. 23. No, I know more about 'I': and 'the virtual I'. 24. The next time when I interact with anyone in the others in the virtual world, I will treat them more like as if they were in the real world. 25. Next, when I do anything crazy and wild another time, I think I should behave more naturally as others are doing the same thing. 26. I should learn to relieve myself, and do the right thing with the right attitude, so that I can interact with others in a better feeling and interaction.

This blog is structured as a recount followed by an evaluation of the worth of the experience recounted. The first paragraph narrates an experience which happened to the writer in *SL*. The second paragraph reflects on its meaning to the writer. In the recount, the writer realises the discomfort of discrepancy between the shy here-and-now or real self, and the desired, more sexually free and active self. The discomfort is decreased by positive, visually detailed and realistic tasks – swimming, and talking about it with another avatar doing the same thing. This writer was explicitly aware of making decisions and taking actions to decrease the discomfort and move towards desired self ('tried to ignore', 'tried to swim', 'tried to relax', 'intended to swim', 'gradually found myself', 'tried to talk' sentences 4-8). This writer realised various emotions in doing so ('shy', 'intense temper', 'not easy', 'bashful', 'excited feeling', 'sense of relieve' sentences 3-8), ad their outcome, a positive appreciation of social esteem-capacity ('found myself be able to' 8). While he achieves a sense of freedom, some elements of the task remain 'impossible' (sentence 8). The recount includes a conversation (9-16) with another avatar who views the naked swim as a first and special experience, but remains shy and asserts that he would not try it again. By contrast the writer's statement of its meaning specifies how the virtual experience impacted his here-and-now self. His avatar left the sea ('I' sentence 17) but the here-and-now self was changed in how it viewed and wanted to interact with here-and-now others ('I' 18, and sentences

19-20). This writer explicitly notices the impact of the virtual self and experiences on the real (21-23). His view of the meaning of his virtual experience is his intention to treat others in a more 'real' (24) and 'natural' way (25). The 'I' of the final sentence is an ought self realising relief (positive affect insecurity-confidence) and rightness (positive judgment social sanction-propriety) at having achieved 'better feeling and interaction'. The reflection, then, articulates a moment during which a desired self has functioned effectively as a self-guide, decreasing the discomfort of discrepancy and moving the here-and-now self, closer to a possible self.

6. Conclusion

Chinese 2L students positively evaluate sexually-active virtual-desired selves. Adept at imagining and managing multiple selves, they can use avatars in decision-making, as self-guides. *SL* is able to mediate effectively between the here-and-now and imagined desired sexual selves, for Chinese students whose Confucian values cause them to feel a sense of discrepancy when it comes to sexual experience. MUVEs offer a sense of self-presence and opportunities for trialing desired and possible selves, in an area of experience fundamental to human happiness. This is potentially particularly significant for students using cross-gender avatars and pursuing same-sex virtual encounters.

Notes

[1] George Veletsianos, 'Cognitive and Affective Benefits of an Animated Pedagogical Agent: Considering Contextual Relevance and Aesthetics', *Journal of Educational Computing Research* 36,4 (2008): 373-377.
[2] Annie S. A. Jin, and Namkee Park, 'Parasocial Interaction with My Avatar: Effects of Interdependent Self-Construal and the Mediating Role of Self-Presence in an Avatar-Based Console Game, Wii'. *Cyberpsychology and Behavior* 12,6 (2009): 723-7.
[3] Konstantinidis Andreas, Thrasyvoulos Tsiatsos, Theodouli Terzidou, and Andreas Pomportsis, 'Fostering Collaborative Learning in *Second Life*: Metaphors and Affordances'. *Computers and Education* 55 (2010): 603-615.
[4] Ulrike, Schultze, and Matthew M. Leahy, 'The Avatar-Self Relationship: Enacting Presence in *Second Life*.' *ICIS 2009 Proceedings*. Paper 12, 2009.
http://aisel.aisnet.org/icis2009/12.
[5] Donald E. Jones, 'I, Avatar: Constructions of Self and Place in *Second Life* and the Technological Imagination'. *Gnovis* 6 (2006).
http://gnovisjournal.org/files/Donald-E-Jones-I-Avatar.pdf.
[6] Dale H. Schunk, and Barry J. Zimmerman, eds., *Motivation and Self-Regulated Learning: Theory, Research and Applications* (New York: Lawrence Erlbaum, 2007).

[7] Ema, Ushioda, 'Language Motivation in a Reconfigured Europe: Access, Identity, Autonomy', *Journal of Multilingual and Multicultural Development* 27,2 (2006): 148-161.

[8] Annie S-A. Jin, 'Avatars Mirroring the Actual Self Versus Projecting the Ideal Self: The Effects of Self-Priming on Interactivity and Immersion in an Exergame, Wii Fit', *Cyberpsychology and Behaviour* 12,6 (2009): 761-765.

[9] See G. Hofstede, *Cultures and Organizations: Software of the Mind* (London, McGraw Hill, 1991); and A. Inkeles, 'Continuity and Change in Popular Values on the Pacific Rim', *Values in Education: Social Capital Formation in Asia and the Pacific Rim*, ed. J. Montgomery (Hollis NH: Hollis Publishing, 1997), 71-91.

[10] Xu Yao, *An Introduction to Confucianism* (Cambridge, Cambridge University Press, 2000).

[11] See R. H. M. Cheng, 'Moral Education in Hong Kong: Confucian-Parental, Christian-Religious and Liberal-Civic Influences,' *Journal of Moral Education* 33.4 (2004).

[12] See Watkins, D. and Biggs, J., eds., *Teaching the Chinese Learner: Cultural, Psychological and Contextual Influences* (CERC, Hong Kong and ACER Australia, 2001).

[13] See M. Martinsons, and P. Hempel, 'Chinese Management Systems: Historical and Cross-Cultural Perspectives,' *Journal of Management Systems* 7.1 (2002): 1-11, Roger G. Tweed and Darrin R. Lehman, 'Learning Considered within a Cultural Context: Confucian and Socratic Modes,' *American Psychologist* 57.2 (2002): 89-99.

[14] See J. Li, 'A Cultural Model of Learning: Chinese 'Heart and Mind for Wanting to Learn,' *Journal of Cross-Cultural Psychology* 33,3 (2002): 248-269.

[15] Crystal, D. (2001) *Language and the Internet* (Cambridge UK, Cambridge University Press).

[16] Human subject research protocols were followed for the collection this data, including gaining signed permission to use these blogs in research publications. At no time were students asked or invited to comment on their sexual activity. It was their choice to write these comments, and this data was an unexpected element of a larger semester-long project on language learning in virtual worlds.

[17] J. R. Martin and P. R. R White, *The Language of Evaluation: Appraisal in English* (UK, Palgrave Macmillan, 2005).

[18] J. R. Martin, *Working with Discourse: Meaning beyond the Clause* (London, Continuum, 2003).

[19] M. O'Donnell, 'Demonstration of the UAM CorpusTool for text and image annotation' *Proceedings of the ACL-08: HLT Demo Session* (Companion Volume) (Columbus, Ohio: Association for Computational Linguistics, , 2008), 13-16.

[20] M. Taboada, J. Brooke, M. Tofiloski, K. Voll and M. Stede, 'Lexicon-Based Methods for Sentiment Analysis,' *Computational Linguistics* 1 (2011): 1-42.

[21] Monika Bednarek, 'Dimensions of evaluation: Cognitive and linguistic perspectives' *Pragmatics* and *Cognition* 17 (2010): 146-175.

Bibliography

Anetta, Len, Marta Klesath, and Shawn Holmes. 'How Gaming and Avatars Are Engaging Online Students'. *Technology Review* 107.3 (2008): 50-55.

Arena, Carla. 'Blogging in the Language Classroom: It Doesn't Simply Happen'. *TESL-E-Journal* 11.44 (2008): 1-7.

Bailenson, Jeremy N., Andrew C. Beall, Jack Loomis, Jim Blascovich and Matthew Turk. 'Transformed Social Interaction: Decoupling Representation from Behaviour and Form in Collaborative Virtual Environments.' *Presence* 13 (2004): 428-441.

Bednarek, Monika. 'Polyphony in Appraisal: Typological and Topological Perspectives'. *Linguistics and the Human Sciences* 3.2 (2006): 107-136.

Boyatzis, Richard E. and Kleio Akrivou. 'The Ideal Self as the Driver of Intentional Change'. *Journal of Management Development* 25.7 (2006): 624-642.

Chae, Seong-Wook and Kun-Chang Lee. 'Empirical Analysis of the Effect of Avatars on Learner's E-Learning Performance: Emphasis on Trust Transference between Avatars and Contents.' *Asia Pacific Journal of Information Systems* 19.4 (2009): 149-176.

Cheng, Roger H. M. 'Moral Education in Hong Kong: Confucian-Parental, Christian-Religious and Liberal-Civic Influences'. *Journal of Moral Education* 33 (2004): 533-551.

Dale H. Schunk and Barry J. Zimmerman, eds., *Motivation and Self-Regulated Learning: Theory, Research and Applications*. New York: Lawrence Erlbaum, 2007.

Donald E. Jones, 'I, Avatar: Constructions of Self and Place in *Second Life* and the Technological Imagination'. *Gnovis* 6 (2006). http://gnovisjournal.org/files/Donald-E-Jones-I-Avatar.pdf.

Dörnyei, Zoltan. *The Psychology of the Language Learner: Individual Differences in Second Language Acquisition*. New Jersey: Lawrence Erlbaum Associates, 2005.

Dörnyei, Zoltan and Ushioda, Ema. *Motivation, Identity and the L2 Self*. Bristol, UK: Multilingual Matters, 2009.

Halliday, Michael. *An Introduction to Functional Grammar*. London UK: Edward Arnold, 1994.

Halliday, Michael and Christian Matthiessen. *Construing Experience through Meaning: A Language-Based Approach to Cognition*. London: Cassell, 1999.

Higgins, E. Tory. 'Promotion and Prevention: Regulatory Focus as a Motivational Principle'. *Advances in Experimental Social Psychology* 30 (1998): 1-46.

Hillis, Ken. *Digital Sensations: Space, Identity, and Embodiment in Virtual Reality*. Minneapolis: University of Minneapolis Press, 1999.

Hoyle, Rick H. and Sherrill, Michelle R. 'Future Orientation in the Self-System: Possible Selves, Self-Regulation, and Behaviour'. *Journal of Personality* 74.6 (2006): 1673-1696.

Lemke, Jay L. 'Resources for Attitudinal Meaning: Evaluative Orientations in Text Semantics'. *Functions of Language* 5.1 (1998): 33-56.

Lundquist, Lita, Heribert Picht and Jacquess Qvistgaard, eds. *LSP Identity and Interface Research, Knowledge and Society*. Copenhagen: Copenhagen Business School, 1998.

Markus, Hazel R. and Nurius, Paula. 'Possible Selves'. *American Psychologist* 41 (1986): 954-969.

Meadows, Mark S. *I, Avatar: The Culture and Consequences of Having a Second Life*. Berkeley, Calif.: New Riders Press, 2008.

Miceli, Tiziana, Sara V. Murray and Claire Kennedy. 'Using an L2 Blog to Enhance Learners' Participation and Sense of Community'. *Computer Assisted Language Learning* 23.4 (2010): 321-341.

Oatley, Keith, Dacher Keltner and Jennifer M. Jenkins. *Understanding Emotions*. Oxford: Blackwell Pub., 2006.

Pang, Bo, Lee, Lillian and Vaithyanathan, Shivakumar. 'Thumbs Up? Sentiment Classification Using Machine Earning Techniques'. *Proceedings of the 2002 Conference on Empirical Methods in Natural Language Processing*. Philadelphia, Pennsylvania, USA, 2002.

Pinkman, Kathleen. 'Using Blogs in the Foreign Language Classroom: Encouraging Learner Independence'. *JALT CALL Journal* 1.1 (2005): 12-24.

Polanyi, Livia and Annie Zaenen. *Computing Attitude and Affect in Text: Theory and Applications*. USA: Springer, 2006.

Ramanathan, Vai and Robert B. Kaplan. 'Genres, Authors, Discourse Communities: Theory and Application for L1 and L2 Writing Instructors'. *Journal of Second Language Writing* 9 (2000): 171 - 191.

Rao, Zhenhui. 'Chinese Students' Perceptions of Communicative and Non-Communicative Activities in the EFL Classroom'. *System* 30.1 (2002): 85-105.

Read, Jonathon, David Hope and John Carroll. 'Annotating Expressions of Appraisal in English'. *Language Resources and Evaluation*, 2010. Viewed 12 May 2010. doi: 10.1007/s10579-010-9135-7.

Roed, Jannie. 'Language Learner Behavior in a Virtual Environment'. *Computer Assisted Language Learning* 16.203 (2003): 155-172.

Sandrock, Paul. 'Creating Intrinsic Motivation to Learn World Languages'. *The Modern Language Journal* 86.4 (2002): 610-612.

Scherer, Klaus R., Angela Schorr and Tom Johnstone, eds. *Appraisal Processes in Emotion: Theory, Methods, Research*. Canary: Oxford University Press, 2001.

Simpson, Brian. 'Identity Manipulation in Cyberspace as a Leisure Option: Play and the Exploration of Self'. *Information* and *Communications Technology Law* 14 (2005): 115-131.

Stevens, Vance. '*Second Life* in Education and Language Learning'. *TESL - EJ 10* (2006). Viewed 12 August 2010. http://tesl-ej.org/ej39/int.html.

Traugott, Elizabeth C. 'Subjectification in Grammaticalisation'. In *Subjectivity and Subjectivisation, Linguistic Perspectives*, edited by Dieter Stein and Susan Wright, 31-54. Cambridge: Cambridge University Press, 1995.

Tweed, Roger G. and Darrin R. Lehman. 'Learning Considered within a Cultural Context: Confucian and Socratic Modes'. *American Psychologist* 57.2 (2002): 89-99.

Vasalou, Asimina, Adam Joinson and Jeremy Pitt. 'Construing My Online Self: Avatars that Increase Self-Focused Attention'. *Proceedings of ACM CHI 2007 Conference on Human Factors in Computing Systems*, 445-448. ACM Press, 2007.

Veletsianos, George. 'Contextually Relevant Pedagogical Agents: Visual Appearance, Stereotypes and First Impressions and Their Impact on Learning.' *Computers* and *Education* 55 (2010): 576-585.

Whitelaw, Casey, Navendu Garg and Shlomo Argamon. 'Using Appraisal Groups for Sentiment Analysis'. *Proceedings of the Conference on Information and Knowledge Management*, 1-7. CIKM, 2005.

Wiebe, Janyce, Theresa Wilson, Rebecca Bruce, Matthew Bell and Melanie Martin. 'Learning Subjective Language' *Computational Linguistics* 30.3 (2004): 277-308.

Williams, Jeremy B. and Joanne Jacobs. 'Exploring the Use of Blogs as Learning Spaces in the Higher Education Sector'. *Australasian Journal of Educational Technology* 20.2 (2004): 232-247.

Xinzhong Yao, *An Introduction to Confucianism*. Cambridge: Cambridge University Press, 2000.

Yashmina, Tomoko. 'Willingness to Communicate in a Second Language: The Japanese EFL Context'. *Modern Language Journal* 86.1 (2002): 54-66.

C. A. DeCoursey is Programme Leader for the MA in English Language Arts at the Hong Kong Polytechnic University. Her research interests include virtual worlds and multimodality in teaching, animation, Appraisal analysis, and Confucian learning styles.

Part II

Experiential and Distributed Learning

VirtualPREX: Developing Teaching Skills in *Second Life*

Yvonne Masters, Sue Gregory, Torsten Reiners, Vicki Knox and Barney Dalgarno

Abstract
Virtual worlds are accepted as alternative learning environments and have been incorporated into the repertoire of higher education teaching and learning strategies for more than a decade. Numerous reports exist regarding the efficacy of this form of learning for both student engagement and enhanced student outcomes. The immersive affordances of these worlds are also being used to enhance another aspect of many higher education courses; work integrated learning. This form of learning, also referred to as practicum, placement, practice teaching and professional experience, is a core component of teacher education courses. Research has highlighted quality preparation for practice teaching (or lack thereof) as problematic, necessitating new approaches to teacher preparation. The active experiential learning affordances of virtual world technologies have led to the development of 3D virtual classrooms and a playground designed to be effective spaces for developing a range of critical teaching skills. Pre-service teachers have opportunities, through interaction in and with the virtual environment, to practise skills and apply concepts in a realistic setting that is risk free. In this chapter, the authors discuss the problems of preparation for practice teaching and the ways in which the virtual world of *Second Life* is being utilised as a site for enhanced teacher preparation.

Key Words: *Second Life*, virtual worlds, practice teaching, work integrated learning, student outcomes, VirtualPREX.

*****

1. Introduction

In Australia, virtual worlds are providing opportunities for a wide variety of learning activities in higher education across a range of disciplines.[1] These opportunities transpire because 'virtual worlds are richly immersive and highly scalable 3D environments'[2] and, along with other emerging technologies, 'are a vital part of the learning environment' which should become 'as readily available as books, desks, and whiteboards'.[3] Virtual worlds have the capacity for simulation and extended interactions.[4] Throughout 2011 and 2012, a team has been conducting a research project incorporating the use of an innovative approach to professional experience preparation known as VirtualPREX (a contraction of virtual world professional experience). VirtualPREX is funded under the auspices of the Office of Learning and Teaching and has been conducted with pre-service teachers from the University of New England and Australian Catholic University.

Pre-service teachers from other institutions will be able to participate in VirtualPREX from 2013 onwards.

It has been well documented that professional experience is a core feature of teacher education courses.[5] In addition, 'the implicit value of this component of teacher education is not contested'.[6] However, concerns have also been raised about inadequate preparation of pre-service teachers prior to school professional experience placements.[7] In a report to the Productivity Commission, Jolley and Maplestone pointed to a number of other issues that were problematic in the organisation of professional experience for pre-service teachers. These issues included: the difficulty in finding adequate school placements and supervising teachers; the stress placed on professional experience placement staff because of this; and the rising costs associated with school placements.[8]

With pre-service teachers calling for even more teaching practice in an already overloaded school placement system,[9] VirtualPREX provides an innovative method in attempting to alleviate these concerns. While VirtualPREX does not seek to replace professional experience in the real-life classroom, it offers opportunities for extra practice and development of skills that have the capacity to build pre-service teachers' confidence prior to undertaking professional experience in the real classroom. VirtualPREX also responds to the criticism in an Australian Commonwealth Government report:

> The problems with practicum have been outlined in nearly every report addressing teacher education in the last decade. The fact that these problems have still drawn so much attention in this inquiry indicates the need for major reform in this area.[10]

It has been suggested that to become better teachers, pre-service teachers need to be supplied with practical teaching skills in their courses.[11] Engagement in VirtualPREX provides pre-service teachers with opportunities to practise their teaching skills, either synchronously or asynchronously, in custom-built virtual classrooms in *Second Life*. Through structured role-play, a pre-service teacher can be presented with a range of teaching scenarios. Role-play and simulations are not new, having been advocated in teacher education for over four decades, most commonly in face-to-face mode in tutorials and workshops.[12] As far back as 1969, Cruickshank described such simulations as a means of presenting a pre-service teacher with 'the most critical problems he [sic] will face in his first year of teaching, in a threat-free, failure-free environment, unlike that of student teaching'.[13] Such simulations provide an opportunity for behaviour management to be practised 'where failure does not impact the learning of real students'.[14] However, while such simulations still occur most often through the medium of face-to-face participation, web-based simulations are becoming more common.[15] Simulations in virtual worlds are now being used in many areas, for example, health and disaster management,[16] where it is difficult, dangerous or simply uneconomical to provide real-life training as an avenue for preparing such learners before they are placed in actual situations. The use of virtual worlds for classroom simulation is a relatively recent addition and there have been a number of studies investigating its use in the area of education, and with pre-service teachers in particular.[17] It is an approach to teacher preparation that is relatively untried in Australia despite an Australian report recommending that the development of a suite of virtual world schools could provide:

> an opportunity to transform the practicum through the use of virtual world simulations so that student teachers are able to experience 'real' teaching situations.[18]

VirtualPREX is seeking to redress this situation.

2. Theoretical Framework: Authentic Learning

VirtualPREX is grounded in the notion of authentic learning which, it has been argued, supports the development of expert thinking, complex communication, reflective judgment, and problem-solving skills in a risk-free environment.[19] Authentic learning occurs in environments that provide enhanced learning opportunities due to the ability to 'focus on a limited, but important, number of variables'[20] in authentic situations.

The VirtualPREX teaching simulations and role-plays have been designed for authenticity, with the intention that pre-service teachers will undertake 'tasks that are identical or similar to those that [they] will eventually encounter in the outside world'.[21] Instead of memorising situations and potential reactions from books, VirtualPREX concentrates on specific areas of the total classroom experience and provides activities targeted at these areas. The learning experienced through the simulations is turned into transferable knowledge thus preparing pre-service teachers for the realities and complexities of real-life classrooms. Some of the challenges in providing authentic learning experiences in VirtualPREX include the specification of boundaries within the simulated environment, the integration of tangible tools for use by the pre-service teachers and establishing a simulation framework that supports the acquisition of skills for responding to (un)expected situations in the classroom.

VirtualPREX is also predicated on the authors' belief that learning should be about *fun*, *play*, and *passion*. Instead of sitting in lectures and retaining 5% of the heard knowledge, pre-service teachers in VirtualPREX engage in active and authentic learning, practising their acquired knowledge which, it has been argued, achieves a salutary 75% retention.[22]

Researchers have found that it is the small, disruptive, everyday interruptions, such as 'talking out of turn' and 'hindering other children' that cause teachers the most concern in managing their classrooms.[23] Managing the classroom and the perceived disconnect between theory and practice are two areas that have been identified as in need of improvement in the preparation of pre-service teachers.[24] Behaviour management has been continuously reported as being of major concern to pre-service teachers.[25] VirtualPREX provides an environment where pre-service teachers can put theory and practice together, utilising and developing strategies they have learned to deal with interruptions in the classroom. In accordance with the nine essential determinants of authentic learning, VirtualPREX concentrates on authentic context and tasks, reflection on the learned lessons and on authentic assessment, without losing sight of the other determinants.[26] The theoretical understanding of this project is balanced with the development and implementation of practical educational processes and tools in order to ensure an authentic experience for the pre-service teacher. The VirtualPREX learning environment incorporates a variety of elements that ensure that pre-service teacher activity will incorporate thinking and problem solving as if performed in a real-world environment. These elements are: the authentic context; the establishment of authentic and challenging tasks; inclusion of expert knowledge for observation and critiques; multiple perspectives for review; opportunities for collaboration; reflection; scaffolding; and assessment.

3. Research Design and Methodology

In 2011, the VirtualPREX team undertook a pilot study to permit preliminary analysis of the efficacy of the research design and to provide data which would inform the revised and expanded design for the major project in 2012. *Second Life*™ was the virtual world of choice for pragmatic reasons: prior ownership of land and researchers' familiarity of use. The specific learning environment consisted of four custom-built classrooms which were created to facilitate the practice of teaching skills by participating pre-service teachers. Forty primary school student avatars and eight teacher avatars were also custom-created for the role-plays allowing the pre-service teachers to experience the role-play both as primary student and school teacher.

Role-plays were developed after a focus group discussion with eight experienced school teachers and principals. The focus group was asked to provide a range of behaviours that are commonly experienced by teachers in real-life classrooms. They were also asked to illustrate these behaviours through specific examples. This discussion was recorded for analysis.

The behaviours described by the teaching practitioners were analysed and melded to provide two groups of 'typical' behaviours. These groups (initially defined as 'good' or 'naughty', but later reconceptualised as 'on task' and 'off task' as shown in Table 1) became the initial basis of the various role descriptions provided to pre-service teachers in the VirtualPREX workshops.

Table 1: Typical Behaviours for Role-plays

'Good' Behaviours	'Naughty' Behaviours
· Good student – ideal student in the classroom · Good student – generally behaves, but does not understand the lesson · Teacher pleaser – always tries to do things for the teacher · Know-it-all – tries to answer every question	· Wanderer – walks around the class a lot, stops and talk to other students · Tattle-tale – 'dobs' on peers and continuously interrupts · Sleeper – stays up too late and continually nods off · Withdrawn student – will not say or do anything · Distracted student – has other things on mind, keeps looking out the window · Rude student – back chats the teacher and rude to other students

In the first phase of the pilot five 2-hour workshops were held in a computer laboratory at the University of New England, Australia, with 72 first year on-campus pre-service teachers (61 female and 11 male) participating. Previously in their course, all pre-service teachers participated in a two-hour tutorial focusing on using the *Second Life*™ environment and a short revision session was provided before the role-plays began. In preparation for the role-plays, each pre-service teacher had been asked to prepare a short teaching scenario or episode (seven minutes) on any subject of their choice. They were also asked to decide the specific year level of primary education that their teaching scenario was designed to meet. The pre-service teachers were divided into groups of six to eight and, in each iteration of the role-play, one pre-service teacher role-played the teacher and the others role-played primary school students with a role assigned to them based on the list shown in Table 1. Each pre-service teacher was to be given the opportunity to act as a teacher in one iteration of the role-play and as a primary school student in the other iterations. The roles as a primary school student alternated between 'naughty' and 'good' for each individual pre-service teacher. Rules of the role-play were outlined to all pre-service teachers in a brief introduction to the structure of the workshop. Depending on the numbers within each workshop, two to three role-plays were conducted, which meant there could be up to three teachers conducting a lesson at the same time. Each group was assigned a different classroom, which were colour-coded: red, yellow, blue, and green, where their role-play would take place. The communication within the role-plays was through typed text (similar to instant messaging), rather than audio, due to the proximity of the pre-service teachers in the computer laboratory.

After the initial analysis of this first phase of the pilot study, the trial extended the opportunity for participation in the role-play scenarios to off-campus (external/distance education) pre-service teachers. The external pre-service teachers who were invited to participate were already familiar with *Second Life*™, eliminating the need for an introductory workshop. Eight off-campus pre-service teachers (6 female and 2 male) accepted the invitation. These off-campus role-plays were conducted with pre-service teachers who were participating from various locations around Australia (in contrast to the on-campus role-plays with all pre-service teachers in the same physical location in a computer laboratory). Another significant modification was that the off-campus pre-service teachers role-playing the teacher used audio for communication while those role-playing the primary school students still used text.

The role-plays of both on-campus and off-campus pre-service teachers were captured in multiple ways – in-world video (machinima), text and screenshots – providing rich data for analysis. Figure 1 demonstrates a role-play in action.

Figure 1: Screenshot of Role-play in Action.
(Available under Creative Commons 3.0 Australia)

All pre-service teachers were asked to complete a survey at the end of their workshop and participated in a reflection on the activity. The survey comprised a range of questions designed to ascertain the following information: demographic details such as age and home location; pre-service teacher confidence in the use of computers and virtual worlds; Likert scale questions about their use of technology; their views about virtual worlds and learning and teaching; and their perceptions of the role-play. Open-ended questions asked about any technical issues or problems encountered during the role-play activity; perceptions about the best or worst part of the activity; and how it could be improved.

In 2012, the role-plays were again conducted with on- and off-campus pre-service teachers. Only minimal analysis of this research has been undertaken so is only briefly documented here (see Section 5: 'Role-Play Developments in 2012').

4. Findings

The pilot project provided both breadth and depth in the data, the analysis of which has informed the major research project in 2012. One Likert scale question asked pre-service teachers to rate the role-play across eight attributes using a 7-point scale from 1 (not at all) to 7 (extremely). The attributes were in order: confusing; difficult; irrelevant; interesting; easy to use; useful; boring; and enjoyable. The weighted (on- and off-campus) mean ratings for each attribute indicated that, despite there being some areas for investigation and improvement in the role-plays, the activity was perceived as beneficial (see Table 2). In this table negative attributes (irrelevant, boring, difficult, confusing) are listed first, followed by positive attributes (useful, easy to use, enjoyable, interesting) .

Table 2: Perceptions of the Role-play – On- and Off-campus Pre-Service Teachers Combined (Weighted Mean: n=80)[27]

Attribute	Mean
Irrelevant	3.13
Boring	3.23
Difficult	3.25
Confusing	3.56
Useful	4.30
Easy to Use	4.60
Enjoyable	4.64
Interesting	4.92

Although the mean responses suggest that, on average, the pre-service teachers perceived that the positive attributes applied to the activity and the negative attributes did not, there was substantial diversity across the responses and there were a number of pre-service teachers who were less positive about the activity. Some of the open-ended responses of the pre-service teachers provided indicators as to why the role-plays elicited some negative feedback such as 'everyone chatting at once' and 'losing track of the conversation'. As the pre-service teachers were using text chat to communicate, if the window where the conversation was being typed and read was not large enough, the gist of the conversation was easily lost. Also, if the pre-service teachers acting as primary school students all spoke (typed) at once, the conversation would not always flow and get out of order, making it difficult to follow. They also felt that it took 'too long to type something ... by then the situation you are responding to is gone' .

Pre-service teachers also identified that the 'behaviour management strategies that involve actions (clapping, hand in the air, etc) which are extremely effective in the classroom but couldn't be used virtually' was an issue. Although all avatars had access to a HUD (Heads Up Display) that provided the option for the avatar to carry out these actions by the click of a button displayed in their window (see Figure 2 of an avatar with the HUD displayed), these comments suggest that some pre-service teachers were overloaded with instructions and interactive virtual world features that they simply did not remember that it was available to be used.

Figure 2: Screenshot of Avatar and the HUD used.
(Available under Creative Commons 3.0 Australia).

Pre-service teachers made a number of comments about the degree to which the role-plays represented the reality of a real classroom, for example, one commented that the environment 'allow[s] less freedom to the avatars which would make it more real as students in a classroom are constantly being monitored', while another commented that 'most of the children in my class were disruptive ... some did not listen to instructions at all'. This latter comment may be a positive comment indicating that the role-play was in fact an authentic experience for the pre-service teacher, or may indicate that the pre-service teachers playing the role of children over-acted their parts to some extent. Nevertheless, unpredictable events like this do occur in a real-life classroom and the teacher does need to develop strategies to deal with them.

Finally, pre-service teachers provided a number of suggestions, including 'better technology', 'longer teaching period' and 'use audio instead of text' which were helpful in identifying possible improvements to the role-play scenarios. All comments provided by the pre-service teachers were taken into consideration by the project team. If it was felt that the suggestion was realistic and something that could be implemented, then this was implemented in the 2012 iteration of the project.

These comments are discussed in the next section on the learnings from the trial and how these have informed the major project that was conducted in 2012.

There were also many positive comments from pre-service teachers, particularly in regard to the efficacy of the role-plays with reference to behaviour management and in terms of preparation for real-life teaching as shown in Table 3. These comments demonstrate that the role-play does have the capacity to enhance the development of teaching skills and to provide an alternative method of preparation to those currently in use.

Table 3: Positive Open-ended Responses

Trying different things to keep the students on task, gave us a chance to practise teaching.
It was fun and interesting. It gave us time to work on behaviour strategies and management of a class.
You had to deal with a number of students, Some were helpful and others were not. They were just down-right annoying. You got to experience that!
I enjoyed being the teacher and having to come up with strategies to deal with students that would not follow instructions.
Being able to take on the roles of different characters, and being able to understand what it is like to have a class of disruptive students.
In a way it reminds you that not every student will want to learn and they will go to any lengths to get out of it.
Enjoyable to see what others did and how they coped with the situation in a safe environment where you could make mistakes and learn from them.

The researchers found the last comment in Table 3 both interesting and encouraging in that this pre-service teacher reported the safety of making mistakes in the VirtualPREX environment. As highlighted earlier, this particular characteristic of simulation activities has been described as a major advantage for practising skills which might otherwise have risks attached.

The data reported in this chapter comprise only a small sample of the entirety of data collected. The sample represents, however, some of the most crucial data that informed the refinement of the role-play for the major project and also the development of accompanying elements of the project such as a schematic for bots (non-player characters) and exemplar machinima. The learning from these data is discussed in the next section.

5. Role-Play Developments in 2012

As outlined via the pre-service teacher comments, the pilot project underscored several aspects of the role-plays where refinement of the process could improve the experience for those taking part. Some of these enhancements, such as using audio instead of typed text, at least for the teacher, could be implemented and might allow for greater role-play facility for the pre-service teachers. However, while audio was used for exemplar machinima (discussed in the next section of the chapter), introducing audio for the second iteration of the role-plays was not undertaken with on-campus pre-service teachers due to the proximity of the pre-service teachers in the computer laboratory and the lack of suitable headset equipment.

In the pilot project pre-service teachers had been informed about a HUD that was available to them (see Figure 2). The HUD permits a range of gestures to be used. The HUD was demonstrated at the start of the workshop, however some pre-service teachers clearly forgot about or felt unable to effectively use this tool given the comments about not being able to make gestures that may have controlled some inappropriate behaviour. In the major project, the HUD was referred to more frequently and was also highlighted more specifically in the introductory remarks. This refinement appeared to assist the pre-service teachers in their use of gestures. There were no comments in the 2012 responses to the survey in relation to an inability to use gestures.

A number of adjustments were made to ensure that the pre-service teachers were more comfortable in their use of the Second Life™ environment before the role-plays commenced so that there would be more effective immersion in the activity. The introduction to *Second Life*™ was held during the week prior to the role-play workshops so it would be fresh. Revision of how to use the *Second Life*™ environment was again given at the beginning of the workshop however pre-service teachers were also supplied with a handout explaining how to undertake the basic activities within the classroom. The pre-service teachers were given a 15-minute period to play within the classrooms before the actual role-plays began.

Significant modifications were made to the classrooms and the avatar primary school children as a result of the feedback from the phase one role-plays. The avatars were changed to look like more realistic school children, changes that included amendments to their size, skin, shape and hair. The avatars were modified to represent a larger range of ethnic backgrounds to provide a more balanced classroom situation. There were equal numbers of male and female avatars assigned to each classroom, but no two avatars looked the same. One comment from survey feedback, stating that 'all avatars should be different, but wear a school uniform', and many verbal suggestions in workshops informed the researchers of the need for this change.

School uniforms were updated to be aligned with a more traditional uniform, consisting of a school blazer and tie for all students. Feedback from pre-service teachers indicated that they preferred this type of uniform as opposed to the cargo pants and polo shirts that the primary school students had worn in the first iteration of uniforms. The shirts in the upgraded uniform were altered so that they were aligned to the colour of the avatar's classroom in which it was assigned.

The classrooms were also moved further apart in the virtual environment to enable local chat to be used when teaching consecutive lessons. When the VirtualPREX project is released to the general public enabling anyone to use the classrooms, it was felt that the classrooms could not be situated so close together otherwise, when talking in local chat, users would be able to hear (see) the conversations of other classes nearby. There was plenty of space available to be able to do this. Also, the classroom colours were changed slightly to allow more light in the classroom. The first iteration of the green classroom was too dark so the classroom was changed to a lighter green t.

Another refinement required was to improve the scaffolding of the role-play and provide different approaches to this in order to permit both synchronous and asynchronous use of the classrooms. The researchers believe that the most crucial refinement for synchronous use of the simulation lies in changing the scaffolding of the role-play. Several pre-service teachers reported that their 'classes' seemed to be composed of only non-responsive 'naughty' children. The researchers present noted that pre-service teachers acting the 'naughty' role did get carried away with their naughtiness. Re-design of the role-plays were undertaken with more careful scripting and the provision of clearer directions. It is possible that the novelty of acting the role of a naughty child was responsible for the excessive behaviours displayed, but for the effectiveness of the role-play this needs to be structured more carefully t.

The researchers felt that defining the roles for the primary school students as 'naughty' and 'good' did not accurately depict what was required of the roles. The role-plays were renamed to 'on task' and 'off task' as would be found in a typical classroom. The roles were also altered to include passive and active roles. A pre-service teacher could be role-playing a passive 'on task' role and would generally get on and do his/her work. However, an active 'on task' role would require the pre-service teacher to participate in the lesson more enthusiastically. The same was true for 'off task' roles. If a student were passively 'off task', s/he would not be disrupting the class, but may not be participating when the teacher requested it. If a pre-service teacher's role was to be actively 'off task' s/he may have been required to actively not participate in a lesson, such as interrupting the teacher.

Finally, as noted above, improvements in the scaffolding of the role-plays were written into the instructions. Pre-service teachers were required to carry out their 'off task' roles only 20% of the time. This gave the teacher role the opportunity to conduct a lesson and only have to deal with 'off task' students for one fifth of the time. Also, in the first (pilot) iteration of role-plays half the class of students were 'good' and the other half 'naughty' roles. In the second iteration of role-plays, 'off task' roles were only assigned to 20% of the student roles. These improvements were noted in pre-service teacher responses to the 2012 survey where they were more thoughtful in the feedback. Statements such as 'being able to consider unexpected occurrences within the classroom and approaches in how they can be overcome' and 'looking at different ways to deal with interruptions' were reported as two benefits of using the VirtualPREX role-plays t.

6. Two Evolving Enhancements

One major innovation in 2012 is the ongoing development of bot supported role-play. Role-play is an important concept in teaching, but is mostly restricted by the need for multiple people (actors) being in the same space at the same time. However, it is possible, using modern software tools, to develop bots. The development of bots permits increased interaction as it is possible to have the bots reflect behaviours shown in role-plays where avatars have been controlled by the pre-service teachers. This interaction can occur either by recording such role-plays or by writing scripts about how to react to certain events. The depth of interaction depends on the underlying systems and their capability of interpreting modification to the environment and approximating the best possible reaction. The stages of interactivity are visually outlined in Figure 3.

In terms of the classroom, the most fundamental script for bots representing students would involve the bot sitting at a specific desk reflecting similar characteristics to a background actor without speaking or acting parts: for example, limited to performing typical tasks such as writing, listening, daydreaming or sleeping (Stage 1). With increasing complexity, bots *listen* for stimuli using sensory receptors and react according to environmental changes: for example, write stories, listen if movies or music is played or gather with others in response to group work (Stage 2). This can be controlled by advanced scripts triggered by key events.

Authenticity is further increased if bots behave according to real-world counterparts and demonstrate an *intelligent* reaction. Rather than requiring specific words, situations are further analysed to find appropriate reactions using past experience, advanced scripts and artificial intelligence (Stage 3). For example, if the student has a short attention span and requires some kind of stimuli, it will observe the teacher for integrated questions, exercises, or keywords of interest. Stimuli will create positive reactions (raising arm and answering the question based on an internal knowledge repository) or initiate negative behaviour (disturbing the class, falling asleep, day-dreaming). In Stage 4, the bots become individuals with a unique character that is recognisable. Students are no longer a nameless person, but become an individual who has certain ways of doing things, emotions, and other specifics that are unique to him or her.

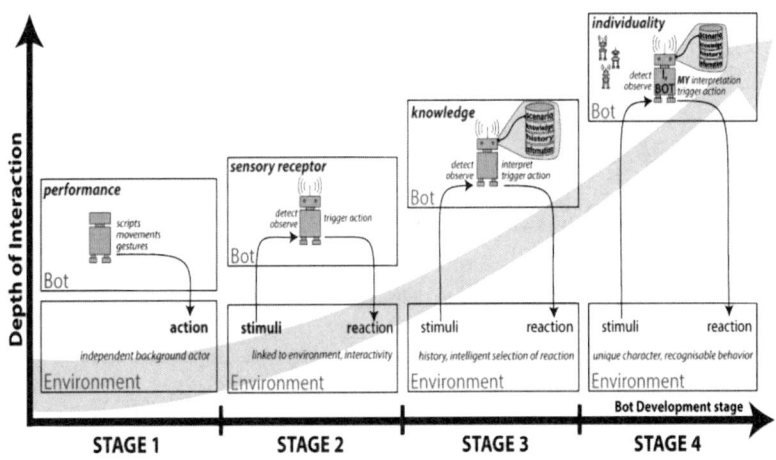

Figure 3: Stages of increased interaction.
(Available under Creative Commons 3.0 Australia).

For VirtualPREX and its focus on role-play with pre-service teachers, the bot development is staged with an increase in interactivity.[28] The inclusion of these types of bots would allow for role-play scenarios played out by a small number of real actors supplemented by these simple non-player characters (Figure 4). At this stage, bots display gestures to imitate students in a classroom.

Next scripts were introduced to increase the authenticity not only of the bots, but also of the environment and the role of the teacher, where one challenge is the interaction with more than two or three students at a time. Filling the classroom with interactive and reactive bots is crucial to increasing the authenticity. Therefore, we implemented simple, but with regard to the context and anticipated teaching scenarios, authentic scripts to emulate (potentially stressful) situations requiring some resolution method.

Figure 4: Teaching the Bots.
(Available under Creative Commons 3.0 Australia).

The schematic for automated role-play, shown in Figure 5, displays how a bot responds to certain stimuli from the teacher such as being spoken to by name or proximity. This schematic allows for bots to automatically move from 'on task' to 'off task' behaviour if there is no acknowledgement of them throughout a lesson. The inclusion of this capacity is intended to approximate what occurs in real-life classrooms. This schematic will be used to develop a range of scripts where different behaviours, requiring different teacher approaches, can be targeted.

The schematic shows the script for bots with three modes; on task, off task, and disruptive. In the beginning, the student is *on task,* but can change to *off task* based on a time period without proper stimuli. If the teacher reacts to the change of mode (using the student's name, moving closer, looking), the student might go back to *on task* or, after an additional time period, change to *disruptive* behaviour t. The time periods between changes follow a defined distribution. Additional stimuli to prevent a change of mode are not shown in the schematic, but include handing out books, assigning exercises or spending some time to explain problems.

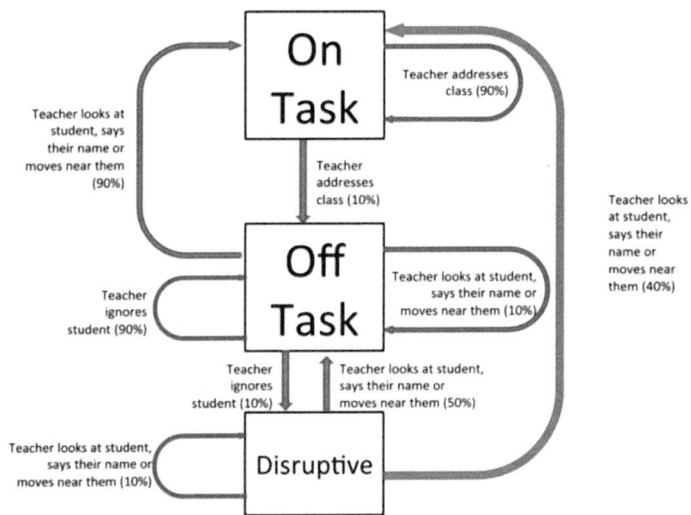

Figure 5: Schematic Outlining Role-play Scaffold for Bots
(Available under Creative Commons 3.0 Australia).

This addition of bots with these capabilities will enhance the experience for off-campus pre-service teachers who cannot always link up with other pre-service teachers for a 'live' role-play. In this scenario they will be able to go into a classroom and 'teach' on their own with bots taking the role of the children. Furthermore, this capacity for asynchronous teaching moves VirtualPREX into a different domain from those simulations which occur in on-campus workshops. It also differs from simulations such as TeachLivE which requires trained actors controlling avatar responses and thus synchronous engagement in the role-play,[29] but is somewhat similar to the approach used by researchers at the University of Nevada t.[30]

A second enhancement to VirtualPREX has been the development of a range of machinima. The first machinima have been created from the University of New England workshops – approximately 150 machinima in total from the combined 2011 and 2012 workshops. They have been developed for a range of teaching and learning purposes including assessment, both formative and summative. The machinima have been divided into several categories based on different learning areas such as English, numeracy, history, etc. This categorisation will enable educators to use the machinima in different ways for lessons or assessment tasks: for example, they can be used to reflect on teaching strategies or be used for peer review. The machinima are available for viewing on the VirtualPREX website (see http://www.virtualprex.com/machinima.html). Assessment of machinima is also found on the above website.

A second aspect of machinima development has been in the area of exemplar machinima (Figure 6). These machinima were semi-scripted and produced by experienced educators using audio.

Figure 6: Screenshot of Exemplar Machinima.
(Available under Creative Commons 3.0 Australia).

The purpose of these machinima was two-fold: to provide examples of sound strategies for classroom management and also to demonstrate to pre-service teachers and educators' ideas on how they could use such machinima. Pre-service teachers could use these machinima for reflective practice and educators could use them to assess pre-service teacher understanding of the efficacy of certain teaching strategies. Machinima were used as they provide a safe form of video without the ethical considerations that arise if filming children in real classrooms. The exemplar machinima are also displayed on the VirtualPREX website t.

7. Future

The pilot project has demonstrated that there are benefits to the VirtualPREX approach to the preparation of pre-service teachers prior to their exposure to real-life professional experience. In 2012, the major enhancement to the project was the updated and more rounded role-play session requirements for pre-service teachers. One other project member institution also undertook role-plays with their pre-service teachers to provide a comparison of experiences. The responses to their role-plays were similar to the responses of University of New England pre-service teachers in the 2012 iteration of the role-plays. In the future, the role-plays will be undertaken through a combination of 'live' role-play (with pre-service teachers undertaking all roles) and automated role-play (with bots). The bot technology can provide further effective support and sustainability for the learner and educator. As sensors and recording mechanisms are established to interact with the bots and observe real-world users or events, we are able to store sessions for immediate or later reuse. Reiners et al. describe several *gaming* mechanisms to improve the effectiveness of the environment for the learner and leverage the learning enhancement and experience in multiple ways; i.e. for reviews, feedback, or repetitive training of certain situations.[31] Among others, these mechanisms include: *rewind* to the start of a learning situation to evaluate other actions; *save points* to keep a bookmark at an interesting situation for later revisits (i.e. with an expert for demonstration); *replay* for review from multiple perspectives for reflection including mechanisms for annotation of the recorded sequences (e.g. to allow the pre-service teacher to record their reflections, or to allow feedback from supervisors). Inclusion of further gaming mechanisms also supports the perception of activities as fun and playful and are more likely to elicit attention and achieve educational results, consistent with gamification principles t.[32]

It is anticipated that self, peer and formal assessment possibilities, enhanced through role-play, bot development and machinima, will extend the current preparation of pre-service teachers for professional experience and create greater self-efficacy in those pre-service teachers.

8. Conclusion

The VirtualPREX project continues beyond 2012 with the classrooms, including bots and the role-play scenarios, becoming available to anyone who wishes to use them from 2013. 2012 saw the refinement of the classroom role-plays, bot scripting and machinima for assessment. The use of 3D virtual worlds for professional experience practice appears promising, particularly for off-campus pre-service teachers who do not typically have the opportunity to test their skills on their peers. Our intention is that pre-service teachers wishing to use the virtual world classrooms to practise their teaching skills will have a full suite of 'how to' information available to them. These will be available from the VirtualPREX website from 2013. More research into the pre-service teacher perceptions of the VirtualPREX classrooms has been undertaken throughout 2012 with the intention of ensuring that a viable 3D role-play classroom has been created and able to be used by others in the future. The efficacy of such use is attested to by a pre-service teacher who commented that 'this activity was highly valuable to my professional skills and confidence because it got me comfortable with teachers and peers, but most importantly the students. I had a rather difficult classroom, but believe I needed the challenge to push myself to strive well in the conditions'.

Notes

[1] Brent Gregory, et al., 'How Are Australian Higher Education Institutions Contributing to Change through Innovative Teaching and Learning in Virtual Worlds?' in *Changing Demands, Changing Directions. Proceedings ascilite Hobart 2011*, eds. Gary Williams, Peta Statham, Natalie Brown, and Ben Cleland (Hobart: The University of Tasmania and ascilite, 2011), 475-90. Viewed 12 December 2011, http://www.leishman-associates.com.au/ascilite2011/downloads/papers/Gregory -full.pdf.

[2] New Media Consortium and EDUCAUSE Learning Initiative, *The Horizon Report, 2007 Edition* (Austin, TX: New Media Consortium, 2007), 18.

[3] Larry Johnson, et al., *The 2010 Horizon Report* (Austin, TX: New Media Consortium, 2010), 4. Viewed 20 February 2011, http://www.nmc.org/pdf/2010-Horizon-Report.pdf.

[4] Steven Warburton, '*Second Life* in Higher Education: Assessing the Potential for and the Barriers to Deploying Virtual Worlds in Learning and Teaching', *British Journal of Educational Technology* 40, no. 3 (2009): 414-26.

[5] Pamela Grossman, *Learning to Practice: The Design of Clinical Experience* (Washington, DC: American Association of Colleges for Teacher Education and National Education Association, 2010); Kari Smith and Lilach Lev-Ari, 'The Place of the Practicum in Pre-Service Teacher Education: The Voice of the Students', *Asia-Pacific Journal of Teacher Education* 33, no. 3 (2005): 289-302.

[6] Richard Taffe and Sally Knipe, 'Professional Experience and Undergraduate's Self-Efficacy for Teaching', in *Teacher Education: Local and Global*, ed. Maxine Cooper (Surfers Paradise: Centre for Professional Development, Griffith University, 2005), 423. Viewed 20 February 2011, http://atea.edu.au/index.php?option=com_jdownloadsandItemid=132andview= finishandcid=556andcatid=80andm=0.

[7] Donald J. Boyd, et al., 'Teacher Preparation and Student Achievement', *Educational Evaluation and Policy Analysis* 31, no. 4 (2009): 416-40; Karen Swabey, Geraldine Castleton, and Dawn Penney, 'Meeting the Standards? Exploring Preparedness for Teaching', *Australian Journal of Teacher Education* 35, no. 8 (2010): 29-46.

[8] Prue Jolley and Angela Maplestone, 'Preservice Teacher Placements - Victoria 2011: Submission to the Productivity Commission Study into Schools Workforce from the National Association of Field Experience Administrators' (NAFEA - Victoria, 2011). Viewed 28 August, 2012, http://www.pc.gov.au/__data/assets/word_doc/0004/111010/sub001.doc.

[9] Sue C. O'Neill and Jennifer Stephensen, 'Teacher Classroom Behaviour Management Preparation in Undergraduate Primary Education in Australia: A

Web-Based Investigation', *Australian Journal of Teacher Education* 36, no. 10 (2011): 35-52.
[10] House of Representatives Standing Committee on Education and Vocational Training. *Top of the Class* (Canberra: Commonwealth of Australia, 2007), 73. Viewed 30 March 2008,
http://www.aph.gov.au/house/committee/evt/teachereduc/report.htm.
[11] Productivity Commission. 'Schools Workforce, Productivity Commission Research Report' (Canberra, 2012). Viewed 31 August, 2012,
http://www.pc.gov.au/_data/assets/pdf_file/0020/116651/schools-workforce.pdf.
[12] Donald R. Cruickshank, 'The Use of Simulation in Teacher Education: A Developing Phenomenon', *Journal of Teacher Education* 20, no. 1 (1969): 23-26.
[13] Cruickshank, 'Simulation in Teacher Education', 24.
[14] Lisa Dieker, et al., 'Virtual Classrooms: Star Simulator Building Virtual Environments for Teacher Training in Effective Classroom Management', *New Learning Technology SALT* 4 (2007): 4.
[15] Dieker, et al., 'Virtual Environments for Teacher Training', 1-22; Jean Ann Foley and Gretchen McAllister, 'Making It Real: Sim-School a Backdrop for Contextualizing Teacher Preparation', *AACE Journal* 13, no. 2 (2005): 159-77; Mark Girod and Gerald Girod, 'Simulation and the Need for Practice in Teacher Preparation', *Journal of Technology and Teacher Education* 16, no. 3 (2008): 307-37.
[16] Douglas Danforth, et al., 'Development of Virtual Patient Simulations for Medical Education'. *Journal of Virtual Worlds Research* 2, no. 2 (2009): 3-11.
[17] Lisa Carrington, Lisa Kervin, and Brian Ferry, 'Enhancing the Development of Pre-Service Teacher Professional Identity Via an Online Classroom Simulation', *Journal of Technology and Teacher Education* 19, no. 3 (2011): 351-68; Donguk Cheong, 'The Effects of Practice Teaching Sessions in *Second Life* on the Change in Pre-Service Teacher's Teaching Efficacy', *Computers* and *Education* 55, no. 2 (2010): 868-80.
[18] Greg Black, Kerrie Smith, and Reece Lamshed, *Hot Topic: ICT in Pre-Service Teacher Training: Strategic ICT Advisory Service* (Adelaide: Education.au Limited; Department of Education, Employment and Workplace Relations, 2009): 33. Viewed 12 December 2011,
http://www.educationau.edu.au/sites/default/files/SICTAS_HT_pre-service.pdf.
[19] Jan Herrington, Thomas C. Reeves, and Ron Oliver, *A Guide to Authentic e-Learning* (London and New York: Routledge, 2010).
[20] Kathleen W. Ingram and M. Katherine Jackson, 'Simulations as Authentic Learning Strategies: Bridging the Gap between Theory and Practice in Performance Technology', in *2004 Annual Proceedings - Chicago of Selected Research and Development Papers: Presented at the National Convention of the Association for Educational Communication and Technology, Volume 1*, eds.

Michael Simonson and Margaret Crawford (North Miami Beach, FL: Nova Southeastern University, 2004), 299.

[21] Jeanne Ellis Ormrod, *Human Learning*. 4th ed. (Upper Saddle River, NJ: Pearson Education Inc., 2004), 396.

[22] Paul Middleton and Maurice Price. *The GP Trainer's Handbook: An Educational Guide for Trainers by Trainers*. (London: Radcliffe Publishing, 2001).

[23] Christie Arbuckle and Emma Little, 'Teacher's Perceptions and Management of Disruptive Classroom Behaviour During the Middle Years (Years Five to Nine)', *Australian Journal of Educational* and *Developmental Psychology* 4, (2004): 59-70; Rebecca Giallo and Emma Little, 'Classroom Behaviour Problems: The Relationship between Preparedness, Classroom Experiences, and Self-Efficacy in Graduate and Student Teachers', *Australian Journal of Educational* and *Developmental Psychology* 3, (2003): 21-34.

[24] Productivity Commission, 'Schools Workforce', 2012; O'Neill and Stephensen, 'Teacher Classroom Behaviour Management Preparation', 35-52.

[25] Judy Peters, 'First Year Pre-Service Teachers' Learning About Behaviour Management', in *AARE International Education Research Conference - 2009*, ed. Peter Jeffrey (Canberra, ACT, 2009), 1-18.

[26] Jan Herrington and Ron Oliver, 'An Instructional Design Framework for Authentic Learning Environments', *Educational Technology Research and Development* 48, no. 3, (2000): 23-48.

[27] Table adapted from Yvonne Masters, et al., 'VirtualPREX - Providing Virtual Professional Experience for Pre-Service Teachers', in *Virtual Worlds in Open and Distance Education*, eds. Sue Gregory, Mark J. W. Lee, Barney Dalgarno, and Belinda Tynan (Accepted, forthcoming).

[28] Torsten Reiners, Sue Gregory, and Vicki Knox. 'Virtual Bots, Their Influence on Learning Environments and How They Increase Immersion', in *Virtual Worlds in Open and Distance Education*, eds. Sue Gregory, Mark J. W. Lee, Barney Dalgarno, and Belinda Tynan (Accepted, forthcoming).

[29] Synthetic Reality Lab, Institute for Simulations and Training, University of Central Florida, *TeachLivE* (TeachLivE, 2012). Viewed 16 January 2012, http://mclserver.eecs.ucf.edu/teachlive/index.php.

[30] Jennifer Mahon, et al., 'Using *Second Life* to Enhance Classroom Management Practice in Teacher Education', *Educational Media International* 47, no. 2 (2010): 121-34.

[31] Reiners, Torsten, et al. 'Operationalising Gamification in an Educational Authentic Environment', paper presented at the IADIS 2012 International Conference on International Higher Education, Perth, Australia, 2012.

[32] Torsten Reiners and Lincoln Wood, 'Immersive Virtual Environments to Facilitate Authentic Education in Logistics and Supply Chain Management', in

Learning Management Systems: Metrics, Standards, and Applications ed. Yefim Kats (Hershey, PA: IGI Global, Accepted, forthcoming).

Bibliography

Arbuckle, Christie, and Emma Little. 'Teacher's Perceptions and Management of Disruptive Classroom Behaviour During the Middle Years (Years Five to Nine)'. *Australian Journal of Educational* and *Developmental Psychology* 4, (2004): 59-70.

Black, Greg, Kerrie Smith, and Reece Lamshed. *Hot Topic: ICT in Pre-Service Teacher Training: Strategic ICT Advisory Service.* Adelaide: Education.au Limited; Department of Education, Employment and Workplace Relations, 2009.

Boyd, Donald J., Pamela Grossman, Hamilton Lankford, Susanna Loeb, and James Wyckoff. 'Teacher Preparation and Student Achievement'. *Educational Evaluation and Policy Analysis* 31, no. 4 (2009): 416-40.

Carrington, Lisa, Lisa Kervin, and Brian Ferry. 'Enhancing the Development of Pre-Service Teacher Professional Identity Via an Online Classroom Simulation'. *Journal of Technology and Teacher Education* 19, no. 3 (2011): 351-68.

Cheong, Donguk. 'The Effects of Practice Teaching Sessions in *Second Life* on the Change in Pre-Service Teacher's Teaching Efficacy'. *Computers* and *Education* 55, no. 2 (2010): 868-80.

Cruickshank, Donald R. 'The Use of Simulation in Teacher Education: A Developing Phenomenon'. *Journal of Teacher Education* 20, no. 1 (1969): 23-6.

Danforth, Douglas, Mike Procter, Robert Heller, Richard Chen, and Mary Johnson. 'Development of Virtual Patient Simulations for Medical Education'. *Journal of Virtual Worlds Research* 2, no. 2 (2009): 3-11.

Dieker, Lisa, Michael Hynes, Christopher Stapleton, and Charles Hughes. 'Virtual Classrooms: Star Simulator Building Virtual Environments for Teacher Training in Effective Classroom Management'. *New Learning Technology SALT* 4 (2007): 1-22.

Foley, Jean Ann, and Gretchen McAllister. 'Making It Real: Sim-School a Backdrop for Contextualizing Teacher Preparation'. *AACE Journal* 13, no.2 (2005): 159-77.

Giallo, Rebecca, and Emma Little. 'Classroom Behaviour Problems: The Relationship between Preparedness, Classroom Experiences, and Self-Efficacy in Graduate and Student Teachers'. *Australian Journal of Educational* and *Developmental Psychology* 3, (2003): 21-34.

Girod, Mark, and Gerald Girod. 'Simulation and the Need for Practice in Teacher Preparation'. *Journal of Technology and Teacher Education* 16, no. 3 (2008): 307-37.

Gregory, Brent, Sue Gregory, Denise Wood, Yvonne Masters, Mathew Hillier, Frederick Stokes-Thompson, Anton Bogdanovych, Des Butler, Lyn Hay, Jay Jay Jegathesan, Kim Flintoff, Stefan Schutt, Dale Linegar, Robyn Alderton, Andrew Cram, Ieva Stupans, Lindy McKeown Orwin, Grant Meredith, Debbie McCormick, Francesca Collins, Jenny Grenfell, Jason Zagami, Allan Ellis, Lisa Jacka, John Campbell, Ian Larson, Andrew Fluck, Angela Thomas, Helen Farley, Nona Muldoon, Ali Abbas, Suku Sinnappan, Katrina Neville, Ian Burnett, Ashleigh Aitken, Simeon Simoff, Sheila Scutter, Xiangyu Wang, Kay Souter, David Ellis, Mandy Salomon, Greg Wadley, Michael Jacobson, Anne Newstead, Gary Hayes, Scott Grant, and Alyona Yusupova. 'How Are Australian Higher Education Institutions Contributing to Change through Innovative Teaching and Learning in Virtual Worlds?' In *Changing Demands, Changing Directions. Proceedings ascilite Hobart 2011*, edited by Gary Williams, Peta Statham, Natalie Brown, and Ben Cleland, 475-90. Hobart, 2011. Viewed 12 December 2011. http://www.leishman-associates.com.au/ascilite2011/downloads/papers/Gregory-full.pdf.

Grossman, Pamela. *Learning to Practice: The Design of Clinical Experience* Washington, DC: American Association of Colleges for Teacher Education and National Education Association, 2010.

Herrington, Jan, and Ron Oliver. 'An Instructional Design Framework for Authentic Learning Environments'. *Educational Technology Research and Development* 48, no. 3 (2000): 23-48.

Herrington, Jan, Thomas C. Reeves and Ron Oliver. *A Guide to Authentic e-Learning*. London and New York: Routledge, 2010.

House of Representatives Standing Committee on Education and Vocational Training. *Top of the Class*. Canberra: Commonwealth of Australia, 2007.

Ingram, Kathleen W., and M. Katherine Jackson. 'Simulations as Authentic Learning Strategies: Bridging the Gap between Theory and Practice in Performance Technology'. In *2004 Annual Proceedings - Chicago of Selected Research and Development Papers: Presented at the National Convention of the Association for Educational Communication and Technology, Volume 1*, edited by Michael Simonson and Margaret Crawford, 297-307. North Miami Beach, FL: Nova Southeastern University, 2004.

Johnson, Larry, Alan Levine, Rachel S. Smith, and Sonja Stone. *The 2010 Horizon Report*. Austin, TX: New Media Consortium, 2010. Viewed 20 February 2011. http://www.nmc.org/pdf/2010-Horizon-Report.pdf.

Jolley, Prue, and Angela Maplestone. 'Preservice Teacher Placements - Victoria 2011: Submission to the Productivity Commission Study into Schools Workforce from the National Association of Field Experience Administrators'. NAFEA - Victoria, 2011. Viewed 28 August 2012. http://www.pc.gov.au/_data/assets/word_doc/0004/111010/sub001.doc.

Mahon, Jennifer, Bobby Bryant, Ben Brown, and Miran Kim. 'Using *Second Life* to Enhance Classroom Management Practice in Teacher Education'. *Educational Media International* 47, no. 2 (2010): 121-34.

Middleton, Paul, and Maurice Price. *The GP Trainer's Handbook: An Educational Guide for Trainers by Trainers*. London: Radcliffe Publishing, 2001.

New Media Consortium and EDUCAUSE Learning Initiative. *The Horizon Report, 2007 Edition*. Austin, TX: New Media Consortium, 2007.

O'Neill, Sue C., and Jennifer Stephensen. 'Teacher Classroom Behaviour Management Preparation in Undergraduate Primary Education in Australia: A Web-Based Investigation'. *Australian Journal of Teacher Education* 36, no. 10 (2011): 35-52.

Ormrod, Jeanne Ellis. *Human Learning*. 4th ed. Upper Saddle River, NJ: Pearson Education Inc., 2004.

Peters, Judy. 'First Year Pre-Service Teachers' Learning About Behaviour Management'. In *AARE International Education Research Conference - 2009*, edited by Peter Jeffrey, 1-18. Canberra, ACT, 2009.

Productivity Commission. 'Schools Workforce, Productivity Commission Research Report'. Canberra, 2012. Viewed 31 August 2012. http://www.pc.gov.au/__data/assets/pdf_file/0020/116651/schools-workforce.pdf.

Reiners, Torsten, Sue Gregory, and Vicki Knox. 'Virtual Bots, Their Influence on Learning Environments and How They Increase Immersion. In *Virtual Worlds in Open and Distance Education*, edited by Sue Gregory, Mark J.W. Lee, Barney Dalgarno, and Belinda Tynan. Accepted, forthcoming.

Reiners, Torsten, and Lincoln Wood. 'Immersive Virtual Environments to Facilitate Authentic Education in Logistics and Supply Chain Management'. In *Learning Management Systems: Metrics, Standards, and Applications*, edited by Yefim Kats. Hershey, PA: IGI Global, Accepted, forthcoming.

Reiners, Torsten, Lincoln Wood, Vanessa Chang, Jan Herrington, Christian Guetl, Hanna Terräs, and Sue Gregory. 'Operationalising Gamification in an Educational Authentic Environment'. Paper presented at the IADIS 2012 International Conference on International Higher Education, Perth, Australia, 2012.

Smith, Kari, and Lilach Lev-Ari. 'The Place of the Practicum in Pre-Service Teacher Education: The Voice of the Students'. *Asia-Pacific Journal of Teacher Education* 33, no. 3 (2005): 289-302.

Swabey, Karen, Geraldine Castleton, and Dawn Penney. 'Meeting the Standards? Exploring Preparedness for Teaching'. *Australian Journal of Teacher Education* 35, no.10 (2010): 29-46.

Synthetic Reality Lab, Institute for Simulations and Training, University of Central Florida. *TeachLivE*. TeachLivE, 2012. Viewed 16 January 2012. http://mclserver.eecs.ucf.edu/teachlive/index.php.

Taffe, Richard, and Sally Knipe. 'Professional Experience and Undergraduate's Self-Efficacy for Teaching'. In *Teacher Education: Local and Global*, edited by Maxine Cooper, 423-429. Surfers Paradise: Centre for Professional Development, Griffith University, 2005. Viewed 20 February 2011. http://atea.edu.au/index.php?option=com_jdownloadsandItemid=132andvie w=finishandcid=556andcatid=80andm=0>.

Warburton, Steven. '*Second Life* in Higher Education: Assessing the Potential for and the Barriers to Deploying Virtual Worlds in Learning and Teaching'. *British Journal of Educational Technology* 40, no. 3 (2009): 414-26.

Yvonne Masters is a Lecturer in Professional Classroom Practice in the School of Education at the University of New England. Yvonne's research interests are professional experience, online learning and virtual worlds, particularly focusing on distance education students.

Sue Gregory is a long term adult educator and Lecturer in ICT in the School of Education at UNE and Chair of the Australian and New Zealand Virtual Worlds Working Group. Since 2007 she has been researching *Second Life* with her students with respect to the various learning opportunities that virtual worlds provide and has been involved in many projects on the efficacy of virtual worlds.

Torsten Reiners is a senior lecturer at Curtin University, Perth, Western Australia. His research and teaching experiences are in the areas of clustering and mining large data sets, online algorithms and incorporation of bio-analogous meta-heuristics in simulations models, Emerging Technologies in Information Systems with focus on interconnected (virtual) environments.

Vicki Knox is currently a project officer at the University of New England on an Australian Learning and Teaching Council funded project on using 3D virtual worlds with pre-service teachers. She has worked for many years as a research assistant in Linguistics, predominantly in the areas of NSM semantics, pidgin and creole languages and second dialect acquisition.

Barney Dalgarno is Sub-Dean, Learning and Teaching within the Faculty of Education at Charles Sturt University. His research interests include: implications of the 'Net Generation' for university learning and teaching; the relationship between interactivity and cognition in multimedia and virtual environments; the impact of electronic whiteboards on Primary and Secondary School teaching practice; and pre-service primary teachers' development in preparedness to use ICT in the classroom.

Acknowledgements
The authors would like to acknowledge the contribution of the following: fellow-researchers Geoffrey Crisp (RMIT), Heinz Dreher (Curtin University) and Matthew Campbell (ACU). They also acknowledge Deanne Gannaway (University of Queensland). Support for this publication has been provided by the Australian Government Office for Learning and Teaching (OLT) and the Australian

Government Department of Industry, Innovation, Science, Research and Tertiary Education through the DEHub Project. The views expressed in this publication do not necessarily reflect the views of the Australian Government Office for Learning and Teaching.

Bringing Playfulness and Engagement to Language Training Using Virtual Worlds: Student Experiences, Results and Best Practices from a Virtual Language Course

Eero Palomäki and Emma Nordbäck

Abstract

Three-dimensional (3-D) virtual worlds (VWs) offer new value creation and business possibilities for globally distributed language training. They incorporate playfulness, social interaction and exploration. In this study, experiences and the best practices of implementing language training were gathered from a language-training case study at Aalto University. A highly graphical VW, Second Life, was used to activate the students and their chemistry vocabulary. Multi-user VWs provide a way for students to practice normal work-life events such as meetings, presentations, or job interviews in a foreign language. In this experiment, 33 intermediate-level students participated in the course, which included a small-talk situation of introducing a new worker into their new workplace. The participating students then completed a laboratory exercise in a foreign language. The course succeeded in motivating the students, and most of them enjoyed virtual learning. The students became engaged in social situations and used foreign language in task-based communication as a tool for achieving goals. They acted more relaxed than in a classroom environment and many felt that the level of interaction was higher than in traditional classroom teaching. The results revealed that it is possible to teach a foreign language with authentic work tasks in a simulated environment. According to the teachers, the students used foreign language more openly in the VW, without worrying about making mistakes. Unfortunately, technological shortcomings were still a hindrance in the effort to implement language training in VWs successfully, and the teachers need pedagogical and technical support.

Key Words: Virtual worlds, language training, case study, best practice, higher education.

*****

1. Introduction

Language education in three-dimensional (3-D) virtual worlds (VWs) is a growing field of distributed education providing opportunities beyond traditional classroom boundaries. VWs can be defined as communication systems in which multiple users share the same 3-D digital space, obtain information, navigate, manipulate objects and interact with each other via avatars.[1] This means that the participants can 'be present' from around the world. VWs enable new value creation and business possibilities for globally distributed language training. They offer opportunities to participate in interactive events, be involved with communities of native speakers and the opportunity to network. Language training can be incorporated into simulating processes and operational applications. Holmberg and Huvila report that the use of Second Life[2] brings advantages (especially to teamwork) when compared to traditional lectures.[3] They note advantageous features such as the physical presence of avatars, the possibility of real-time communication, and the existence of a shared local space. These features lead to a more realistic feel of presence than can be achieved with discussion forums or chat rooms. This is in line with Jones, Morales, and Knezek who noted that Second Life brings the good sides of face-to-face education to distance education.[4]

Graham defines the term 'blended learning system' to mean a combination of face-to-face instruction with computer-mediated instruction.[5] The term seems relevant to the use of VWs in education. The reported advantages are that blended learning allows more effective pedagogical practices, greater flexibility (i.e., with adult students), and the possibility to achieve cost-effectiveness.[6] Eschenbrenner et al. identified the advantages of using 3-D VWs in education to be: a risk-free environment, enhanced collaboration and communication, engagement of learners, utilization of an alternative space for conducting courses and associated tasks, and visualization of difficult content.[7]

VWs have been described as more immersive and engaging than traditional technologies.[8] Immersion has reportedly led to improvements of abstract mental activities and help in creating conceptual understanding.[9] Immersion can activate the students and their vocabulary around a certain subject by providing visual representations of the vocabulary and incorporating playfulness, social interaction and exploration. As VWs are multi-user environments providing a way to build quite realistic scenes, they fit well in emergency scenario training. These scenarios can act as a platform or tool for language training, as the participants need to be active and use the language to escape or follow pre-defined protocols in an emergency situation. Other useful situations include normal work-life events like meetings, presentations or job interviews in a foreign language. There are some existing services already using VWs for language training. One of them is English City by a UK school called Language Lab.[10] It claims 1,000 paid student subscribers and 50,000 users in over 70 countries.

Increased engagement is one benefit attached to the use of VWs in education. According to Mason, students are more engaged in learning tasks and spend more time thinking and discussing the subject material.[11] Richter, Anderson-Inman, and Frisbee noticed that immersion into another world is a unique feature of VWs and that learning through an avatar is more interactive and experiential than education conveyed through symbols and words.[12] VWs can increase enthusiasm for learning and introduce students to an experience that they may never have realized otherwise.[13] Holmberg and Huvila also found this to be true for students who spend a lot of time in areas that include speakers of foreign languages.[14] The students have practiced their written and spoken French there. Holmberg and Huvila suggest there is some potential in this kind of motivation. As learners are allowed to interact with information using avatars, this facilitates constructivist-based learning activities according to Dickey.[15] Dickey states that the interaction with virtual objects can be helpful in developing a stronger conceptual understanding, depending on the content. This can be seen as an advantage for language training, where conceptual understanding is of considerable importance.

Another suggested benefit of VWs, is enhanced collaboration and communication. VWs provide a platform for collaborative and cooperative learning that is valued in the socio-constructivist paradigm.[16] The creation of an avatar has been found to increase the individual user's sense of tele-presence or co-presence, to improve communication, as well as social and educational experiences in VWs.[17] Bronack, Riedl, and Tashner list the benefits of VWs in education to be 'a sense of presence, immediacy, movement, artifacts, and communications unavailable within traditional Internet-based learning environments.'[18] They also describe that they were able to interact with students in 'more fluid and natural ways',[19] allowing students to select their own paths of learning, resources, and activities, and are 'encouraging cross-class collaboration.'[20] His students reported the interactions with other students to be stimulating and the experience to be enriching. Furthermore, it has been reported from a course that was partly held in Second Life that barriers for participation in discussions in Second Life was lower than in face–to–face lectures according to 83 percent of the respondents.[21]

2. Case Description: Language Course at Aalto University

In this case study, experiences and best practices were gathered from two parallel language course implementations at Aalto University.[22] The courses were mandatory Swedish courses for the Finnish students, and they included basic Swedish grammar and technical vocabulary of the students' major subject, chemistry. They are geared toward intermediate-level students.

The goals of the case study were to find out: 1) how to motivate students to use foreign language more freely and openly (a major challenge in current teaching), 2) how to activate technical vocabulary in a real workspace context and authentic work-life tasks, and 3) how to change student attitude towards using a foreign language as a tool for achieving goals, not just as a study subject. This study explored how to motivate language learners and their technical vocabulary with playfulness, social interaction, and exploration using a highly graphical VW. In this experiment the students used foreign language in a small-talk situation of introducing a new worker into their new workplace, which was followed by their taking part in a laboratory exercise. The learning results, the students' experiences, and the results of two teacher interviews are reported. In addition a support course model for teachers is created based on the results of the empirical part.

A virtual chemistry laboratory called LabLife3D[23] was used as a learning environment. LabLife3D is housed in the archipelago of Aalto University in the VW Second Life and is freely accessible for visitors. There are laboratory equipment modeled from real-life photographs and the layout is planned with the help of subject experts. Two interactive learning scenarios have been created into the laboratory. In the microbiology scenario the students work with viruses in a cleanroom facility, and in the chemistry scenario they practice laboratory safety measures. The students used this virtual laboratory as a context for foreign language usage. Although the participants in this study were students, the environment and tasks are comparable to work life challenges and work life language training. In total, four VW sessions were held in each group between February and April 2011. See Table 1 for structure and content of the VW sessions of the course.

Table 1: Structure and content of the VW sessions of the course.

Session 1
• Software (VW client) training in a foreign language • Groups of 20 and 13, a total of 33 students
Session 2
• Group exploration and diary reporting of far-away places • In pairs, total of 20 students
Session 3
• Introduction to a virtual laboratory – Role-play: new employee orientation • Groups of 3-4 students, total of 33 students
Session 4
• Activity in a workplace setting – performing a microbiology laboratory experiment • Groups of 3-4 students, total of 14 students

The teachers reported problems with nearly graduated students whose degree programs had only one Swedish course remaining. They had already begun their careers, and were expected to come to the campus for two hours of Swedish lessons. That proved problematic, and the teachers hoped to test out new distance learning solutions in addition to the old ones they were using. Shy students were another problem they had, since they find it difficult to give a presentation in front of other people. The third related issue is that the students were set to be divided into subject groups in autumn 2011, and the teachers wondered how to teach chemistry vocabulary and conversation skills more efficiently. These are the reasons why the teachers wanted to try out virtual worlds. Through their own interest they had contacted some people from Aalto University Second Life virtual world group; because they felt they needed some help to implement the courses. The need and excitement came from the teachers.

The decision to use VWs in these courses was made only after the Swedish courses had begun. Thus, the students in the courses didn't know that there was a four time virtual training part included, when they chose to participate in the course. Both courses included work-at-home sessions, where the students would do exercises independently. The virtual training part replaced some of those sessions. The teacher of course 1 told the students that these sessions were mandatory (course 1), while another offered students the option of volunteering for a virtual training session (course 2). Counted together, 33 students participated.

3. Research Methods and Design

For the analysis of the language course we used a questionnaire with open-ended questions about students' experiences in one of the courses (n = 16), and a questionnaire for measurement of immersion in both of the courses (n = 33). All Second Life sessions were recorded, but these recordings have been excluded from this analysis. After sessions 3 and 4, the students had a vocabulary exam from the word list they were given between sessions 2 and 3. The exam was held for both of the courses and for a comparison group (control group) that used traditional learning methods.

The transfer from the traditional classroom teaching to virtual language training sets requirements and challenges for teachers. The two teachers participating were interviewed about their experiences after the course. They were asked how they felt before, during, and after the course to give some insight into how the teachers think about using this new technology. Both of the teachers have been interested in computers for a long time and have around 10 years of language teaching experience.

One of the interviews (the teacher of course 1) was a face-to-face interview in a cafe, and the other was a phone interview (the teacher of course 2). During the interviews, the interviewer wrote notes at the same time, but both interviews were recorded in order to enable transcription and as a backup. The interview was a semi-structured interview. The interview structure is shown in Appendix C.

4. Student Questionnaire Results and Analysis

The course succeeded in activating the students. They had an interaction inside the VW using tools familiar to them, such as chat and Skype. The environment helped to provide them with ideas, vocabulary, places to visit, and the arrangement of interactive situations and tasks. Based on the feedback, the students felt quite immersed (M = 2.94 on a scale 1 - 5, SD = 0.72) in the environment and felt more open and free to communicate than in a traditional classroom. Students made jokes and laughed a lot during the classes, and the atmosphere was relaxed. Most found this way of studying interesting, but some didn't like it. A more detailed mapping of student experiences is presented in Table 2.

Table 2: Student feedback on the virtual language course.

Category	Summarized student comments
Expectations	☐ 13 % had bad expectations, but were positively surprised ☐ 81 % did not have any expectations
Playfulness	☐ 31 % thought that it was more playful than classroom lectures ☐ 63 % were more relaxed than in classroom lectures
Freedom / exploration	☐ 63 % liked the exercise where they could venture out freely and chat with their friends better ☐ 19% liked the prepared task better
Interaction and activation	☐ 38 % considered the amount of interaction to be more, 25 % less, 13 % same amount, 13 % said that it depends on the situation ☐ 56 % were more active, 25 % were less active, 19 % said that it depends on the situation
Technical problems	☐ 67 % encountered technical problems in Second Life, e.g., the program crashed, the audio did not work or the computer rebooted
Learning outcomes	☐ 44 % learned to discuss better in Swedish, 38 % learned new words, and others mentioned only the use of Second Life (18 %)
The purpose of use	☐ 69 % would use it for discussions (learning of communication in a different language) ☐ 19 % would use it for learning vocabulary ☐ 12 % would use it for meeting people
Future use	☐ 38 % think that VWs will be used in the future for teaching, 25 % think that VWs will be used, but that it will require further development before it can be used, and 19% think VWs will not be used ☐ 47 % would recommend language learning in VWs for their friends, 27 % would recommend it after the technology has been developed further and 20 % would not recommend it

The overall attitude towards virtual teaching from the students was positive. They liked the freedom in the adventure exercise (63 %) and they found the tasks as a good way to practice conversation skills. The students felt engaged and most students (56%) said that they were more active than usual. Several students (38 %) considered the level of interaction to be higher in the VW compared to classroom teaching, although there were also students that considered the amount of interaction to be less (25 %). One student described the amount of interaction as 'dependent on the training situation, Second Life doesn't force interaction like a classroom does'. According to this view, the virtual learning situation did not enhance interaction per se, which implies for careful planning of the training tasks in order to activate the students.

Most of the students (63%) felt more relaxed in the VW compared to classroom teaching. The students liked the exploration task, text chat, and diaries of the existing locations inside the VW and felt that the atmosphere was more genuine of a real language usage situation than in a classroom. However, several students mentioned that they would have perceived more value in tying the exercises to their own field of work and the work environment. Furthermore, some students mentioned that the ability to speak to native Swedish speakers would be the ideal way to learn the language.

Half of the students would recommend the course for their peers (47 %), and additional 27 % would recommend it after some technological improvements would be made. Most (63 %) think that VWs will be used in the future for language training. They felt that it was a nice variety for traditional teaching and especially a good way to practice conversation skills (69 %), but no one wanted it to replace traditional classroom teaching completely. A student mentioned that he 'believe that VWs will become more common in teaching in the future, but as a help tool' and another student thought 'VWs can be used as a voluntary supplementary aid'. The use of VWs in language teaching is thus mainly restricted to an additional aid to traditional classroom teaching. When the students were asked to compare the VW classes to normal classroom teaching, their experiences varied from good to bad. Some comments of the students were; 'it felt more difficult to concentrate on teaching', 'it is more difficult when you don't see the others face-to-face and more time goes to the regulating everything', 'in a way it is nicer when you can participate from wherever', 'variety is refreshing, there is something good in both', 'the talk atmosphere was more real' and 'VW- classes are more free, but at the same time additional stimuli were disturbing'.

When it comes to learning outcomes, 44 % of the students mentioned that they learned to speak better in their foreign language (Swedish), others (38 %) learned new words, and some students (18 %) merely mentioned that they have learned to use Second Life. These subjective learning outcomes go hand-in-hand with the applications for which students would use VW-teaching. Most students (69 %) would use VW-teaching for discussions in order to learn communication skills in a foreign language, others (19 %) for learning of vocabulary and some (12 %) for meeting new people. The learning results were also objectively measured with a vocabulary test. The starting level was assumed to be uniform, because of the highly specific vocabulary. The list of words to be learned was given to the students at the beginning of the virtual training part of the course. They were not specifically told that there was a test coming. The test results are shown in Table 3.

Table 3: Vocabulary test results from the two courses and a control group.

	Course 1 (n = 12)	Course 2 (n = 20)	Control group (n = 20)
Average score (0-10)	5.8	3.5	3.5
Standard deviation	2.5	2.0	2.0

We can see from the results that course 1 got better results than the control group, and that course 2 got an identical result with the control group. Based on this limited sample, it cannot be argued that virtual training provides better learning results than traditional classroom teaching.

5. Teacher Interview Results

This chapter will report the results of the teacher interviews. One driver for the teachers has been the upcoming change of student groups in language courses. In autumn 2011 the courses were changed to include only students of certain subjects. This made it possible to use subject-specific vocabulary, and trains students to use a foreign language in professional situations. It could be said, that this is the purpose of university language training. As virtual worlds make it possible to have the training sessions in a chosen environment, such as in a factory, in a meeting room, or in a chemistry lab, teachers can transfer the classroom learning experience to an environment relevant to the specific student group.

The teachers found creating the 3-D virtual training course time-consuming and demanding. But in the interviews they also brought up that now, with the help of the existing 4-session course structure, it is easier to arrange the virtual teaching again in the future and modify it to their needs. Also, they might need to learn new ways of working and teaching in the first implementation, but after this course they are already more experienced. They both reported that it was quite difficult to acquire any training from the university for the needed software skills or pedagogical methods.

They also reported that virtual worlds added variety to their teaching. Also the student feedback reported that students felt that some variety had been added to the course. Teachers felt that learning to use this kind of teaching tools improves them in the professional sense.

Distributed learning is one reason they tried virtual teaching. After the course they felt that this way of teaching would work in a fully distributed course without classroom sessions. However, in that case the students should know how to use the software before the course. The teachers would like to have the first introduction session in a classroom. They thought that this way of learning would be good for technology students.

One change the teachers want to make is adding more virtual world sessions to the course. In the case of the session discussed herein there were four sessions, but they would like to have five or six sessions spread more evenly through the course. This would allow more opportunities for the students to utilize their new virtual world skills.

Teachers didn't comment on whether they felt students needed to meet in the real world, but expressed that generally this might make cooperation easier. The teachers noticed that the students tried to fill quiet times by speaking up. Combining good and not-so-good students in to the same group seemed to help spark up the discussion. In technology school there are many shy students that find it hard to give presentations in a foreign language in front of other students. Virtual worlds allow them to use the language more easily, as the avatar acts as a shield for them. Such alternative roles for students are also used in some alternative teaching methods such as suggestopedia. The teachers felt that some of the shy student groups could adopt this kind of tool. Such students could get the conversation going in the virtual environment and then transfer the skills and courage to the real world. The students could also use the tool to connect to native speakers from another country.

The teachers' interviews reported that the amount of interaction in the virtual worlds were equal to that of everyday classroom teaching. However, the student feedback showed signs that the students had more courage to talk during the exercises than in the classic classroom setting. This could be related to the fact that many of the sessions were held in small groups of only 2-3 persons, and so the rest of the classroom could not see or listen to their conversations. Also, these exercises were presented as practice situations for the students, and the students were told that they would not be graded. Instead the result of these sessions was measured in the end in the form of the amount of learned words. This is also in more in line with the view that the other teacher had, that language should be a tool and not the object; hence she tries to encourage the students to speak and use the language, even though they make mistakes. This virtual tool suits this ideology well in her opinion, as it made the situations more real and authentic, and the students have to manage themselves in these situations using the language as a tool. It didn't matter so much, if their language was not perfect, as long as they used it to achieve the goal of introducing a new worker or performing some practical chemistry laboratory tests. The teacher felt that in these sessions there was more intimate, genuine and authentic interaction using the foreign language than in a classroom.

The teachers have been using other online tools before virtual worlds. However, they feel the earlier tools do not begin best for the task, and have been looking for alternatives. They have been using Skype as well, for real-time audio conversations, but they feel that the virtual worlds offer the advantage of students feeling the presence of others (in the form of avatars) also in the quiet moments while thinking of what to say.

One of the teachers emphasized the role of planning in making the learning environments the best possible quality. The most important tasks are course planning, session planning, and continuous reporting during the course. This way the teacher stays up-to-date on how the students are doing and if they are completing the tasks. She also felt that good instructions and task-type-selection makes the learning situations more student-driven. This encourages the students to take responsibility for language usage, helping them to complete any given tasks. All in all, both teachers wanted to continue using the virtual worlds in their future teaching.

6. Discussion and Best Practices

Our results showed VWs being a suitable tool for language learning. Students' experiences were positive overall, and most of the students found the learning experience to be more relaxed (63%), interactive (38%) and motivational (56%) than traditional classroom lectures. These findings are in line with Eschenbrenner et al. and Richter et al. among others.[24] The findings also indicate that the goal of motivating students to use foreign language more freely and openly was reached. Students noticed improvements in their discussion skills in foreign language (44%) and most students (69%) would use VWs for this aim. Learning outcomes from the vocabulary exam were furthermore the same or slightly better than the results of the control group that used traditional learning methods. This could indicate interaction with virtual objects being helpful in developing a stronger conceptual understanding, also stated by Dickey.[25] This shows that our second aim of activating technical vocabulary in a real workspace context with authentic work-life tasks was achieved, at least to some extent. However, this would need more data to be confirmed. Moreover, the quite high level of immersion (M = 2.94 on a scale 1 - 5, SD = 0.72) experienced among the students could have contributed to the higher learning outcomes. This is in line with results of Bowman et al. (2009), which found immersion to be valuable in the improvement of memorization performance. This means that students' vocabulary was successfully activated in a real workspace context. However, it should be asked whether the vocabulary exam is the right way to measure the learning results. As the students claimed, they might have improved their discussion skills in having ad-hoc discussions, gained some courage to have discussion in a foreign language, and learned to identify and connect vocabulary with real-looking objects in the laboratory. A simple vocabulary test does not measure this learning, but can only indicate that some learning has taken place. Minogue, Gail Jones, Broadwell, and Oppewall challenge paper and pencil as a method of evaluation and call for the development of alternative evaluation methods for interaction in VWs.[26] We suggest that evaluation could take place already at the time of the task, and could be thought to be a goal-based scenario. The students would advance together towards a shared goal, and the speed or end product could be evaluated. The students could also fill out a self-evaluation or a diary report.

The teachers liked the students having two different kinds of tasks: one classroom assignment and one pair assignment. In the classroom contact sessions teachers and experts were helping the students. One of the teachers found the teaching sessions to be a little confusing, and would like to prepare the students better before the sessions. For example, students need time to familiarize themselves with the environment and the vocabulary. In addition, she noted that if this preparation were optional, not everyone would do it. In the pair assignment the students used the environment on their own time, working in pairs. They reported later to the teacher about their adventures using a diary. There are exercises for both session types. Role-playing and the chemistry practical exercise are not suitable for classroom sessions, as only one group can reasonably do them at a time. As the students liked the free exploration and the diary task, it might not be necessary to create any places in the VW but only use existing places. Sessions 3 and 4 were completed on the university premises in order to validate the research setting and allow data collection. The participating students suggested that this kind of arrangement did not allow them to take part from off campus, hence making a strong advantage of distance learning void. One thought that the environment could be used to have conversations with real natives, otherwise it is not useful. These comments remind the teachers to ponder for which type of exercises the environments are good tools and plan accordingly.

There were two main challenges in implementing the course: the problems with technical support in a centrally managed IT environment and the lack of pedagogic support for the teachers. The Second Life software needs quite frequent updates in order for the students to be able to log into the VW. It was required for the course personnel to periodically check if there were new updates, and then ask IT support to install them on the centrally managed classroom computers; otherwise the students might not be able to log in. In the first session of course 1 the software was not the latest version, which might have been the reason for some of the problems encountered. The older version might have been the cause of the blue screen errors and rebooting of the computers during the lessons. It disturbed the lecture when half of the computers in the classroom had to be rebooted. However, the students were quite patient, but the problem affected their experiments with virtual language learning negatively to some extent.

Another challenge was the lack of experience of the teachers to plan and implement a course utilizing VWs. The teachers had hoped to have some support from the university or a peer group that could give them ideas for planning the training. They liked the possibility to plan the course together with their peer and a VW expert. In fact, they stated that extra resources during the planning and implementation phases were crucial in getting the course implemented successfully. Often a qualified expert is not available in a university environment, but the university could support the teachers by providing such an expert for one or two sessions. This would help them get a better understanding of what kind of activities could and should be used in VWs. The teachers also reported that it was hard to find work time for the extra planning that the usage of VWs requires. However after having planned a course once, they can use the same structure again in future courses.

The interview results revealed the consensus that support is needed for the implementation process of the new tool as a part of an existing course. The teachers liked the process of creating ideas in a group with someone who has experience of virtual world teaching. At the same time, they felt that they got support from their peers, as there was two of them present in this case study. Now, the teachers added the virtual training sessions as a part of their old course. This is not the only good way to do it: it is possible to plan a completely new course using virtual world environments. However, in the interviews it became clear that the teachers would have had a lot of trouble changing the course independently. If some support were to be offered, it should focus on how teachers can organize the course independently.

Based on the aforementioned need for support, a course was planned in cooperation with the participating teachers. The course includes five sessions, and it enables a teacher who is new to virtual language training to plan their own course or at least get some initial ideas of how they could utilize virtual training in their own work. The implementation process of adapting a new technology is quite fast, and this course has been planned to make this process easier and faster. This course was planned especially for language teachers. The basic idea was to involve the teacher in the virtual world, give them experiences of training situations planned and implemented by others, and to challenge them to plan and implement a training situation of their own. The five sessions and their goals are described in Table 4.

One of the important side results of the project was the creation of motivation inside Aalto University to push the educational use of VWs forward in the university. Collaboration was created between the language center of the Aalto University School of Science and Technology and the Virtual and Mobile Work research unit, as well as between the language center and the LabLife3D project, which provided help in the use of their virtual laboratory in language training. It takes time for the experience of using VWs in training to reach maturity, and this process received some healthy momentum by way of this case at Aalto University. The use of VWs is going forward with more students participating than before. A similar virtual language course will be held again this semester at Aalto University and a tandem language course between Swedish native speaking students and Finnish native speaking students is planned to take place in Second Life next autumn. Students´ motivation and thresholds to participate in foreign language discussions in VWs is a subject that should be investigated more in order to shed light on how VWs add value to the pedagogical aspect. We believe that VWs and aspects such as anonymity can lower the threshold for discussing in a foreign language, which in turn can lead to more interaction, more words exchanged and a higher quality of education. Our result supported this: more interaction was tracked and the atmosphere was more relaxed than in normal classroom teaching.

Table 4: Training course for language teachers. Sessions, classroom/virtual, and the session content and goals.

1 Introduction and pedagogy – Classroom

To familiarize the teachers with the software. They are asked to complete a set of actions, so that after the session they all have a virtual world account, can log in to the world, use voice and text chat functions and travel around a given virtual world. Additionally there is a presentation about pedagogical approaches to virtual world teaching, and a few pedagogical lenses (tools) that the teachers can bring up when developing ideas of possible teaching methods.

2. Searching for locations and visiting them in groups – Virtual

In the second session the teachers travel in small groups of 2-3 persons around five locations in the virtual environment. They discuss the places and their suitability as educational environments in voice or text chat. The list of places is provided for them, but they can replace a given place with a choice of their own if they wish.

3. Arrange an interesting teaching session - Classroom

From the five places the groups visit, they have to choose one, where they plan a teaching session together with their group to be held for the other groups.

4. Teaching sessions - Virtual

Here the groups from the previous session carry out their short teaching sessions. This gives the groups their first experience of facilitating training in a virtual environment, and gives observing groups a chance to see examples of how other groups approach virtual training.

5. Feedback and brainstorming for own course – Classroom

The course's virtual-world-training expert gives feedback from the group teaching sessions and their feedback is shared with the whole group. After the feedback, the groups brainstorm ideas one-by-one for the courses of the teachers in each small group. This way the teachers get peer support and ideas from others from their own course implementation.

Notes

[1] Eva-Lotta. Sallnäs, 'Effects of Communication Mode on Social Presence, Virtual Presence, and Performance in Collaborative Virtual Environments,' *Presence* 14.4 (2005): 434-449; Nick Yee and Jeremy Bailenson, 'The Proteus Effect: The Effect of Transformed Self-Representation on Behavior,' *Human Communication Research* 33.3 (2007): 271-290.

[2] Second Life, 'Second Life Official Site - Virtual Worlds, Avatars, Free 3D Chat,' Accessed 3 September 2013, http://www.secondlife.com.

[3] Kim Holmberg and Isto Huvila, 'Learning together Apart: Distance Education in a Virtual World,' *First Monday* 13.10 (2008).

[4] James Greg Jones, Cesareo Morales and Gerald A. Knezek, '3-Dimensional Online Learning Environments: Examining Attitudes toward Information Technology between Students in Internet-Based 3-Dimensional and Face-to-Face Classroom Instruction,' *Educational Media International* 42.3 (2005): 219-236.

[5] Charles Graham, 'Blended Learning Systems: Definition, Current Trends, and Future Directions,' *Handbook of Blended Learning: Global Perspectives, Local Designs*, ed. Curtis Bonk and Charles Graham (San Francisco, CA: Pfeiffer, 2006).

[6] Charless Graham, S. Allen and D. Ure, 'Blended Learning Environments: A Review of the Research Literature,' (Unpublished Manuscript, Provo, UT, 2003).

[7] Brenda Eschenbrenner, Fiona Fui-Hoon Nah and Keng Siau, '3-D Virtual Worlds in Education: Applications, Benefits, Issues, and Opportunities,' *Journal of Database Management* 19.4 (2008): 91-110.

[8] Molly Wasko, et al., 'Stepping into the Internet: New Ventures in Virtual Worlds,' *MIS Quarterly* 35.3 (2001): 645-652.

[9] Doug A. Bowman, et al., 2009. 'Higher Levels of Immersion Improve Procedure Memorization Performance,' In *Proceedings of Joint Virtual Reality Conference*, 121-128. doi: http://dx.doi.org/10.2312/EGVE/JVRC09/121-128.

[10] Languagelab.com, 'Virtual Environments, Real Training,' Accessed September 3, 2013. http://www.languagelab.com.

[11] Hilary Mason, 2007. 'Experiential Education in Second Life,' In *Proceedings of the Second Life Education Workshop 2007*, 14-18.

[12] Jonathon Richter, Lynne Anderson-Inman and Mindy Frisbee. (2007). 'Critical Engagement of Teachers in Second Life: Progress in the SaLamander Project,' In *Proceedings of the Second Life Education Workshop*, 2007, 19-26.

[13] Andrea Foster, 'Professor Avatar,' *Chronicle of Higher Education* 54.4 (2007): A24-A26.

[14] Holmberg and Huvila, 'Learning together Apart:'.

[15] Michele D. Dickey, 'Three-Dimensional Virtual Worlds and Distance Learning: Two Case Studies of Active Worlds as a Medium for Distance Education,' *British Journal of Educational Technology* 36.3 (2005): 439-451.

[16] Michele D. Dickey, 'Brave New (Interactive) Worlds: A Review of the Design Affordances and Constraints of Two 3D Virtual Worlds as Interactive Learning Environments,' *Interactive Learning Environments* 13.1-2 (2005): 121-137; Michele D. Dickey, 'Three-Dimensional Virtual Worlds and Distance Learning', 439-451.

[17] Mark Peterson, 'Learner Interaction Management in an Avatar and Chat-Based Virtual World,' *Computer Assisted Language Learning* 19.1 (2006): 79-103.

[18] Stephen Bronack, Richard Riedl and John Tashner, 'Learning in the Zone: A Social Constructivist Framework for Distance Education in a 3-Dimensional Virtual World,' *Interactive Learning Environments* 14.3 (2006): 220.

[19] Ibid., 230.

[20] Ibid.

[21] Holmberg and Huvila, 'Learning together Apart: Distance Education in a Virtual World'.

[22] The project program of TIVIT Oy, Next Media, has a vision to renew the business environment of Finnish media and help to elevate the Finnish media business to the status of being a major international player. This case was partly funded by NextMedia.

[23] Aalto University, 'LabLife3D: A Virtual Chemistry Lab Created at Aalto University inside the Virtual World Second Life.' Accessed September 3, 2013. http://sites.google.com/site/lablife3d/.

[24] Eschenbrenner, et al., '3-D virtual Worlds in Education: Applications, bBenefits, Issues, and Opportunities,' 91-110; Richter, et al., 'Critical Engagement of Teachers in Second Life,' 14-18.

[25] Dickey, 'Three-Dimensional Virtual Worlds and Distance Learning,' 439-451.

[26] James Minogue, et al., 'The Impact of Haptic Augmentation on Middle School Students' Conceptions of the Animal Cell,' *Virtual Reality* 10.3-4, 293-305.

Bibliography

Bowman, Doug A., Ajith Sowndararajan, Eric Ragan and Regis Kopper 'Higher Levels of Immersion Improve Procedure Memorization Performance.' *Proceedings of Joint Virtual Reality Conference*, 121-128. doi: http://dx.doi.org/10.2312/EGVE/JVRC09/121-128.

Bronack, Stephen, Richard Riedl and John Tashner. 'Learning in the Zone: A Social Constructivist Framework for Distance Education in a 3-Dimensional Virtual World.' *Interactive Learning Environments* 14.3 (2006): 219-232.

Dickey, Michele D. 'Brave New (Interactive) Worlds: A Review of the Design Affordances and Constraints of Two 3D Virtual Worlds as Interactive Learning Environments.' *Interactive Learning Environments* 13.1-2 (2005): 121-137.

———. 'Three-Dimensional Virtual Worlds and Distance Learning: Two Case Studies of Active Worlds as a Medium for Distance Education.' *British Journal of Educational Technology* 36.3 (2005): 439-451.

Eschenbrenner, Brenda, Fiona Fui-Hoon Nah and Keng Siau. '3-D Virtual Worlds in Education: Applications, Benefits, Issues, and Opportunities.' *Journal of Database Management* 19.4 (2008): 91-110.

Foster, Andrea. 'Professor Avatar.' *Chronicle of Higher Education* 54.4 (2007): A24-A26.

Graham, Charles, S. Allen and D. Ure. 'Blended Learning Environments: A Review of the Research Literature.' (Unpublished Manuscript, Provo, UT, 2003).

Graham, Charles. 'Blended Learning Systems: Definition, Current Trends, and Future Directions.' *Handbook of Blended Learning: Global Perspectives, Local Designs*, edited by Curtis Bonk and Charles Graham. San Francisco, CA: Pfeiffer, 2006.

Holmberg, Kim and Isto Huvila. 'Learning together Apart: Distance Education in a Virtual World.' *First Monday* 13.10 (2008).

Jones, James Greg, Cesareo Morales and Gerald A. Knezek. '3-Dimensional Online Learning Environments: Examining Attitudes toward Information Technology between Students in Internet-Based 3-Dimensional and Face-to-Face Classroom Instruction.' *Educational Media International* 42.3 (2005): 219-236.

Mason, Hilary. 2007. 'Experiential Education in Second Life.' In *Proceedings of the Second Life Education Workshop* 2007, 14-18.

Minogue, James, M. Gail Jones, Bethany Broadwell and Tom Oppewall. 'The Impact of Haptic Augmentation on Middle School Students' Conceptions of the Animal Cell.' *Virtual Reality* 10.3-4, (2006): 293-305. doi: 10.1007/s10055-006-0052-4.

Peterson, Mark. 'Learner Interaction Management in an Avatar and Chat-Based Virtual World.' *Computer Assisted Language Learning* 19.1 (2006): 79-103.

Richter, Jonathon, Lynne Anderson-Inman and Mindy Frisbee. 'Critical Engagement of Teachers in Second Life: Progress in the SaLamander Project.' In *Proceedings of the Second Life Education Workshop*, 2007, 19-26.

Sallnäs, Eva-Lotta. 'Effects of Communication Mode on Social Presence, Virtual Presence, and Performance in Collaborative Virtual Environments.' *Presence* 14.4 (2005): 434-449.

Wasko, Molly, Robin Teigland, Dorothy Leidner and Sirkka Järvenpää. 'Stepping into the Internet: New Ventures in Virtual Worlds.' *MIS Quarterly* 35.3 (2001): 645-652.

Yee, Nick. and Jeremy Bailenson. 'The Proteus Effect: The Effect of Transformed Self-Representation on Behavior.' *Human Communication Research* 33.3 (2007): 271-290.

Appendix A - Feedback Form for Students

1. Had you used Second Life or other similar virtual world before this course?
2. Did you feel that the amount of training with the platform was enough? What could have been done differently?
3. How much time did you use to change the appearance of your avatar?
4. Did you use Second Life in addition to the required sessions during the course?
5. Did you practice for the exercises or the vocabulary in Second Life alone or with a friend outside of the required sessions?
6. What would you have done differently during the course to support your learning better?
7. Would you recommend this kind of course to a friend? Why or why not?
8. Did you encounter problems during the Second Life sessions? Other critical feedback?
9. What did you think you learned in the Second Life sessions?
10. Were you more active than in traditional classroom lectures?
11. For what would you like to use Second Life in language learning? Conversations/meeting people/learning vocabulary/other?
12. Would you have liked to use other spaces for learning in Second Life in addition to the virtual laboratory?
13. How would you compare the Second Life exercises to traditional classroom teaching?
14. What expectations had you previously had about virtual language teaching?
15. Was the situation more playful than in a classroom? Were you more relaxed or more nervous?

16. Was there more or less interaction than in traditional classroom teaching?
17. How did you like the free travelling and diary reporting compared to the ready-made lab environment and the exercise there?
18. Do you think that virtual language teaching will be used in the future?
19. Do you think that learning to use virtual worlds is useful for your future work life?
20. Of what use has Swedish been to you outside of this course?
21. In what situations do you think that you will use Swedish in the future?

Appendix B - Immersion Questionnaire

Mark the answer that is similar to your opinion

A) How well did you know the members of your group before this session?
1. Not at all   2. Not so well 3. Quite well 4. Very well

B) How much had you cooperated with your group members before this course?
1. Not at all   2. Not so much   3. Quite a bit 4. Very much

C) How much experience had you had in 3D virtual worlds (for example World of Warcraft) before this course?
1. None at all 2. Not so much   3. Quite a bit 4. Very much

D) How much experience with Second Life had you had before this course?
1. None at all 2. Not so much   3. Quite a bit 4. Very much

E) Respond to the statements about your Second Life experience (1 = Not at all, 5 = Very much)
a. How participatory was the experience?1 2 3 4 5
b. How intensive was the experience? 1 2 3 4 5
c. To what extent did you feel that you were inside Second Life? 1 2 3 4 5
d. To what extend did you feel immersed in Second Life? 1 2 3 4 5
e. To what extend did you feel that Second Life was around you? 1 2 3 4 5

F) Respond to the statements about your interaction with the other group members inside Second Life. (1 = Completely disagree, 5 = Completely agree)
a. The interaction aspect of the exercise was pleasant. 1 2 3 4 5
b. Everyone had the same opportunity to take part in the interaction aspect of the exercise. 1 2 3 4 5

Appendix C - Teacher Interview Structure

Background
Computer usage skills:
Previous Second Life usage:
Have you used SL in your teaching before?
How long have you done language training?

Before course
Expectations
    -Why join this case?
    -What had you expected from virtual teaching?
Course Planning
    -What help did you get? What more would you have needed?
    -How was the planning done?
    -What were the goals of the course and the virtual training sessions?
    -What differences were there when compared to the planning of a more traditional teaching exercise?
    -Quality of the preparation?
    -Time usage?

During the course
    -Organization
    -Student reactions and first impressions
    -Ongoing evaluation through the course
    -How were the students when compared to classroom teaching?
    -Were the sessions playful?
    -How would you compare the amount of interaction of the students to classroom teaching?
    -Was there explorative teaching present?

After the course
    -How would you describe the learning results?
    -How do you feel about virtual teaching after the course?
    -How do you see the future of virtual language training?

General topics
    What did you learn?
    What would you do differently?
    What would you change?

- More freedom for students or controlled exercises?
- Would you combine other distance learning online tools?

Was the amount of sessions suitable?
How about the relationship of the sessions conducted remotely to the sessions conducted at school?
What added value did the virtual training give to the course or to the teaching?

What would be the biggest obstacle for you to continue/start using virtual training in your teaching?
How could you overcome it? What would you need?

What kind of support do you wish you had had?
How could we support other teachers better when they have to implement such training?
Who would be a suitable student target group?
How could the university support the program better? Before, during, after, other training?

What kind of problems came up? What were major ones?
What was good, where did we succeed?
Could the teacher handle the situations by themselves or will they need another technical facilitator?
    -If yes, what skills would the facilitator need? Language / technical?

How was the activity level of the students?
Did you observe learning results? What about when compared to the comparison group?

Second Life as an Environment
What was good/bad about Second Life as an environment?
Did you feel that the sound worked?
Were there ready places for teaching sessions in the second life world?
What kind of place would you want for you, if you would want your own space/virtual class room?
Would you need some kind of internal tools of the virtual world for teaching?

Describe how the following activities would suit your language training sessions:
- travelling
- meeting native speakers
- cooperation with other educational organizations

- self-paced tutorials
- displays and exhibitions
- immersive exhibitions
- role play and simulations
- data visualizations and simulations
- historical recreations and re-enactments
- living and immersive archaeology
- machinima construction (short film created by recording video of a 3-D virtual world)
- treasure hunts and quests
- language and cultural immersion
- creative writing

Eero Palomäki (MSc Tech) is a doctoral student at Aalto University, Finland. He has enthusiasm for technology combined with business expertise. His special interest is technology-mediated knowledge sharing in multi-cultural settings. He is also interested in virtual and mobile work, education, training, and emerging technological solutions such as virtual worlds.

Emma Nordbäck (MSc Tech) is a doctoral student at Aalto University, Finland. Her research interests include virtual teams, virtual environments, technology-mediated communication and leadership. Her background is in user-centered design processes and work psychology. In her master's thesis she studied decision-making in virtual teams.

Fusing Virtual, Digital and Real-World Experiences for Science Learning and Empowerment

Audrey Aronowsky, Beth Sanzenbacher, Johanna Thompson and Krystal Villanosa

Abstract

Science entails asking questions and making observations, two activities that teenagers practise, if unknowingly, in their daily lives. Yet science is perceived by teenagers as inaccessible. Two museum programmes have successfully fused digital, virtual, and real-world activities to increase scientific content knowledge and engender positive attitudes towards science among teenagers. I Dig Science employs the 3D virtual world *Second Life* (*SL*), satellite communication, and real-world experiences to explore evolution and environments. Activities centre on a synchronous palaeontology expedition in Africa. *SL* replicates field research on the end-Permian mass extinction, allowing collaboration on activities that test hypotheses, mimic true excavation site tasks and enable the creation of virtual museum exhibits. Daily satellite calls from the real-world expedition team give teenagers a primary source of information and a venue to discuss their own hypotheses with experts. Museum activities also give teenagers the opportunity to examine fossils as primary data sources. Conservation Connection uses the 2D virtual world Whyville, video blogging, social networks, and real-world experiences to connect teenagers in Chicago, Illinois, USA and Suva, Fiji around the topic of coral reefs. Teenagers explore coral reef biology through Whyville. Using the social network FijiReef, teenagers exchange blog posts and videos with each other and marine experts, sharing knowledge gained and researching threats to reef ecosystems. Visits to museums, aquaria, and live reefs allow teenagers to observe threats to reefs and learn about current conservation efforts. Combined, these elements provide teenagers with tools to collaborate and carry out conservation of Fijian reefs. These multi-faceted approaches to science learning draw upon the unique way that virtual worlds and digital media, when combined with real-world activities, create a holistic environment in which youth engage in the scientific process, learn key concepts, and experience positive affect changes towards science.

Key Words: Virtual worlds, palaeontology, science learning, teenagers, marine ecology, museum.

*****

1. Introduction

A. Science Competencies of Teenagers in the United States

Within the field of education, it is well known that teenagers in the United States significantly trail their counterparts abroad with regard to science, technology, engineering and mathematics (STEM) competencies. Results from the Trends in International Mathematics and Science Study, produced by the National Center for Education Statistics, show that out of 29 countries, teenagers in the United States rank 17th and 24th respectively on science and maths tests. Furthermore, teenagers in under-resourced countries are now outperforming teenagers in the United States in both maths and science. This is especially alarming given that the sustainable growth of any country – economic and otherwise – increasingly depends on a workforce with expertise in STEM.[1]

Addressing a problem as complex as this requires the cooperation of multiple industries and educational institutions as well as a cohesive agenda. For its part, the Field Museum of Natural History (FMNH) continues to develop its portfolio of education programmes targeted towards young learners to engage them in STEM-related topics. It is our desire to encourage those that are still developing their interests in science, to support those that are already interested in science, and to impact the career trajectory of those about to enter university. Education programmes such as Conservation Connection (ConConn) and I Dig Science (IDSci), both of which place a strong emphasis on STEM, deliver a suite of virtual, digital and real-world activities that provide young people with opportunities to learn science content and develop STEM-related skills, empowering them across multiple settings – from home to school to museum.

B. Impact of Digital Technologies on Science Achievement

Given the lower levels of STEM competencies among American teenagers, many experts are calling for the development of new approaches in the instruction of STEM-related content. These approaches should allow teenagers to 'conduct investigations, directly observe natural phenomena, or work to formulate scientific explanations for these phenomena.'[2] Cognitive research suggests that through these activities, teachers will be able to further develop their students' understanding of science concepts and processes while engendering motivation for science learning.[3] The incorporation of digital technologies, such as virtual world simulations and games, into informal science learning experiences has great potential to revolutionise science learning and science education. This is due to the multiple affordances of digital media. 3D and 2D simulations allow learners to observe representations of natural phenomena that would otherwise be impossible to observe – a process that helps them to formulate scientifically correct explanations for these phenomena. Simulations and games can motivate learners with challenges and rapid feedback and tailor instruction to individual learners' needs and interests.[4]

Virtual world simulations and games have, under controlled circumstances, proven effective instructional tools that can have a positive impact on science content acquisition, behaviour, and attitude towards science among teenagers.[5] Still, in many ways digital media learning as a field remains formative and, despite emerging evidence, current research is somewhat limited. Nevertheless, FMNH takes an optimistic stance towards digital technologies as evidenced by the two education programmes described within this chapter.

C. Natural History Museums as Critical Sites for Scientific Inquiry-Based Learning

Informal learning institutions, specifically natural history museums, are uniquely positioned to engage teenagers in interest-driven learning that heavily leverages both digital media and science content. Past studies have demonstrated that informal learning institutions have characteristics that make them significant sites for inquiry-based learning;[6] socially-mediated learning;[7] and constructivist learning.[8] Given that young people today are already engaging with digital technologies, the challenge for informal learning institutions is how to support teenagers in the digital learning nodes and ecologies to which they belong and are already engaged.[9] One way to support teenagers in their use of digital technologies is to expose them to content and future career paths that align with their interests. For FMNH (an informal learning institution whose core research areas include anthropology, botany, geology, and zoology), this means leveraging digital technologies to engage interested teenagers in science and STEM-related careers. With extensive experience in developing and delivering digital education programmes to teenagers, FMNH is poised to strengthen its presence in the digital sphere so that we may play a critical role in developing STEM-related competencies in young people.

2. Digital Learning Programmes at The Field Museum of Natural History

Two museum digital learning programmes have successfully combined digital, virtual and real-world activities to increase scientific content knowledge and skills, and engender positive attitudes towards science among teenagers. These programmes exemplify FMNH's problem-based learning approach, in which learning activities are centred on a scientific problem. Participants are encouraged to work together as active learners, guided by experts who serve as mentors while using digital technologies to bridge time zones and geographic distances. In IDSci, the central problem was the cause and effects of the largest mass extinction in Earth's history: the end-Permian extinction in which an estimated 90% of all species went extinct. Teenagers were challenged to discover what happened during this event and what might have caused the catastrophe. In ConConn, the central problem was the degradation and loss of coral reef ecosystems. Earth has lost a large proportion of its original coral reefs and less than half of these vital marine ecosystems are classified as healthy. Under the umbrella of this problem, teenagers at FMNH were connected to teenagers in Fiji to learn about coral reef biology, ecology and conservation. Together, they were challenged to evaluate the condition of Fijian reefs and develop strategies to conserve Fijian reefs.

IDSci was an out-of-school programme for youth ages 13-17 in Chicago, Illinois and New York, New York, and ConConn was an after-school programme for teenagers ages 13-17 in Chicago, Illinois and Suva, Fiji. IDSci focused on evolution and environments through the study of palaeontology and a virtual fossil expedition in *Second Life* (*SL*). ConConn focused on marine biology and conservation using virtual and real coral reefs. Although these programmes used different digital platforms and had different science content foci, their scientifically-accurate simulations, games and activities provided platforms for teenage participants to gain and apply skills in a scientific context. Numerous studies have shown that providing opportunities for young people to participate in the scientific process is critical to their future enjoyment of and engagement with science.[10] In these programmes, participants experience science by mimicking how researchers generate solutions to real-world questions, providing real-life 'scientific discovery' moments and opportunities for 'higher-level' engagement.[11]

IDSci (Figure 1) used a suite of participatory virtual, digital and real-world activities in which teenagers could collaborate, tinker, learn, and co-create to explore scientific topics in depth and experience the process of scientific research. The activities in IDSci provided opportunities for teenagers to see how science is done on a day-to-day basis, collect data and collaborate with peers and experts to create a hypothesis and disseminate their results.

The major learning goal of IDSci was for teenage participants to understand evolution and environments by employing scientific inquiry and problem-solving skills. Activities developed to achieve this goal took place within the context of palaeontological fieldwork, which provided a sense of adventure and discovery that attracted teenagers who might otherwise be reluctant to engage with science content. Participants were challenged to discover the causes, effects and implications of the end-Permian extinction, the largest mass extinction in Earth's history. Focusing on the end-Permian extinction was ideal because it required teenagers to develop a detailed grasp of the factors that drive evolution and encouraged the synthesis of data and concepts related to geology, biology, ecology, and climatic and environmental change. Additionally, it emphasised the important contribution that palaeontology can make to conservation efforts in the modern world by helping participants to better understand modern extinction events and climatic change. This focus also directly connected with cutting-edge research being conducted by a multi-national team of palaeontologists, which used the fossil record preserved in Tanzania, Zambia and Brazil to investigate regional differences in how the end-Permian extinction and subsequent recovery proceeded in terrestrial communities.[12]

Figure 1: IDSci Programme – a) palaeontologists excavating fossils in Tanzania, b) teenagers assembling fossils in *SL*, c) teenagers on a behind-the-scenes museum tour, d) teenagers participating in the programme using *SL*. © The Field Museum

IDSci leveraged *SL*, satellite communication, and real-world experiences for programme participants to explore and understand evolution with activities centred on a synchronous palaeontology expedition. The programme has been successfully piloted as I Dig Tanzania (2008), I Dig Zambia (2009), I Dig Brazil (2010), and continued in summer 2012 (although this chapter does not reference happenings from summer 2012) with the second iteration of I Dig Tanzania. Participants were typically divided into four groups with each group consisting of teenagers from

Chicago and New York. Thus, *SL* functioned as a participatory learning environment where teenagers in different cities collaborated in real time.

In *SL*, teenagers participated in activities that replicated the palaeontologists' field research on the end-Permian mass extinction in a virtual environment designed to mimic the geographic area in which the field research was taking place. The virtual dig site consisted of four vertical, or stratigraphic, layers that represented the middle Permian to the middle Triassic Periods of time (~265-245 million years ago). These stratigraphic layers contained different sediments (rocks), fossil plants and fossil animals that are common to the different environments of those time periods. Activities included digging for fossils and sediment in different stratigraphic layers, recording of fossil and sedimentary data in a field notebook, and interacting with local wildlife. Engaging in these activities enabled programme participants to collect data similar to what the palaeontologists were collecting in the field and craft valid hypotheses. Participating teenagers also used *SL* to test hypotheses about the Permian and Triassic environments by performing physical and chemical tests with the sedimentary and fossil data they collected. Similar to real scientific collaboration, participating teenagers in different groups were only able to access part, but not all, of these data. This resulted in the need for programme participants to communicate and collaborate across groups to uncover the entire story. Google documents and a virtual bulletin board in *SL* were used to record, tabulate and share data acquired by all groups. Teenagers also met at their virtual campsites and near the virtual bulletin board to review the collective data and discuss findings to craft their theories about the end-Permian extinction.

Daily videos and satellite calls from the expedition gave participants a primary source of information, which they used not only to complete activities but also to gain an extremely personal and realistic view of science. Scientists in the field shared their fossil discoveries and the day-to-day aspects of fieldwork, such as asking local chiefs in the expedition region for permission to excavate, what food they ate, and a description of their camps. Satellite calls were also an important venue for programme participants to ask questions and discuss their hypotheses and theories on the end-Permian extinction with experts. After these calls and throughout the programme, participants produced blog posts and videos to share their experiences and knowledge gained with peers and experts which further helped them to craft their theories.

Guided tours of and activities in the exhibitions and behind-the-scenes areas at museums helped to tie the virtual, digital, and real-world experiences together for participants. It was through these experiences that teenagers learned how fossils are prepared for museum collections, used in research and presented to the public. An example of a real-world IDSci activity included providing teenagers with the opportunity to examine real fossils and skeletons as primary data sources. Teenagers compared their virtual fossil to real fossils and skeletons of modern animals (such as turtles and lizards) to research the diet and locomotion of the ancient animal they uncovered in *SL*. This allowed them to better understand the process of evolution and how different species are related while further refining their hypotheses on the end-Permian mass extinction.

Participants were challenged to present their hypotheses and theories by creating interactive virtual museum exhibitions on end-Permian extinction and evolution. The virtual exhibitions, built in *SL*, used the digital assets teenagers created throughout the programme as well as assets from the scientists. They also used virtual fossils, photographs, original artwork, and videos to reconstruct each of the four stratigraphic layers they excavated and researched. The virtual exhibition space was set up vertically in *SL*, to mimic the vertical layers of time on which their data collection was centred. Cross-location groups were assigned one level of the vertical exhibition space. Final exhibitions showcased each group's discoveries, tools, and theories on the cause of the mass extinction. The cumulative event for programme participants was a collaborative presentation of their exhibition to the scientists and their peers, disseminating their results for review. In these presentations, teenagers were challenged to explain the findings showcased on their exhibit level. Blog posts and group discussions with experts encouraged participants to synthesise findings across stratigraphic levels and city locations to develop the full picture of what happened during the end-Permian mass extinction and why. Synthesis of their virtual world data and interpretation informed by real-world museum collections led teenage participants to the same conclusion that scientific experts have crafted over their years of investigation: climate change played a significant role in the largest mass extinction in Earth's history and should be monitored carefully for impact on our modern world.

The fusion of virtual, digital, and real-world components within IDSci gave participating teenagers new experiences with, and potentially a new impression of, science. Preliminary evaluation of the IDSci programmes found that all programme participants increased their understanding, knowledge, and appreciation of palaeontology, evolution, extinction, ecology, and scientific methodology based on comparison of pre- and post-test results. Programme participants also further developed their problem-solving, critical-thinking, analytical, digital, and 21st century skills.[13] Additionally, the programme was successful in encouraging teenagers 'to explore career landscapes and workplace literacies that they may not have previously considered.'[14] Daily participant-authored blog posts provided the most authentic examples of teen learning and impressions. The blog post excerpts in Table 1 below demonstrate the positive attitudes towards the programmes and science, the personal connection to palaeontology and workplace literacies gained, and the use of data collected from experiments and discussions with scientific experts to reconstruct past environments.

A. I Dig

The suite of participatory virtual, digital and real-world activities in the IDSci programme made the scientific process accessible and familiar, which increased content knowledge, heightened interest in science, and engendered positive attitudes towards science among participants. The combination of activities allowed teenagers to experience science by mimicking how researchers generate solutions to real-world questions, and providing real-life scientific discovery moments as well as opportunities for higher-level engagement.

Table 1: Blog excerpts from the three pilot IDSci Experiences

Number	Blog Excerpt
1	'One of the biggest changes that I am proud of is that I am more interested in science because before I used to think that it was boring and no fun but then I learned so many new things that it got me thinking about science and has me looking at it from a different point of view, which is that science is more important to me.' – I Dig Tanzania Teen, 2008
2	'I learned about the amount of work it took to go on a field dig. Which is a ridiculous amount of preparation with all the food and supplies. I learned where you should look to find fossils, and the best place to look is in places with large rock outcroppings with little or no vegetation so the fossil can be easily seen. Also I learned what you need to study (Biology and Geology) to become a paleontologist.' – I Dig Zambia Teen, 2009
3	'From the Permian to Triassic periods animals grew smaller and became herbivores as the smaller animals that could eat meat died. Only Plant eaters could survive as the meat eaters couldn't find food. (The only species that we found remaining was the *Lystrosaurus*. They survived because of the variation within the species: some of their family members had traits that could endure the new dry environment.) Plants also change between eras. Plants stopped having spores and instead grew seeds. Seeds do not require as much water and therefore this also shows us the climate was in transition.' – I Dig Brazil Teen, 2010

B. Conservation Connection

ConConn (Figure 2) was a multi-faceted digital learning programme designed to engage and educate teenagers in biology, ecology and conservation by learning from both peers and experts in the field. The virtual world, social network, and real-world activities of ConConn allowed teenagers in the U.S. and Fiji to learn about coral reefs and the problems that confront them as well as to take action and address real problems impacting Fijian reefs and the communities that surround them.

Figure 2: ConConn Programme – a) WhyReef, b) FijiReef Ning, c) teenagers on a field trip to village in a locally managed marine area, d) overfishing article published in the *Fiji Times*. © The Field Museum

WhyReef (http://reef.whyville.net), a coral reef simulation and suite of gaming activities in the 2D virtual world of Whyville, was used for teenage participants to gain equivalent knowledge in coral reef biology, ecology and conservation. WhyReef was designed by FMNH and partner Numedeon, Inc. (the proprietors of Whyville) to accurately depict the species and interactions of an Indo-Pacific coral reef within the graphical limitations of Whyville. The core learning activities in WhyReef are (1) the Food Web Games in which learners explore who eats whom and (2) the Count and Identify activity in which learners help scientists to monitor the reef by counting and identifying all 50 species on a regular basis. Given that WhyReef is based on authentic science conducted by FMNH researchers, the food web and identification games are scientifically accurate and can serve as common primers for global players.

WhyReef consists of a central Reef Station linking two virtual coral reefs: the North Reef and the South Reef. These two reefs are critical to the learning goals around which WhyReef was designed because two reefs allow FMNH to impact one reef while the other remains healthy and serves as a point of comparison for players. Periodically, FMNH scientists and teachers alter the appearance and species composition of one reef to simulate a major disturbance to that ecosystem, for instance the overfishing of top predators or the bleaching of corals. The healthy reef serves as an experimental control and allows learners to compare the species and conditions that they observe in the two ecosystems during gameplay. These disturbances are never announced or promoted in advance, rather over the course of several weeks, conditions gradually change and the citizens of Whyville must recognize, identify, and address the problem on their own. When the reef is at its most impacted state, FMNH launches a series of activities called Save the Reef. Save the Reef activities include a Reef Simulator module that allows players to test hypotheses about the reef perturbation, Save the Reef campaigns in which players can write or sign online petitions, management plans which players can vote on to save the reef, editorials that players can write for the Whyville Times online newspaper, or donations of virtual currency to be used towards rehabilitating the reef. FMNH leveraged these activities to give ConConn participants in both countries a large and ready forum for airing their opinions about what was wrong with the virtual reef and how it might be helped. ConConn participants utilised what they learned after engaging in these activities to craft their real-world plans for raising awareness about the plight of Fijian reefs.

The FijiReef Ning social network was used by all teenage and expert participants (including marine biologists, conservationists, and underwater photographers) to share and provide feedback on ideas, blog posts, photos, videos, and projects. Because real-time collaboration was not possible between participants (due to the 17-hour time difference between Chicago and Suva), the FijiReef Ning became the virtual social hub where participants in the U.S. and Fiji collaboratively learned about coral reef biology and ecology, and the problems that confront them. Teenagers authored blog posts and produced videos as an active way to learn about topics in coral reef biology, ecology and conservation and each other. These blog posts and videos were then shared with peers and experts to communicate knowledge gained and to obtain valuable feedback to increase that knowledge. While each set of teenagers in the U.S. and Fiji did not work on the exact same video or activity, their blogs and videos were designed to be complementary so they were able to share ideas, critique each other's work, and learn from their peers and experts.

Fusing virtual and real experiences was an effective combination for facilitating knowledge gains and empowering youth to engage in science in this programme. By engaging in real-world activities, teenage participants were able to connect knowledge gained in virtual and digital settings to the real world, gather data and information from their local communities to share with their international peers, and then use those data and experiences to inform their conservation plans. WhyReef and interaction with local experts gave programme participants a large knowledge base, and the FijiReef Ning was an invaluable repository for the teenagers' real-world observations and data. Teenagers in both locations went on four field trips that capitalized on the resources unique to their location. During these experiences, they were able to engage with and learn about local aqueous environments and participate in hands-on science. Teenagers in Chicago participated in a fish dissection in the Museum's Fishes Wet Lab, received a personalised tour of the Wild Reef exhibition at Chicago's Shedd Aquarium, performed DNA extractions on clips from coral reef fishes in The Field Museum's Pritzker DNA Discovery Center, and explored their local aquatic environment on a trip to the Indiana Dunes National Lake Shore. Teenagers in Fiji also participated in a fish dissection, went on an investigative trip to a local fish market, visited a nearby village in a locally managed marine area, and explored their local aquatic environment with a snorkel trip on a coral reef.

As a final project, teenage participants attempted to make a real-world impact on Fijian reef conservation efforts. Both groups decided that creating educational outreach pieces would be the most effective method for them to address the threats to coral reefs and encourage locals in Fiji to take action. Participants in Fiji wrote an article to raise awareness of the dangers of overfishing by outlining the causes, effects and possible solutions. This article was published in the *Fiji Times* (see Figure 2.d). Participants in Chicago wrote an editorial for the *Fiji Times* that called attention to the problem of abandoned fishing vessels, and also produced a public service announcement on the effects of rubbish on coral reefs and how that impacts human food supplies (http://www.vimeo.com/27538531).

Through the multi-faceted digital and real-world activities of ConConn, participants showed their understanding of the interconnectedness of reef species and how food webs are important gauges of energy flow. Programme participants were also able to comprehend the causes of coral degradation and the main threats to reefs, and showed a deep understanding of the importance of reefs not only for the health of the ocean but also for the health of all animals, including humans. Teenage participants also learned about the varying problems with implementing strategies to conserve and preserve reefs, from cultural roadblocks to economic ones. They were quite astute at seeing the problem from varying points of view and understanding which stakeholder groups may resist conservation plans. Final projects showed that participants gained an understanding of the interactions within a reef ecosystem, how humans are impacting these interactions, and ways to solve these problems to keep the reef ecosystem healthy. Incorporating global perspectives on local issues allowed participating teenagers to have a more holistic understanding of these issues.

3. Comparisons
A. Differences in Virtual World Utilisation

IDSci and ConConn both utilised a suite of virtual and digital technologies to invigorate science for teenagers and demonstrate the relevance of science to their daily lives. However, despite using similar technologies across programmes, these technologies were utilised in different ways. IDSci employed the 3D virtual world, *SL*, as a synchronous collaborative space for teenagers in different American cities. *SL* functioned as a participatory learning environment because teenagers from different cities were paired into cross-location groups and used *SL* for their problem-based learning activities and to build their cross-location relationships. Cross-location teams were possible because there is only a one-hour time difference between New York and Chicago, so the program was able to run synchronously across locations. *SL* also facilitates easy and versatile artefact construction and was therefore able to serve as a place where teenagers could construct their virtual museum exhibits to summarize what they learned. Finally, *SL* served as a vehicle for cross-location communication and team building, because teams used instant messaging to relay information to one another.

In contrast, ConConn used the 2D virtual world of Whyville as an introductory activity to give teenagers in different countries a common base for launching their investigations and discussions. In ConConn, the virtual world served as a digital primer promoting common knowledge, terms, and experience. Participants engaged in the same activities and played the same games in WhyReef, but were never in the virtual world synchronously given the 17-hour time difference between Chicago, USA and Suva, Fiji. This significant time difference meant that cross-location communication was limited to exchanging comments and artefacts on the FijiReef Ning with a one-day lag between most posts and replies. The artefacts created by learners in ConConn included videos, image montages, blog posts, and articles for publication in newspapers. Thus, artefact creation took place in the real world (filming videos or writing articles) and cross-location collaboration took place in the FijiReef Ning rather than in the virtual world as in IDSci. Artefact creation in Whyville was minimal and limited to avatar accessories (face parts, *sensu* Whyville) in the ConConn program.

B. Differences in Technology and Participant Experience

Given that IDSci depended on a synchronous cross-location experience and utilised a 3D virtual world, the technology necessary to implement the programme (computers and bandwidth) was much greater than for ConConn. IDSci technology included high-quality computers for all participants with excellent graphics cards, high bandwidth internet access (via LANs in both locations), and a satellite terminal for broadcasting from Africa. Whereas technology utilised in ConConn included laptop computers in Chicago and older desktop computers and modem internet access in Fiji. ConConn depended on the participation of Fijian teenagers, so the programme was designed to be implemented with the basic technology and bandwidth available in Fijian schools.

Given the more sophisticated technology and the fairly complex controls involved in utilising *SL* (as compared to the point-and-click commands for Whyville), teenage participants in IDSci had a steeper learning curve to master *SL* than did the ConConn participants using Whyville. The simplicity of the Whyville controls meant that ConConn teenagers could spend a greater amount of their time on video scripting and production, digital photography, and web and expert research. In addition to *SL*, IDSci participants also used Skype to communicate across locations, produced videos, and learned web applications such as Google Maps, Google Docs, and Blogger. Ultimately, ConConn participants became better versed in their programme's full suite of technology, with all participants able to use Whyville, script and produce videos, post and comment on blogs, and conduct informed research. Participants in IDSci tended to divide tasks and become experts at a subset of their programme's technology. For example, when designing their virtual exhibitions, teenagers specialised into (1) those who had a robust understanding of the synthesised data and provided content direction, (2) those who were the most skilled and comfortable using *SL* to build the virtual exhibition, and (3) those who gained other digital skills to develop assets (videos, original artwork) for inclusion in the exhibition. Despite these differences in technology, both programmes provided teenage participants with an array of digital experience and exit interviews showed a marked increase in 21st century skills.

C. Differences in Real-World Activities and Experts

The integration of real-world activities and experts was key to the success of each programme; however, the framework for integration differed greatly by programme. In IDSci, the real-world activities melded seamlessly with digital activities encouraging participants to synthesise their theories and take part in the scientific process. Real-world activities elucidated the process of scientific research at a natural history museum and provided content knowledge applicable to virtual world artefact construction and final presentations. Thus, in IDSci, knowledge gained in real-world activities was brought into the virtual world for dissemination and discussion. For example, when teenage participants were tasked with learning the biology of their fossil animals, they seamlessly used and compared their virtual and real-world assets while discussing their findings with experts. Participants used laptops to access their virtual fossils in *Second Life*. They would move back and forth between their laptops and tables full of real fossils and skeletons, comparing anatomical features to discover how the fossil animal they excavated and discovered moved and what it ate. While comparing the real and virtual fossils, they engaged with the participating palaeontologist to ask pertinent questions and clarify points of confusion. The knowledge gained during this activity was then incorporated into their final theories and the virtual museum exhibition.

Due to the differences in programme design, timing, and technology discussed above, the activities in ConConn allowed participating teenagers to apply knowledge gained from all three spheres – virtual, digital and real, in real-world settings. In ConConn, knowledge and skills gained as a global team in virtual, digital and real-world settings were disseminated and applied in the real world. For example, participating teenagers first learned about reef ecosystems and food webs through game play and simulations in the virtual world, WhyReef. They furthered their knowledge about reef ecosystems through blogs, videos and interaction with experts to learn how seemingly small disturbances in food webs can have large impacts on the health of the ecosystem. Armed with this new knowledge, the Fijian teenagers went to a local fish market to interview fishermen about their catches and how these catches have changed over the past 10 years. The Fijian teenagers then shared this information with the Chicago participants, and through further blogs and videos created on this topic and shared between both sets of teenagers, the Fijian participants were able to synthesize all that they learned to craft their overfishing article for the *Fiji Times*.

The roles of experts in each programme also differed. In IDSci, teenage participants worked with a small group of experts on a regular basis and became very familiar with them. This close working relationship between experts and teenagers closed the gap from expert-novice to peer-peer over the course of the programme. Due to the asynchronous nature of ConConn and the goal of producing real-world conservation plans, a more diverse group of experts including marine biologists, graduate students, scientific officers, conservation programme directors, photographers, and teachers joined the programme for specific activities and shorter durations. Teenagers formed close relationships with each other and with mentors in their home location, but relationships with other experts stayed at the student-teacher level.

4. Conclusion

Science can often be obscure for youth and blended experiences can promote science learning by grounding technology-based activities (digital and virtual) with real-world interactions, mentors, and artefacts. As these two programmes demonstrate, these fusions can happen in different ways and to different degrees while still yielding positive learning outcomes. The goals of IDSci were for teenage participants to engage with the scientific process in order to learn about palaeontology and evolution within the context of discovering the causes of the end-Permian mass extinction. The goals of ConConn were to learn about coral reef biology and ecology, and to implement coral reef conservation plans. Each programme was designed to accomplish these goals for the given participants and technologies available. Despite the differences in the virtual, digital and real-world experiences, each programme created a holistic environment in which teenagers participated in the scientific process, learned key concepts, and experienced positive affect changes towards science.

Notes

[1] Alan I. Leshner, 'A Wake-Up Call for Science Education', *The Boston Globe*, last modified January 19, 2009, http://www.boston.com/bostonglobe/editorial_opinion/oped/articles/2009/01/12/a_wake_up_call_for_science_education/; A. Aronowsky, B. Sanzenbacher, J. Thompson, and K. Villanosa, 'Worked Example: How Scientific Accuracy in Game Design Stimulates Scientific Inquiry', *International Journal of Learning and Media* 3, no. 1 (2011): accessed February 10, 2012, http://ijlm.net/10.1162/ijlm_a_00065.
[2] National Research Council, *Learning Science through Games and Computer Simulations* (Washington DC: National Academies Press, 2011).
[3] Ibid.
[4] Ibid.
[5] National Research Council, *Learning Science*; Aronowsky, 'Worked Example'.
[6] Scott G. Paris, ed., *Perspectives on Object-Centered Learning in Museums* (Mahwah, New Jersey: Lawrence Erlbaum Associates, Publishers, 2002).
[7] John H. Falk and Lynn Dierking, *Learning from Museums: Visitor Experiences and the Making of Meaning* (Walnut Creek, CA: Altamira Press, 2000).
[8] G. Hein, *Learning in the museum* (New York: Routledge, 1998).
[9] J. Goodlad, *A Place Called School: Prospects for the Future* (New York: McGraw-Hill, 1984); John Seely Brown, 'Learning, Working and Playing in the Digital Age', (presentation at the Conference on Higher Education of the American Association for Higher Education, 1999), accessed November 18, 2009, http://serendip.brynmawr.edu/sci_edu/seelybrown/seelybrown.html.
[10] H. Gibson and C. Chase, 'Longitudinal Impact of an Inquiry-Based Science Program on Middle School Students' Attitudes toward Science', *Science Education* 86, (2002): 693-705; N. G Lederman, 'Students' and Teachers' Conceptions of the Nature of Science: A Review of the Research', *Journal of Research in Science Teaching* 26, (1992): 771-783.
[11] Aronowsky, 'Worked Example'.

[12] K. D. Angielczyk, C. A. Sidor, S. J. Nesbitt, R. M. H. Smith, and L. A. Tsuji, 'Taxonomic Revision and New Observations on the Postcranial Skeleton, Biogeography, and Biostratigraphy of the Dicynodont Genus Dicynodontoides, the Senior Subjective Synonym of Kingoria (Therapsida, Anomodontia)', *Journal of Vertebrate Paleontology* 29, (2009a): 1174-1187; K. D. Angielczyk, C. A. Sidor, R. M. H Smith, S. J. Nesbitt, J. S. Steyer, and J. Fröbisch, 'Permian and Triassic Tetrapod Faunas and Paleoenvironments of Tanzania and Zambia: Implications for the Permo-Triassic Transition', *Geological Society of America Abstracts with Programs* 41, no. 7 (2009b): 242; C. A. Sidor, K. D Angielczyk, D. M. Weide, R. M. H Smith, and L. A. Tsuji, 'Tetrapod Fauna of the Lowermost Usili Formation (Songea Group, Ruhuhu Basin) of Southern Tanzania, with a New Burnetiid Record', *Journal of Vertebrate Paleontology* 30, (2010a): 696-703; C. A. Sidor, J. S. Steyer, K. D. Angielczyk, R. M. H Smith, and S. C. Tolan, 'New Information on the Permian and Triassic Vertebrate Faunas of the Luangwa Basin, Zambia', *Journal of Vertebrate Paleontology* 30, supplement to 3 (2010b): 165A.

[13] C. Steinkuehler and E. Alagoz, 'Out-of-School Virtual Worlds-Based Programs: A Cross-Case Analysis', *ICLS 10 Proceedings of the 9th International Conference of the Learning Sciences* 2 (2010): 304-305.

[14] Ibid., 304-305.

Bibliography

Angielczyk, K. D., C. A. Sidor, S. J. Nesbitt, R. M. H. Smith and L. A. Tsuji, 'Taxonomic Revision and New Observations on the Postcranial Skeleton, Biogeography, and Biostratigraphy of the Dicynodont Genus Dicynodontoides, the Senior Subjective Synonym of Kingoria (Therapsida, Anomodontia)'. *Journal of Vertebrate Paleontology* 29 (2009a): 1174-1187.

Angielczyk, K. D., C. A. Sidor, R. M. H. Smith, S. J. Nesbitt, J.-S. Steyer and J. Fröbisch. 'Permian and Triassic Tetrapod Faunas and Paleoenvironments of Tanzania and Zambia: Implications for the Permo-Triassic Transition'. *Geological Society of America Abstracts with Programs* 41, no. 7 (2009b): 242.

Aronowsky, A., B. Sanzenbacher, J. Thompson and K. Villanosa. 'Worked Example: How Scientific Accuracy in Game Design Stimulates Scientific Inquiry'. *International Journal of Learning and Media* 3, no. 1 (2011): Accessed February 10, 2012. http://ijlm.net/10.1162/ijlm_a_00065.

Brown, John Seely. 'Learning, Working and Playing in the Digital Age'. Presentation at the Conference on Higher Education of the American Association for Higher Education, 1999. Accessed November 18, 2009. http://serendip.brynmawr.edu/sci_edu/seelybrown/seelybrown.html.

Falk, John H. and Lynn Dierking. *Learning from Museums: Visitor Experiences and the Making of Meaning.* Walnut Creek, CA: Altamira Press, 2000.

Gibson, H. and C. Chase. 'Longitudinal Impact of an Inquiry-Based Science Program on Middle School Students' Attitudes toward Science'. *Science Education* 86 (2002): 693-705.

Goodlad, J. *A Place Called School: Prospects for the Future.* New York: McGraw-Hill, 1984.

Hein, G. *Learning in the Museum.* New York: Routledge, 1998.

Lederman, N. G. 'Students' and Teachers' Conceptions of the Nature of Science: A Review of the Research'. *Journal of Research in Science Teaching* 26 (1992): 771-783.

Leshner, Alan I. 'A Wake-Up Call for Science Education'. *The Boston Globe.* Last modified January 19, 2009. http://www.boston.com/bostonglobe/editorial_opinion/oped/articles/2009/01/12/a_wake_up_call_for_science_education/.

National Research Council. *Learning Science through Games and Computer Simulations.* Washington DC: National Academies Press, 2011.

Paris, Scott G., ed. *Perspectives on Object-Centered Learning in Museums.* Mahwah, New Jersey: Lawrence Erlbaum Associates, Publishers, 2002.

Sidor, C. A., K. D. Angielczyk, D. M. Weide, R. M. H. Smith and L. A. Tsuji, 'Tetrapod Fauna of the Lowermost Usili Formation (Songea Group, Ruhuhu Basin) of Southern Tanzania, with a New Burnetiid Record'. *Journal of Vertebrate Paleontology* 30 (2010a): 696-703.

Sidor, C. A., J. S. Steyer, K. D. Angielczyk, R. M. H. Smith and S. C. Tolan. 'New Information on the Permian and Triassic Vertebrate Faunas of the Luangwa Basin, Zambia'. *Journal of Vertebrate Paleontology* 30, supplement to 3 (2010b): 165A.

Steinkuehler, C. and E. Alagoz. 'Out-of-School Virtual Worlds-Based Programs: A Cross-Case Analysis'. *ICLS 10 Proceedings of the 9th International Conference of the Learning Sciences* 2 (2010): 304-305.

Audrey Aronowsky is the Scientific Program Manager for the Biodiversity Synthesis Center at The Field Museum. She works closely with the Education, Information Technology, and Research departments in the Museum for specific digital projects.

Beth Sanzenbacher is the Outreach Coordinator for the Biodiversity Synthesis Center at The Field Museum. She develops, manages and facilitates several different digital learning projects, which provide immersive environments for youth to learn and experience science.

Johanna Thompson is a Digital Learning Specialist for the Education Department at The Field Museum. She develops, manages and facilitates several different digital learning projects, which provide immersive environments for youth to learn and experience science.

Krystal Villanosa served as the Digital Learning Manager at The Field Museum for 5 years and oversaw the development of digital learning programmes aimed at teenagers. She has recently left this position to pursue her doctorate in Learning Sciences from Northwestern University in Chicago, Illinois.

Part III

Managing Experiential Learning

Mixing Virtual, Real-World and Digital Communication Elements to Create Successful Global Teams

Audrey Aronowsky, Beth Sanzenbacher, Johanna Thompson and Krystal Villanosa

Abstract

Coral reef biodiversity loss has reached a critical moment as a result of human activity. In order to address this issue, awareness-raising and action must be both local and global. The museum-run digital learning programme Conservation Connection created a virtual community and brought together teenagers in Fiji and the United States to ignite their interest in the connections between species survival, biodiversity, conservation, and human communities. It may serve as a model for creating global teams in order to create change and spur progress. Two groups of teenagers were brought together using a mix of virtual world simulations and games, video production, social networking, and real-world activities. Via gameplay in WhyReef, a 2D virtual coral reef in Whyville.net, participants immersed themselves in the simulated coral reef ecosystem to gain actionable knowledge of reef biology. They used a Ning-based social network, FijiReef, to share videos and blog posts about coral reef biodiversity and conservation. The social network served as a platform for teenagers to connect, collaborate, and share with each other and experts. Additional content acquisition was made possible through real-world field trips to interact with marine ecosystems and experts, the results of which were shared between the two groups of participants. Implementation of real-world conservation plans was the product of this mix of distanced digital interactions. By blending digital technologies and real-world activities, Conservation Connection was able to mimic a progression of engagement often used to foster real-world teams. The resulting global team, based on a generative culture of content creation, allowed members in disparate locations to enter into active, social, and meaningful relationships with science mentors, their environment, and each other.

Key Words: Science, museum, marine biology, conservation, global team, team building, virtual world, social networking, video blogging, cross-cultural communication, coral reefs.

*****

1. Introduction
A. Biodiversity Loss and Threats to Coral Reefs

Biodiversity loss and species extinction are approaching, or may have already reached, a critical moment. Many scientists agree that the Earth is experiencing its 6th mass extinction; though unlike previous extinctions, this one is caused by human activity.[1] The International Unions for Conservation of Nature (IUCN) estimates that the current species extinction rate is 1,000 to 10,000 times higher than expected natural extinction rates.[2] Coral reefs are hotspots for biodiversity but are in imminent danger. For example, there are currently 845 known species of reef-building coral and of that number, 231 species (almost one-third) are facing extinction.[3] Global issues, such as climate change, habitat loss, and pollution due to economic growth are key factors in biodiversity loss.[4] Biodiversity provides innumerable medical, social and economic resources, and its preservation is vital for human survival.[5] Millions of people and several global organisations (e.g., the United Nations, The Nature Conservancy, the World Wide Fund for Nature) have recognised this crisis. These organisations find it imperative to work locally and coordinate globally to find practical solutions to the issues that result in biodiversity loss worldwide.[6]

Natural history museums and other informal learning institutions can use both their frequent interaction with the public and their status as trusted sources to impact both science education and awareness of this biodiversity crisis. Digital learning programmes for youth at The Field Museum of Natural History (FMNH) aim to introduce the tools, such as critical thinking and problem-solving, necessary to understand the consequences of biodiversity loss, and to engage youth in the global connections between species survival, biodiversity, conservation, and human communities.

B. Building a Global Team to Address Environmental Issues

Global teams can be created through a generalised progression of goal-centred engagement (Figure 1) that starts by providing a base of common information about the problem (inform), followed by asking potential team members to become involved (recruit). For potential team members who choose to be involved, engagement progresses from being tasked with activities (recruit), to individualised action (act), to group action and reaction (collaborate), to the final stage wherein the group is functioning as a goal-oriented team and trying to enact change (empower). For a team of *learners*, the progression is usually guided-- expert-to-novice in the early phases and peer-to-peer in later phases as learners take control of the process.

Conservation Connection (ConConn) was a digital learning programme designed to engage and educate teenagers in ecology and conservation by working as a team with both experts in the field and peers. The programme's virtual world, social network, and real-world activities allowed teenagers in the United States and Fiji to become a global team by providing them with common experiences, the ability to share isolated experiences, and a forum for discourse.

1a. Generalized Ladder of   1b. Iterative Virtual
Community Engagement   Community Engagement

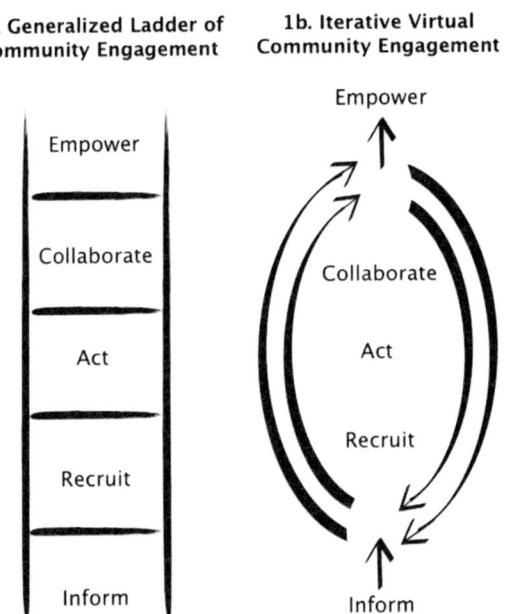

Figure 1: Forms of Community Engagement – 1a. represents a generalised model widely used for community engagement. Here the word recruit is defined as bringing people to a cause. 1b. represents how this model was adapted for Conservation Connection to engage teens in an iterative process and create a virtual global team. Here the word recruit has two definitions: 1) enlisting people to address a cause and 2) tasking team learners to engage in structured activities.
© The Field Museum

In the case of ConConn, team-building centred on the goal of Fijian coral reef conservation. A blending of virtual, digital, and real-world activities steered the progression of engagement. Coral reef biodiversity loss is a global issue and will require action by global teams. Thus, FMNH developed ConConn to engage teenagers in the stewardship of coral reefs using the cross-location, collaborative problem-solving necessary to effect change. FMNH partnered with a secondary school in Chicago, IL, USA and a secondary school in Suva, Fiji to create a team of teen participants, separated by geography but working together towards a common goal. The ConConn curriculum provided teenagers with knowledge about coral reef ecosystems and the threats reefs face, guided them through an iterative process of sharing and collaboration, and asked them to explore potential solutions to this problem. ConConn used a combination of virtual worlds, social networking, blog posting, video production and vlogging, and real-world activities. By fusing virtual and real-world experiences, the team of teen participants successfully engaged in science and civic action to protect Fijian reefs and raise awareness of environmental impacts in their local communities.

2. Components of the Programme

Figure 2: ConConn Programme – a) WhyReef, b) FijiReef Ning, c) Real-World Activites, d) Final Projects. © The Field Museum

A. WhyReef

In order for both sets of teenagers to effectively and efficiently collaborate on conservation plans for coral reefs, it was imperative that teen participants gained equivalent knowledge in coral reef biology, ecology, and current conservation techniques (the initial 'inform' phase of the progression). To ensure that the inform phase was participatory rather than passive, ConConn participants engaged in gameplay in WhyReef, a coral reef simulation with an accompanying suite of activities accessed through the 2D, low-bandwidth, web-based virtual world of Whyville.net. WhyReef was utilised as the primary source of information because of its content, ease of use, and its ability to provide an immersive experience for teen players. Gameplay also allowed teenagers to virtually experience the charismatic ecosystem that they were tasked to help. Within WhyReef, teenagers identified and monitored populations of 50 unique reef species, observed who-eats-whom in the reef, and experimented to discern how human events can impact reefs. WhyReef contains two simulated reefs, North and South, which allows players to compare the appearance and condition of two separate reef environments. During the course of the programme, one reef was degraded by an overfishing event. This virtual event served to make team members aware of the severity of the problems facing coral reefs and to encourage members to act and collaborate (recruit phase). Teen participants were asked to identify the cause of the catastrophe and to affect the state of the unhealthy reef through civic action and group intervention. WhyReef was important in building this virtual global team because it ushered team members through the information and recruitment phases, and allowed programme participants in Chicago and Suva, none of whom had ever seen a living coral reef, to understand the intrinsic and economic value of this ecosystem and the importance of the programme's ultimate goal.

B. FijiReef Ning

In order to deepen learning about coral reef ecosystems and to create effective conservation plans for real reefs, a low barrier, online space was required for programme participants to move through the act and collaborate phases of the progression. ConConn used a Ning-based customizable social network called FijiReef to encourage team members to collaborate and learn from coral reef experts and mentors including museum teachers, marine biologists, conservationists, and underwater photographers.

In FijiReef, teenagers created and shared blog posts, photos and videos as an active way to become involved with and learn about coral reef biology and conservation (recruit/act phases). Experts also contributed through blog posts, photos and videos. Participant-authored content was shared with experts and peers to obtain valuable feedback that augmented content knowledge (act/collaborate phases). The Coral Reef Documentary activity serves as a good example of this process. Through this activity, teenagers in each location were challenged to make a short documentary about a specific coral reef species using WhyReef as their primary source of information. Chicago and Fijian teenagers then shared their video with peers across the Pacific and experts for review and comment. Both teenager and expert feedback focused on the scientific accuracy of the content as well as video quality. Teenagers were then tasked with editing their videos, incorporating feedback they received and new information they acquired from expert interviews, expert photos and blog posts, and real reef specimens from museum collections. The addition of new information allowed teen participants to learn more about their species and broaden the content of their videos. The iterative process of video production allowed teenagers to learn from their peers' videos and incorporate new ideas and themes into their own work to make their product more dynamic and familiar to each other. This iterative process of challenges, drafts, commenting, and modification using feedback was repeated for all of the digital activities and cycled team members through the recruit, act, and collaboration phases to strengthen team ties and move the team closer to their ultimate goal of empowerment to effect change on Fijian reefs (see Figure 2b). Challenges used in this process were designed to facilitate teenager-expert interactions, facilitate participant exchange across locations, increase participant understanding of the complex interactions within reef ecosystems, and increase participant understanding of the importance of reefs to Fijian society and the global community.

C. Real-World Activities

An important component of ConConn was the inclusion of real-world activities and field trips that drew upon the strength of each location's resources and opportunities. Teenagers in Chicago participated in a fish dissection, received a guided tour of the exhibition *Wild Reef* at the Shedd Aquarium, performed DNA extractions on samples from Fijian coral reef fishes, and explored their local aquatic environment on a trip to the Indiana Dunes National Lake Shore. Teenagers in Suva participated in a fish dissection, took an investigative trip to a local fish market, visited a nearby village in a marine protected area, and explored their local aquatic environment with a snorkel trip on a coral reef. These activities enabled both sets of teenagers to learn more about the issues facing local communities and gather information to share with their peers. As such, the real-world activities, while done thousands of miles apart, served the early phases of the team-building progression (inform, recruit, and act). An example of this was the Fijian participants' trip to the village of Navakavu, a locally-managed marine protected area. From the teen participants' work in WhyReef and FijiReef, they were well-versed in reef biology and in the problems that confront reefs, such as pollution. However, after visiting this village, Fijian teenagers witnessed the very real impact that pollution can have on a reef. They were able to hear first-hand from village elders of the problems they face in keeping their reefs free of pollution coming from the capital city of Suva, where the participants lived. Fijian teenagers posted videos and blogs about their experience for the Chicago team members, who were then able to relate this experience to a previous discussion they had with a marine biologist about ocean rubbish and pollution. *Because* real-world activities were done separately by Chicago and Fijian participants and shared in the digital space, the act of sharing and describing these separate experiences served to unify the global team. Sharing and comparing real-world experiences allowed both sets of teenagers to see the very real threats of pollution on a personal, local and global scale, and the need for action, a critical step for successful empowerment.

D. Final Projects

Fijian and Chicago teen participants successfully became a global conservation-focused team through an iterative progression of the inform, act, and collaborate phases. They used knowledge and skills gleaned from virtual, digital, and real-world activities to make a real-world impact through their final projects. Final projects were peer-generated and directed, and had the goal of assisting Fijian reef conservation efforts. Fijian teen participants wrote an article that was published in the Fiji Times to raise awareness about overfishing that outlined the causes, effects and possible solutions to this problem. Chicago programme participants published a letter in the Fiji Times that highlighted the problem of abandoned fishing vessels with a call to action on the part of Fijian citizens and government. Chicago teenagers also produced a public service announcement on the effects of rubbish on coral reefs. This video informed the public that ocean rubbish can negatively impact a reef. With a strong link between reefs and fish populations, littering in the ocean can also have a negative impact on humans. In addition to the final projects, and perhaps, more importantly, teen participants in both locations made personal changes in their behaviour, such as not littering, because they saw these actions not only as detrimental problems for their local communities, but also for communities across the globe. The team of ConConn teenagers became true stewards of coral reefs by seeing reefs not only as a resource for a local village but as a vital component of the Earth's ecosystem. It is our hope that real-world adult global teams addressing the same issue will have the same measure of success.

3. Discussion

A. Conservation Connection as a Model for a Global Team

ConConn blended a suite of digital technologies with real-world activities to build a global team of teenagers with a shared knowledge base to effect change in the real world. Team building was important for giving diverse and disparate members a common set of goals and common motivator while leveraging individual preferences and skills to achieve those goals. In the case of ConConn, the goals were to heighten awareness of coral reefs among a finite group of teen participants, increase their knowledge of coral reefs and the threats they face, and use this newly acquired content to become effective stewards of coral reefs in Fiji. The common motivator was a desire to stop or reverse the current degradation of Fijian reefs.

The major element ConConn leveraged to build an effective global team was digital technology. The virtual world simulation of WhyReef provided both sets of teen participants with the opportunity to acquire common knowledge and language around coral reefs. The social network FijiReef served multiple purposes in that it was a 1) site for teenagers to acquire digital assets for their projects; 2) a platform for teenagers to share what they learned; 3) a safe space for teenagers to receive feedback from their peers and mentors; and 4) a hub that documented all of the activities of ConConn, both digital and real world. Additionally, when both sets of teen participants engaged in real-world activities in their own local communities, the FijiReef Ning allowed for their local activities to further develop relationships with team members abroad. For example, 1) single location role-playing activities resulted in blog posts in which teen participants shared their opinions promoting cross-location discussion and 2) single location field trips resulted in shared videos and still images that gave team members insight into a different culture allowing for comparison. Ultimately, the FijiReef Ning provided all team members with an online forum that satisfied the range of activities involved in global team building: informing, recruiting, acting, collaborating, and empowering.

In addition to digital technology, global team building was also aided by curriculum tasks. In creating online profiles and introducing themselves to their counterparts abroad, teenagers engaged in networking, making connections to both their peers and mentors. In producing videos and uploading content to the FijiReef Ning, teenagers mimicked real-world asset sharing. In reviewing peer work and providing as well as receiving feedback, teenagers engaged in a critique and review process. In taking local field trips and familiarizing themselves with their physical environments, teenagers performed research and made observations of their surroundings, which they then shared with one another.

The core components of the ConConn experience can be used as a model for other team building educational programmes, particularly those centred around a global environmental or conservation issue. The model will be useful to investigators who perform much of their research or data gathering in a country other than their own. The ConConn model can also provide a way to link their research location and their institutional home while broadening the impact of their research programme through the engagement and education of local youth in two countries. To implement a similar programme, an investigator would need to identify a compelling problem upon which to centre the team building. They would need to recruit partner schools in their home and research locations. Equipment requirements are fairly minimal, although both schools would need computer laboratories. Using a customised Ning platform for sharing and discourse is low cost and flexible. Low resolution portable video cameras such as the Flip models (now discontinued) are a low cost way to enable youth to produce and share media easily and using low bandwidth. ConConn used a virtual world simulation to provide learners with a common knowledge base, but other digital, virtual, or real-world activities can substitute for this component so long as the activities meet the goal of informing and engaging students using active learning (i.e. problem-solving or inquiry).

B. Complexities of Global Teams as Highlighted by Conservation Connection
Building a global team is a complex task. Obstacles can arise from differences in regional customs, logistics (time and location differences), and language. In the case of ConConn, the two most impactful issues arose from regional customs (Fiji is more male-dominated than the United States and has cultural differences related to time). Because the major goal and final project for ConConn was actionable conservation to aid Fijian reefs, the programme project team selected Marist Brothers Academy as its Fijian partner school. By involving teenagers from Marist, an all-male private secondary school with many students from influential families, the programme included Fijian students with great potential to enact positive change; however, these teenagers were all male and were a sharp contrast to the Chicago partner school, which was female-dominated. Regional attitudes about time also played a role in the ability of the two groups to operate smoothly. Many studies have addressed the fact that western cultures live by a 'clock' while other cultures, such as South America and the Pacific Islands, have a more laid-back approach to time. Despite an awareness by programme teachers from both Fiji and the United States about their counterpart's differing approach to time, it was sometimes difficult to stay in sync with respect to the curriculum. The impact of cultural differences related to time were most noticeable in information sharing and planning between teachers, necessitating extra work to keep the two-meeting-per-week programme model intact.

Logistics also had a great impact on ConConn. The global team consisted of youth and mentors in Chicago, IL, USA and Suva, Fiji; locations that are 17 hours apart. Today's youth often expect instantaneous gratification from their digital technology, so the 17-hour time lag could have hampered discussions via the FijiReef Ning. However, programme teachers in each location were careful to manage participant expectations and daily activities so that teenagers barely noticed the day-long delay in receiving answers to their questions from team members in the other country. The widely disparate locations impacted team building because it was cost-prohibitive to have any meaningful face-to-face group training or follow-up. For this grant-funded project, one teacher from Fiji was designated to visit Chicago for training, however, during the course of the programme, this teacher's role was significantly decreased. Only two experts were able to visit teen participants in both locations during the course of the programme.

Language barriers were occasionally obvious in ConConn and may have impacted the programme. Two manifestations of this barrier included youth using regional slang or colloquialisms and the Fijian tendency to avoid saying 'no.' In Fiji, it is considered rude to say no, so some Chicago team members were disappointed when Fijian team members said yes without meaning it.

4. Conclusion

This global team, based on a generative culture of content creation, increased participant understanding of biodiversity and global citizenship, and allowed team members in disparate locations to enter into active, social, and meaningful relationships with each other, science mentors, and their environment. It is our hope that the ConConn model can be used by other scientists, teachers, and non-governmental organisations to engage and connect youth around the world around issues of global importance.

Notes

[1] 'Human Footprint too Big for Nature', *World Wildlife Fund*, last modified October 24, 2006, http://wwf.panda.org/index.cfm?uNewsID=83520; Russell A. Mittermeier, Will R. Turner, Frank W. Larsen, Thomas M. Brooks, and Claude Gascon, 'Global Biodiversity Conservation: The Critical Role of Hotspots', *Biodiversity Hotspots* 1 (2011) : 3-22.
[2] IUCN, 'Species Extinction: The Facts', *The IUCN Red List of Threatened Species for 2007*, accessed February 8, 2012,
http://cmsdata.iucn.org/downloads/species_extinction_05_2007.pdf.
[3] Richard Black, 'Alarming Plight of Coral Reefs', *BBC News*, last modified July, 10, 2008, http://news.bbc.co.uk/2/hi/7498502.stm.
[4] Mittermeier, 'Global Biodiversity Conservation', 3-22.
[5] Michael R. W. Rands, et al., 'Biodiversity Conservation: Challenges Beyond 2010', *Science* 329 no. 5997 (2010) : 1298-1303.
[6] Rands, et al., 'Biodiversity Conservation', 1298-1303; Tamar Ron, 'A Proposed Alternative Institutional Approach to Meeting International Biodiversity Targets', *IUCN*, last modififed December 10, 2010,
http://www.iucn.org/involved/opinion/?6676/A-proposed-alternative-institutional-approach-to-meeting-international-biodiversity-targets.

Bibliography

Black, Richard. 'Alarming Plight of Coral Reefs'. *BBC News*. Last modified July, 10, 2008. http://news.bbc.co.uk/2/hi/7498502.stm.

'Human Footprint too Big for Nature'. *World Wildlife Fund.* Last modified October 24, 2006. http://wwf.panda.org/index.cfm?uNewsID=83520.

IUCN, 'Species Extinction: The Facts*'. The IUCN Red List of Threatened Species for 2007.* Accessed February 8, 2012. http://cmsdata.iucn.org/downloads/species_extinction_05_2007.pdf.

Mittermeier, Russell A., Will R. Turner, Frank W. Larsen, Thomas M. Brooks and Claude Gascon. 'Global Biodiversity Conservation: The Critical Role of Hotspots'. *Biodiversity Hotspots* 1 (2011): 3-22.

Rands, Michael R. W., William M. Adams, Leon Bennun, Stuart H. M. Butchart, Andrew Clements, David Coomes, Abigail Entwistle, Ian Hodge, Valerie Kapos, Jörn P. W. Scharlemann, William J. Sutherland and Bhaskar Vira. 'Biodiversity Conservation: Challenges Beyond 2010'. *Science* 329 no. 5997 (2010): 1298-1303.

Ron, Tamar. 'A Proposed Alternative Institutional Approach to Meeting International Biodiversity Targets'. *IUCN.* Last modified December 10, 2010. http://www.iucn.org/involved/opinion/?6676/A-proposed-alternative-institutional-approach-to-meeting-international-biodiversity-targets.

Audrey Aronowsky is the Scientific Program Manager for the Biodiversity Synthesis Center at The Field Museum. She works closely with the Education, IT, and Research departments in the Museum for specific digital projects.

Beth Sanzenbacher is the Outreach Coordinator for the Biodiversity Synthesis Center at The Field Museum. She develops, manages and facilitates several different digital learning projects, which provide immersive environments for youth to learn and experience science.

Johanna Thompson is a Digital Learning Specialist for the Education Department at The Field Museum. She develops, manages and facilitates several different digital learning projects, which provide immersive environments for youth to learn and experience science.

Krystal Villanosa is the Digital Learning Manager for the Education Department at The Field Museum. In this position, she partners with internal and external stakeholders and oversees the development of digital learning programmes for youth, specifically teenagers, with the ultimate goal of engaging them in science.

Facilitating Community in the Virtual Learning Environment

Shana Garrett

Abstract
Working with students can be a challenging and often rewarding experience given their experiential differences and the virtual learning environment. In a traditional classroom, there are many opportunities to learn more about your students via classroom interactions, one on one conversation, non-verbal observations, as well as social engagements. However, in the virtual environment, such subtleties as face to face interactions are non-existent, as well as other modalities that leave several missed opportunities to create viable connections. In the virtual environment, the importance of communication and approaches to establishing communities are based on a creative vision of constructing a virtual environment that is dynamic and engaging in an effort to establishing and developing a positive working relationship for the online student.

Key Words: Virtual learning, online student, connections, communication, establishing communities.

*****

1. Introducing Experiential Learning in Virtual Worlds

As an online facilitator and administrator, a successful hybrid approach to working with students has developed through a multi-disciplinary methodology consisting of several strategic psychological approaches from which an online community supports virtual world pedagogy. By utilizing this informal community of practice, the institution and instructor shift the educational methodology from instruction to facilitation, lending the academic achievement to not only reinforcing the positive learning experience, but is also utilizing the team community approach to reinforce and support the individual community members in participating in class. More importantly, this approach assists the virtual student in staying connected during the course as well as serving an information intervention when challenges arise during the learning session.

Several key techniques used in the pilot project were cultivate to educate various staff members who work in tandem with the students in an effort to partner with the faculty members so there is an additional layer of connection and community to the virtual student. Having a separate training initiative has worked extremely well with at-risk students in both attention probation cases as well as those students who are experiencing beneficial to the team working at the institution to support the pedagogical efforts.

Virtual learning environments hold a multiplicity of definitions and descriptions yet it all culminates into one persistent process of offering academic courses within an online platform.

The key words here are:

- *Virtual Learning Environment:* Learning environments differ in their utilization of communication, concepts of space-both physical and time, as well as characterized by the types of interaction and the barriers to shared information. A virtual learning environment:

  ... involves a combination of physical and virtual interaction, social imagination, and identity. They may be distinguished from physical communities in the virtual communities can extend the range of the community and individual can tailor their personal communities. The online interactions make possible forms of interaction that can be both more flexible and more durable than face –to-face interactions. The ability to come to identify with a group online, and support to do so, actually provides a scaffold for a different and enhanced sense of possibility for individuals...[1]

- *Community of Practice*: CoP is a group of individuals who share a common interest, concern, or come together to fulfil goals. The focus is often on best shared practices and sharing knowledge that advances the fruition on the community goal. According to founder of Communities of Practice Etienne Wenger:

  ... Communities of Practice are dynamic social structures that require 'cultivation' so that they can emerge and grow[2].

- *Appreciative Inquiry:* A psychological approach to learning from mistakes in order to modify thoughts and behaviors in order to strengthen weakness and ensure increase success.

According to Johnson and Leavitt:

  ... Instead of focusing on deficits and problems, the Appreciative Inquiry focuses on discovering what works well, why it works, and how success can be extended throughout the organization. It is both the visions, and the process for developing this vision, that create the energy to drive change throughout the organization.[3]

- *Distance Education:* Has existed in various forms for many years but is traditionally referred to as utilizing forms to communicate and teach that are not physically located on campus, visa vie conducted face-to-face. Examples of distance education can be see virtual interactions, video chats, and the standard asynchronous and synchronous method within a virtual learning management system. For Meyer and Kezar, states that

States have come to support distance education as a way to expand access to rural residents and working adults, because neither population had been well served by higher education. Actions by legislatures and governors have been particularly supportive of distance education, for their own reasons.

2. Online Learning Environment and Imparting the Concept of Community of Practice

Online learning has faced numerous challenges and questionable efficacy since its beginning in the higher education industry. Given its obvious differences in methodology and delivery, this diversity of systems have only increased its challenge and misunderstood significance within the academic standing of quality education. However, persistence and dedication of challenge the norms has resulted in distance education gaining in popularity and familiarity within the higher education industry.

Communication is a key element in the virtual learning environment although it's not provided in the conventional form of face to face but rather in various forms which can also been seen as effective communication. However, online education is not for all learners and some can find themselves as a distinctive disadvantage as it relates to understand the curriculum, bonding with classmates, and truly identifying with the online experience. But before the weighing of pros and cons of online learning as an alternative means to obtaining an education, one must look to the infrastructure of the online learning environment as well as administrative and support staff who are creating the courses, programs as well as the institutional culture.

The Online Learning Community is a shared virtual space of engaged communications around experience and knowledge while promoting an academic readiness and social engagement. It differs from the traditional educational experience of being in a face to face environment where verbal and nonverbal communication is the primary method of instruction. The virtual learning environment has created a shift in the educational approach and philosophy. The learner has now become the focus of the educational process and the recipient of the products of that process. Instructors are in the best position to know how to meet the needs of their students because the virtual classroom puts them on a level field of communication. The instruction should drive the vision of a virtual community for students to partake and actively participate with the instructor and classmates whereas traditional classrooms are more instructor driven lectures and receptive audience.

Teaching vs. Facilitation- Delivery techniques are now a focal objective in the virtual classroom. Faculty are now promoters of information and guide studies through the process of gathering information, testing, and creating meaning and application to their world. Faculty serve as mentors to students to empower them to know they can change their lives. The social pedagogies of communities of practice afford a method to engage into a student's instinct motivations: to be a part of a community and to share what they know with that community.

Community of practice is a concept developed by Etienne Wenger which proposes a phenomenon of individuals coming together to work for a united goal and/or objective. Taking this basic premise a step further, this community commits to the process and development of the community through continual investment of purpose.[4] The three primary components of communities of practice are domain, community, and practice. Domain refers to the shared interest among individuals which is represented by a chosen membership of mutual interests.[5] By valuing the collective input and commitment, the domain sustains the membership within the community. The second element of this event is referred to as a community. This element functions to sustain the members around the focus of the group.[6] Specifically, individuals within this assembly engage in pursuits and discussions sharing information to create relationships to support the shared community. Lastly, the third component is referred to as practice. This element is the developed repertoire of resources, albeit shared experiences, stories, efforts, approaches- all that contribute to the concept of a shared practice.[7]

Communities of Practice and the Online Learning Environment cross paths on several levels of collaboration and engagement. The first key distinguisher is the learning management systems, or the virtual classroom design used to focus the student into the engagement assignment, such as discussion boards. Questions are developed based on weekly curriculum goals that support the learning objectives in order to encourage student participation but to also demonstrate relevancy. By designing the virtual classroom in such a method, the interactions offer opportunities for students to engage in the materials as well as other learners which inevitably support the learning process.[8]

3. Impact of Application: Institutionally, Faculty Participation and Student Support Services

As an institution, the application of community within the virtual learning environment is created and supported on three basic levels: school, faculty, and student support. The strategies are built upon determining benchmarks, clear processes and setting procedures that support an online learning environment.

For this study, the analysis came from looking at student engagement within the virtual learning environment as well as retention rates as it pertained to student progression. The more opportunities within the learning environment to engage the student, the stronger the impact on the stronger the retention of their participation and persistence. When students can recognize their contribution to the virtual learning environment, their focus transfers from their personal barriers to bonding with other students within the community.[9] Peer engagement and support reinforces the level of connection.

A. For the Institution

Curriculum plays a key role in building Discussion Boards that support a strong and interactive class community. This covers such items as Preadmission Assessments and Learning-Style Assessments in order to build a collaborative approach utilizing social learning theory. Examples can be seen in lectures, guided discussion, role-playing and case studies utilizing YouTube videos or *Second Life*.

B. For the Faculty

Faculty are the experts within the subject matter and facilitator of the CoP. It is critical that faculty are engaged in a positive and collaborative effort with Curriculum in course development as well as revisions and corrections as warranted by faculty and student feedback. Faculty are also on the front lines, so to speak, as it relates to having the Institution's academic presence, setting clear performance expectations as well as open lines of communication. Faculty have imparted several Best Practices to convey an engaged community: (1) short lectures with video or audio podcasts, (2) weekly coaching and reminder announcements, (3) explanations and interactions with students. Lastly, Faculty are dependent upon consistent and solid technology in both the LMS but with administration as well.[10] Open lines of communication are necessary for any effective community of practice.

C. For the Student

Students need to feel supported and motivation in order to engage in the CoP. Having a Student Portal and Student Services team that is engaged in this practice is key to any successful online program. Social media has been a compelling platform for education given its social engagement practices which are easily referable to the distance education.

4. Meaningful Educational Experience in the Virtual Learning Environment

For the virtual learning environment, Discussion Boards are these interactive tools promote substantive discussion and critical thinking that activate engagement while also sustaining the community. Within this active dynamic of interaction, students are also participation in social collaboration and building of a community specific to their assignment, course, or program. Through these daily interactions, these experiences validate experiences and respect for differences of opinion.

Supporting students in their own reflection and inquiries is a critical component to building an online community through which learning is an active process. Faculty utilize their industry experience to transcended the obvious and engage the student in understanding how will this assignment help today, tomorrow, or two months from now. This simple interaction connects virtual students to focus on one task that joins them into a discussion of experiences, ideas, and solutions. Connected students do not abandon their dream of an education if they are engaged and nurtured within a community of inquiry and support.

One such example of a virtual CoP is the Academic Recovery Program. The ARP was designed to assist students struggling in their academic performance: attendance probation and/or academic probation. This program was developed to focus on students who are experiencing academic difficulties within the on ground or online classroom, which often leads to probation or suspension. By encompassing appreciative inquiry and specialized training of staff, this multi-disciplinary approach assists students to recover academically and fulfil their educational dream. This specialized CoP was created in an effort to reduce the number of failing grades and loss of students by course and overall program. It has been suggested that given the anonymity and remoteness of online classes, the withdrawal rate is higher for online student than those enrolled in face to face classes.[11] The multi-disciplinary intervention includes participation from advising, curriculum/course revisions as well as faculty involvement. Specialized training has been developed for the various departments utilizing various therapeutic approaches such as appreciative inquiry, cognitive behavioural coaching, etc.

Creating this specialized academic and student advocacy approach, improvement has been documented in areas such as improve course designs, statistical significance in passing grades, as well as addressing and minimizing obstacles to student which had led to improved persistence. More importantly, this endeavour revealed the existence and high value students placed in the importance of belonging to a community in which they shared a common interest and goal-academic achievement.[12]

One of the core concepts utilized in the ARP is the concept of collaborative change known as Appreciative Inquiry (AI). The focus of (AI) is positive in nature and strives to focus on strengths and accomplishments of the individual rather than focus on the negative, challenging barrier prohibited them from succeeding. AI is approach, the focus shifted to learning from successes. AI is unconventional in its concentration on ascertaining what works well, why it works, and how success can be achieved by the individual.[13] AI allows for individuals to discover, comprehend and reflect from their successes in order to respond positively to challenges and difficulty situations.

The Academic Recovery Plan is designed to identify and strengthen student engagement and performance while introducing the remote student to a virtual environment of students experiencing similar academic challenges.

5. Conclusions

Student empowerment is the fundamental means to academic achievement and challenges within the remoteness of online education. That factor is truly one of the biggest challenges students face in their academic journey. By a collective approach from the Institution, Faculty and Administrative support, real learning is about the connection students make to the bigger picture in their lives- both academically and experientially. Building a virtual community, either on the academic or social level, is one of the most effective means by which a sense of community and belonging is instilled in the remote student. Combining the concept of Community of Practice with Appreciative Inquiry has served to engaged and encourage a robust level of participation from students but staff as well. Best learning comes from personal experience and the foundation for this can be located in creating sustainable relationships built upon familiarity and camaraderie across the organization.

Perspectives in online education have changed from being a hierarchical structure to an open learning community from which everyone can contribute and sustain.

Notes

[1] K. Ann Renninger and W. Shumar, eds., *Building Virtual Communities: Learning and Change in Cyberspace* (Cambridge, England: Cambridge University Press, 2002), 7, viewed on 30 September 2012, http://www.questia.com.
[2] Mark Bell, 'Toward a Definition of "Virtual Worlds",' *Journal of Virtual Worlds Research* 1.1 (2008): 3.
[3] Ibid.
[4] Etienne Wenger, *Communities of Practice: Learning, Meaning and Identity* (Cambridge University Press; UK: Cambridge, 1998).
[5] Ibid.
[6] Ibid.
[7] Ibid.
[8] A. Perreault, H. Waldman and J. Zhao, 'Overcoming Barriers to Successful Delivery of Distance-Learning Courses,' *Journal of Education for Business* 77.6 (2002): 313.

[9] L. A. Bressler, M. E. Bressler and M. S. Bressler, 'The Role and Relationship of Hope, Optimism and Goal Setting in Achieving Academic Success: A Study of Students Enrolled in Online Accounting Courses,' *Academy of Educational Leadership Journal* 14.4 (2010): 37.

[10] M. E. Exter, N. Korkmaz, N. M. Harlin and B. A. Bichelmeyer, 'Sense of Community within a Fully Online Program: Perspectives of Graduate Students,' *Quarterly Review of Distance Education* 10.2 (2009): 177.

[11] Alison Rossett and Lisa Schafer, 'What to Do about E-Dropouts: What If It's Not the E-Learning but the E-Learner?' *TandD* 57.6 (2003): 40.

[12] Spellman, Natasha, 'Enrollment and Retention Barriers Adult Students Encounter,' *Community College Enterprise* 13.1 (2007): 63.

[13] G. Johnson and W. Leavitt, 'Building on Success: Transforming Organizations through an Appreciative Inquiry,' *Public Personnel Management* 30 (2001): 129.

Bibliography

Bell, Mark. 'Toward a Definition of "Virtual Worlds".' *Journal of Virtual Worlds Research* 1.1 (2008): 1- 5.

Bressler, L. A., M. E. Bressler and M. S. Bressler. 'The Role and Relationship of Hope, Optimism and Goal Setting in Achieving Academic Success: A Study of Students Enrolled in Online Accounting Courses.' *Academy of Educational Leadership Journal* 14.4 (2010).

Chang, Shujen L. 'Online Learning Communities with Online Mentors (OLCOM): A Model of Online Learning Communities.' *Quarterly Review of Distance Education* 5.2 (2004).

Darnell, P. 'Building Online Learning Communities.' *Adult Learning* 19 (2008).

Exter, M. E., N. Korkmaz, N. M. Harlin and B. A. Bichelmeyer. 'Sense of Community within a Fully Online Program: Perspectives of Graduate Students.' *Quarterly Review of Distance Education* 10.2 (2009).

Johnson, G. and W. Leavitt. 'Building on Success: Transforming Organizations through an Appreciative Inquiry'. Public Personnel Management 30 (2001).

Meyer, K. A. *Quality in Distance Education: Focus on On-Line Learning.* San Francisco: Jossey-Bass, 2002.

Perreault, A., H. Waldman and J. Zhao. 'Overcoming Barriers to Successful Delivery of Distance-Learning Courses.' *Journal of Education for Business* 77 (2002): 313.

Renninger, K. Ann and W. Shumar, eds. *Building Virtual Communities: Learning and Change in Cyberspace.* Cambridge, England: Cambridge University Press, 2002.

Rossett, Alison and Lisa Schafer. 'What to Do about E-Dropouts: What If It's Not the E-Learning but the E-Learner?' *TandD* 57.6 (2003): 40.

Spellman, Natasha. 'Enrollment and Retention Barriers Adult Students Encounter.' *Community College Enterprise* 13.1 (2007).

Wenger, Etienne. *Communities of Practice; Learning, Meaning and Identity.* Cambridge University Press; UK: Cambridge, 1998.

Shana Garrett began her leadership within education at Pepperdine University and has gained experience as both as a faculty member, curriculum developer, and senior leadership administrator throughout her fifteen years of higher education experience. She has over twenty years of experience in business operations, non-profit organizations and project/program management.

'That ever-ephemeral sense of "being" somewhere': Reflections on a Dissertation Festival in *Second Life*

Clara O'Shea and Marshall Dozier

Abstract

The MSc in E-learning at the University of Edinburgh is a fully online distance programme with around 150 students that have come from around 35 countries. In this chapter we discuss the Dissertation Festival which took place in 2011 and was developed as an opportunity for students undertaking their dissertations to reflect on their process, and to share ideas, issues, inspirations and feedback with tutors and peers. The Festival took place in *Second Life* (*SL*) on a specially designed island. The island captured the Festival atmosphere with banners, kites, a sunny, meadow-like environment and playful elements like sushi and champagne. Each presenting student contributed a poster, oral presentation with slides, and haiku to this naturalistic exhibition and meeting space. Festival events included a champagne poster viewing session, synchronous presentation sessions and a week-long exhibition of the students' work. The Festival was more successful than we had anticipated, with participants commenting particularly on its 'specialness'. We engaged in generative, rich dialogue with participants to explore what this 'specialness' was and what it means to be part of a community in an online, distance programme. In our analysis, we explored this further asking what it means to be 'here' at the University of Edinburgh and in what ways the Festival encompassed, challenged or shaped ideas of location and identity in distance learning. Our findings suggest that reports of 'specialness' related to a sense of community, shared purpose, shared membership, and the celebratory nature of the festival. The roots of this are linked to the wider practices and ethos of the MSc E-learning and specific practices for engagement in *SL*. We have also identified different layers of cues that helped shape the interactions within the festival itself, from the affordances of the constructed environment, the arrangement of 'props' like posters and scripts, through to modelled behaviours, all of which supported a peer-group interaction with a flattened hierarchy.

Key Words: Space, place, virtual worlds, *Second Life*, presence, connection, community, online learning, distance learning.

*****

1. Introduction

This chapter explores the interplay between a virtual world, programme values, learning community practices and academic identity. It considers the design, development and enactment of experiences within a virtual world, examining how the materiality of the world and the sociocultural context participants bring *to* and bring out *of* the world support learning for online postgraduate students.

The MSc in E-learning[1] is a fully online, distance programme at the University of Edinburgh, which can be taken full-time, over a one year period, or part-time, over a two to five year period. The programme has around 150 students drawn from 35 countries, most of whom are taking a part-time route and balancing their study with full-time work and a range of other personal commitments. Most students tend to do one course per semester, occasionally with a semester off during a busy work period.

The programme comprises 120 credits of coursework (a 40 credit introductory course, 20 credit research methods course and three 20 credit courses of the students' choosing) and a 60 credit dissertation. The programme has a strong ethos of student participation, one where students work across multiple media and modes of representation[2] and develop advanced skills in transliteracy.[3] The courses tend to be collaborative, dynamic and 'hard fun',[4] with a high level of pedagogical, technological and pastoral support from tutors and from within the student community. Comments, such as these from the most recent iteration of one of our courses, are typical:

> This course offers a great opportunity to mix with people from a wide variety of teaching backgrounds and a chance to share experiences and explore new ideas and reflect on old ones.

> For me, the design of the course was as good as the content, and so I was learning at different levels. I gained so much more from this course than I expected – it was an exceptionally positive learning experience.

The programme's core foundation course (*An Introduction to Digital Environments for Learning* or IDEL for short) specifically aims to scaffold[5,6] students' introduction not only to the main technologies they will encounter on the programme, but more importantly, to the ways of thinking and practising in the diverse field of digital education.[7] During IDEL, students have a personal tutor who helps steer them through this transitionary period and offers a range of guidance and advice through the student's personal, private blog space (scaffolding which instantiates Vygotsky's zone of proximal development).[8] Alongside their blog, students engage in a range of shared activities, some synchronous, others asynchronous (the IDEL course uses discussion board forums, 'twittorials' in Twitter, wikis and synchronous sessions using Skype text, Skype voice, *Second Life* and video conferencing tools like Adobe Connect or Collaborate).

2. The Problem

By the time students have reached the dissertation stage, they have completed courses which draw differently on a range of digital environments, but which nonetheless take a similar approach to encouraging constructive, critical conversations in and about digital environments. In contrast, then, the dissertation can be a lonely process as students design and carry out their own, individual research projects. Although they have a dissertation supervisor who supports them throughout each stage of their dissertation journey, the sense of shared purpose within courses and the collaborative, community aspect of their learning is diminished as they move to a very self-directed investigation of a personal or professional interest. As one student explained, there can be an element of "isolationness' not 'seeing' and knowing what others are doing'. Although students may be connected across different media (Facebook, Twitter, and the programme's own social network site 'the Hub'), that same student went on to articulate:

> It's hard to explain – Some of us [are] on FB, but I feel I'm 'interfering' their time asking about dissertation, where [as] when you face to face and in Uni/education environment, you tend to ask them how their study get on... if you get what I'm meant to say here. :)

Peer interaction and a sense of community are seen to be important in mitigating isolation and leading to greater rates of course completion in online distance learning courses.[9] So, there are two potential issues at stake in the dissertation process. Firstly, a sense of isolation, and secondly, from that isolation, a lack of opportunity to fully participate in the learning community, to articulate their arguments to peers and tutors, to test what makes for a convincing argument and to benefit from feedback that would come from that interaction.

3. Our Solution: The Dissertation Festival

Our solution to this problem was to create an event that included both synchronous and asynchronous elements, that encouraged dissertation students to articulate their arguments in multiple ways (using different genres and modalities), that allowed for a sharing and exchange of ideas in a community space dedicated to the MSc in E-learning programme's ethos of hard fun.

In creating a space for the Dissertation Festival, we took a sociomaterial approach[10] to our design, and, as will be seen, to our analysis of the events. A sociomaterial approach does not see pedagogy and technology as distinct, rather it acknowledges that 'the medium *is* the pedagogy'[11] that technology is not neutral, and that it is not a collection of decontextualised practices.[12] Instead, technology is another participant in the network, one that is not distinct from the human. To take a sociomaterial approach is to make a shift away from seeing meaning as either attributed to particular technologies or objects or seeing them as traces of culture; instead it is to see such things as 'continuous with and in fact embedded in the immaterial and the human'.[13] This kind of approach can help contextualise the learning and social processes that occur in digital environments by acknowledging the role of the material, the way it is entangled with people, practices and purposes and by acknowledging that 'Both the scope and the limits of pedagogic methods are influenced by the media involved'.[14]

For us, the sociomaterial approach's emphasis on the way materials participate in the social, and indeed are necessary for the social to be enacted, usefully aligned with the concept of 'affordances'. Gibson[15] coined the term 'affordances' as the relationship between the 'actionable properties' in the environment and an organism. He argues that:

> ... an affordance is neither an objective property nor a subjective property... [it] cuts across the dichotomy of subjective-objective and helps us understand its inadequacy. It is equally a fact of the environment and a fact of behaviour. ... An affordance points both ways, to the environment and to the observer.[16]

For Norman, however, the emphasis is on 'the perceived and actual properties of the thing, primarily those fundamental properties that determine just how the thing could possibly be used'.[17] Norman, though later claiming his intention was to focus on *perceived* affordances,[18] positions affordances as a property of the thing ('When affordances are taken advantage of, the user knows what to do just by looking'.[19] However, Bloomfield et al make a strong argument for seeing affordances as collective accomplishments, in which the perceived affordances of particular technologies are engaged with by a range of social actors within particular cultural contexts, and where the 'action possibilities emerge out of the ever-changing relations between people, between objects, and between people and objects'.[20] For us, this focus on affordances as an on-going exchange usefully aligned with our sociomaterial approach.

As we considered what technologies to use to help create the Dissertation Festival, it was clear to us that *Second Life*[21] – as a place that has been used for tutorials, Christmas parties and virtual graduation – might act as contextual cues, prompting particular possibilities for action, and play a role in shaping emergent behaviours at the Festival. In designing the space and activities of the Dissertation Festival, we took advantage of the relationship between the affordances of the material and the interaction of the community.

4. Methods

Before turning to a detailed discussion of the Dissertation Festival design, process and analysis, it is useful to take a moment to discuss our methodology. However, it should be noted that we did not set out to do a formal research project when we set up the Dissertation Festival: we initially sent emails to Festival participants to get feedback on whether the Dissertation Festival had been of benefit and might be improved, and we asked about place and space because of a separate concurrent project.[22] It was only when participants' initial responses indicated that something 'special' had happened that we decided to follow up the feedback more deeply and look systematically at participants' experiences. Not having designed a specific methodology into the project in advance, we therefore have taken what has been described as a 'generic qualitative' approach.[23] With the aim of being utterly clear in our approach, we have followed the stipulation of Caelli *et al.* to state explicitly our theoretical position, how we have 'congruence between methodology and methods,' how we have tried to achieve rigour, and finally our 'analytic lens'.[24]

We have taken a constructionist stance in this piece of research, with the 'view that all knowledge, and therefore all meaningful reality as such, is contingent upon human practices, being constructed in and out of interaction between human beings and their world, and developed and transmitted within an essentially social context'.[25] In line with this constructionist stance, our qualitative approach has allowed us to gain insight into participants' experiences and views of the event, recognising that each person will have an equally valid and probably different perspective. As is described in more detail below, the bulk of the data were generated by semi structured interviews with open-ended discussion, consistent with an aim of exploring participants' individual experiences and thoughts. We used thematic analysis[26] to generate conceptualisations of the participants' experience of the Dissertation Festival, bringing rigour to the themes by testing and re-testing the emergent themes initially as part of the interviews, and then in three separate iterations of coding by the researchers. As discussed in more detail below, we have used a sociomaterial approach as an analytic lens informing the thematic analysis and interpretation.

A. Dissertation Festival Participants

There were a total of 18 participants over the week who attended events or left comments on student work, not including the two authors (who were the Festival organisers): four student presenters, eight student attendees, five tutor attendees and one external attendee not associated with the programme. Most participants only attended one or two of the synchronous sessions. There may have been other visitors to the event space who did not leave artefacts of their presence (and we did not use a visitor tracking script).

B. Consent

At the beginning of their time on the MSc E-learning programme, students are asked for permission to use suitably anonymised materials generated on the programme as research data (this includes forum postings, assignments, and discussion transcripts). Permission to use the external participant's input was sought by email along with the interview questions. Permission to use data that emerged in a non-programme forum (e.g. Facebook) was sought as it appeared.

C. Data Generation

Following the Dissertation Festival, the four presenters and seven of the attendees (six students and one tutor) responded to email interview requests. Interviewing by email allowed us to have multiple asynchronous dialogues with respondents living in different time zones, and permitted reflective discussions between the researchers and the individual respondents over periods of up to a few days. Other studies conducting interviews by email have shown that email is an effective way of interacting with difficult-to-reach participants[27] and of exploring complex issues.[28] We consciously took an active approach to the email interviews, aiming 'to provide an environment conducive to the production of the range and complexity of meanings that might occur to all interview participants'[29] by engaging not just with follow-up questions, but by testing and inviting ideas, interpretations and conceptual links so that the respondents were also active in constructing meaning. We took the stance that meaning-making would come from the interactions between interviewers and interviewees,[30] that the account of the Dissertation Festival would be jointly assembled. The initial emails asked three broad questions:

1. What worked and what could we do better for next time?
2. Did the Festival help at all on your MSc journey?
3. We're thinking a little bit about notions of space and place – that a distance learner's sense of location and connection to an institution is perhaps differently felt or imagined than campus-based students. Is there anything in that idea you can relate to your experience of the Festival?

Although we acknowledge that our questions could be considered 'leading', we argue that interviews of this type are not intended to be neutral information gathering techniques[31] and that it is through the responsive, conversational and joint exploration between interviewers and interviewee that rich meaning-making can be achieved.

Additional, unanticipated, data from social media were collected and utilised. Triggered by the experience of attending the Dissertation Festival, dialogues (with three presenters and one student attendee) about the dissertation process emerged in Facebook and the programme's blog site.

Images of the event were taken as either screenshots or in-world pictures by the researchers and participants. While Prosser and Loxley[32] distinguish between these two types of visual research data (researcher-created and participant-created), we took all images as *community created*, seeing, as we do, both ourselves as researchers and members of the community taking part in the Festival. The chat texts in *SL* were logged automatically and saved for analysis, as is the case for most tutorial transcripts across the programme.

D. Data Analysis

Each author separately looked through all the data and developed an initial set of themes; we then discussed the emergent themes, agreed on thematic categories that felt most relevant, developed hierarchical groupings and merged some themes. After we agreed on the thematic categories, we returned to the data sources for fresh examination and interpretation. Some themes had been identified as areas of interest in advance (notions of space and place), a few had emerged during the active email interviews but most themes came out of the author analysis. Themes and concepts that had early testing in the email interviews were re-tested in this process. The coding was managed using the online qualitative analysis system Dedoose.[33]

5. Dissertation Festival Design

A. The Programme in *SL*

The MSc in E-learning has a specific allocation of land within the wider University of Edinburgh *SL* presence, known as 'Holyrood Park'.[34] This land is a peninsula away from the main University area, with branching areas designed as natural, open and welcoming tutorial spaces such as a forested space with logs around a fire, a beach tent made with a high roof and colourful gauze, a flower garden with a circle of cushions and an open air cafe. This pastoral design intentionally avoided replicating 'Real Life' edifices in a virtual world, where enclosed rooms and lecture halls are unnecessary, to encourage us all to re-think what constitutes a learning environment.

All students on the programme have a scaffolded, two week introduction to *SL*, which includes basic orientation sessions, optional building sessions and text and voice tutorials. The space is then used throughout the programme, not only as a tutorial space in some courses (using either text or voice), but also as a place of programme-wide events and celebrations, such as alumni seminars, Christmas parties and virtual graduation.[35] The multiple uses and naturalistic setting blur the formal/informal distinction that might be more clearly demarcated in other programme spaces, such as our VLE.

The physical campus can be symbolically and materially significant for online students. Research with our own students[36] has shown that online distance students 'need their own version of the 'spatial certainties' of bounded, campus space' and that 'The university, like any 'object' is always enacted across multiple topologies, 'dependent for [its] constancy on the intersection of different spaces' (Law, 2002: 98)'.[37] Within our programme, one apparent constant is the *SL* campus. As one of our interviewees explained:

> The Holyrood Park space in *SL* has come to feel like the primary, and most 'authentic', meeting space on the MSc. I say most authentic because it feels more so than with video conferencing, say for example with Wimba. There is something static about video conferencing, in that there is no feeling of shared space, and freedom of movement within it. *SL* seems to create a sense of ease through emulating the three dimensions of the real world. I think this is also entirely related to the aesthetic design of Holyrood Park, but also at a fundamental level, it is the sense of embodiment and place that makes it instinctive.

B. The Festival Space

We felt the Dissertation Festival required a space both a part of and apart from the usual tutorial spaces, creating a familiar but unique space for this one shared purpose. We raised a small island just off the peninsula and landscaped it in a similar naturalistic way, with a wildflower meadow theme. Bunting, fluttering kites in the shape of koi fish, and flowers all helped set the festival tone.

Posters, haikus and slideshow presentations were clustered in free-floating circular frames that glowed with a gentle, semi-transparent colour unique to each presenter. To a certain extent, the poster objects emulated the familiar poster display section of real-life conferences or academic building-corridors.

At one end of the island, visitors were greeted with bunting that declared the nature of the space (*The MSc in E-learning Dissertation Festival 2011*), as well as a small information point that offered a notecard with a more detailed explanation about the Festival and a timetable of events. At the other end of the island, a number of logs were clustered near a large floating screen where the presentations would be given. The logs could be formed into a circle or a very loose row-like configuration, depending on the needs of the specific events. Also at this end of the island was a table laid out with fruit, sushi and champagne which visitors could help themselves to and eat or drink by 'wearing' as 'attachments' to their avatar.

Image 1: Dissertation Festival Island. © 2013. Image courtesy of the authors

Image 2: A Poster Cluster. © 2013. Image courtesy of the authors

The intention with each of these design choices was to exploit the affordances of *SL* and of specific objects. For instance, the logs controlled avatar poses (as all such objects can do in *SL*) so that avatars appeared to be sitting in relaxed and informal styles. The clusters for each student's work ringed the perimeter of the island, offering a sense of boundary without excluding the possibility of panoramic views of the sea or across to the main programme space. Our hope had been that this specific configuration of objects and their affordances alongside the familiar use of the space for tutorials (and special events like end-of-semester parties or virtual graduations), would help create an atmosphere of celebration – of a shared but also excitingly new space that brought programme members together for a unique reason. Afterwards, one student who presented work noted:

> I think that Marshall's design had a lot to do with the non-stress environment – it would be interesting to see if having lines of wooden straight-backed chairs has an effect. It may also have something to do with how the avatars sit / slouch / loll when seated – none of that looks very formal at all

Image 3: Virtual Champagne and Sushi. ©2013. Image courtesy of the authors

C. The Festival Activities

The Festival focused on synchronous events that emulated real life seminar presentations of research in progress. The first of these events was a champagne poster viewing session to start the Festival (on the Monday). This was followed by a dialogue on dissertations – a roundtable chat between current dissertation students, tutors and other students on the programme about the dissertation process. This ranged from debriefing the research process, queries about writing up and brainstorming ideas for research for would-be dissertation students. The final event type was a presentation session in voice with complementary chat. There two presentation sessions, each which included a 10-15 minute presentation by one student, followed by discussion on their presentation, and then another 10-15 minute presentation by a second student, with conversation afterwards.

We did have an asynchronous element for the week of the Festival: each cluster of student materials (poster, presentation and haiku) included a comment board, where visitors could leave brief thoughts, questions and ideas that the student could then respond to later. Each comment was visible to the public. Several attendees came to view the displays and leave comments outwith the synchronous events.

This series of events was designed to encourage engagement with other students and tutors. This is a key factor in students developing their 'academic literacy'[38] or 'connoisseurship'.[39] By this we mean, as Royce Sadler[40] outlines it, coming to understand quality, what makes a 'good' dissertation in this case, in a way similar to that of the programme tutors. For this, as Hounsell argues, 'practice in recognising and judging work of varying standards is indispensable',[41] more so than simply seeing exemplars of good work or model answers. Instead, opening up the process of creating a piece of work, feeding back on the work-in-progress and doing so for an array of work in various stages of readiness may engage students more in the exercise of their judgement and the developing understanding of 'quality'. In thinking about how to create this kind of opportunity for our students, we were inspired by more traditional, face-to-face events for postgraduates such as departmental poster conferences, presentations and seminars and by the argument that multimodal work can encourage new ways of thinking about arguments.[42]

6. Experiences of the Festival

The Festival was well attended, given the size of the programme, with dissertation students, students not yet at the dissertation stage, tutors and an external visitor attending events. The champagne poster viewing session was a busy occasion, with festival go-ers discovering the space together: the opening minutes of chat were peppered with comments and a sense of delight at each event, such as 'oo pancha, can I have some sushi?', 'I love the 'kites'', 'already at the champagne i see' and so on.

The 'dialogue on dissertations' which kicked off the week was lively, with current dissertation students discussing their experience and asking tutors and peers for advice about the write up. Students at the coursework stage also found this dialogue useful, with one saying that after the summer break she was 'feeling all MSc-y again'. A student presenter said:

> The session did feel like a group of friends rather than a formal lecture-situation even though I've only met one person (Clara) once – it felt a lot like the friendship I found in the message boards (but on steroids)

Four students presented their dissertation work, each at a different stage of progress. The oral presentations had many elements of a traditional seminar, including introduction and moderation of the event by the authors and approximately ten minutes of oral presentation followed by 20 minutes of discussion with the audience.

Image 4: Student Presenting. © 2013. Image courtesy of the authors

Each presenting student was asked to send a haiku, a poster, and the slides accompanying their oral presentation, all of which were used to create an exhibit for each student's project. Each element was chosen as a complementary way of facilitating students' development and communication of the ideas – and areas of uncertainty – in their project. The haiku, being a mere 17 syllables long, challenged students to identify the very heart of their argument. The poster allowed students to give a deeper exposition of their aims, methods and findings thus far, considering the diagrammatic relationships in their work. The oral presentation with slides was an opportunity to discuss context, methods, findings, concerns and to seek feedback from audience members. This example haiku nicely captures the essence of the research question and also findings:

> Online MBAs
> teach leadership skills ... don't they?
> It's all in the blend.

Our intention had been for all participants to use voice (presenters and audience). However, the affordance of text chat, and, we suspect, the informal and playful atmosphere developed during the events, created an adaptation of the traditional face-to-face seminar presentation format. As the presenters spoke, audience members used the text chat to indicate agreement, disagreement and those non-verbal cues not implicitly communicated online. These included nods, laughs (of the '/me smiles' or simply 'LOL' variety), or comments on the presentation ('that's quite a population!', 'grounded theory approach then' or 'transcription sucks!'). The text chat effectively substituted for body language that a presenter can use as a cue in a face-to-face situation, as one of the students in the audience observed:

> It's a most unnerving experience on teleconferences when you are talking and everyone else is absolutely silent. I hate that! Having a little text ticker showing that people are listening and understanding is kind of like the proof and reassurance that the RL people behind the avatars aren't AFK [away from keyboard] or bored.

The audience also started asking questions in the text chat ('how did you choose those 6 people?', 'did they get offered 'lack of opportunity'?'). Some presenters chose to engage with these questions and comments during the presentation while others relied on the Festival organisers to collate them and raise them during the discussion session. These text comments were not unidirectional – participants also responded to one another's comments, creating something akin to a twitter backchannel at a conference. Text became a way to both make up for perceived missing physical cues but also of exploiting advantages of the technology. Although there was tutor concern this use of chat might undermine presenters' 'flow', the presenters themselves said things like:

> I think using voice and instant messaging worked really well, allowing a kind of back channel for comments. This also allowed the speakers to ad lib a bit in response to comments, which made things quite dynamic. In fact, I thought that the *SL* presentation format worked so well, I wondered why more of the courses on the MSc didn't utilise this idea.

7. Did the Festival Address the Problem?

This is a difficult question to answer. As discussed above, the two primary aims of the Festival were to address an isolation that students in the dissertation phase of the programme can feel, and to give opportunities for students to develop their work by discussing and getting feedback. Of the four students who presented, two submitted their dissertations at the next submission deadline, two realised they had further work to do and chose to aim for a later deadline. All four spoke well of the

Festival. For those close to submission, it was a chance for affirmation, fine tuning and making connections with others. For those further from a deadline, the chance to articulate their work multimodally, to present their arguments and to engage in conversation with others helped them realise the work that lay ahead. For other students, tutors and visitors, the Festival was a chance to reconnect with an academic community, engage in ideas and dialogue, and have a little fun (and sushi). Finally from a programme perspective, the Festival did create an opportunity for participative, multi-modal, collaborative community building based on furthering academic connoisseurship and transliteracy that we believe marked a turning point in the way we address the dissertation process.

In some ways, it was this communal engagement that seemed the most successful element of the Festival. Participants referred to the 'specialness' of the festival, and there was a suggestion that the space of the festival transcended into a 'place'. Is there a way to 'capture' this specialness? Was it a result of design or implementation? Would the Festival still be 'special' with another cohort? And what does this tell us about location, identity and community online? We think the sociomaterial approach might help theorise and understand why this particular aspect of the Festival worked so well.

8. Transforming a 'Space' into a 'Place'

A sociomaterial approach[43] can reveal some of the dynamics which transformed a 'space' into a 'place', providing a useful lens through which to examine the 'specialness' of the Dissertation Festival. 'Space is not the equivalent of 'place'',[44] for while space can be sedimented and static, place is dynamic and multiply produced. Place, as Al-Mahmood[45] discusses, is space endowed with meaning and significance. Place comes into being through the enactments between the different aspects of the network, both human and non-human. As Sheller and Urry argue:

> Places are thus not so much fixed as implicated within complex
> networks by which hosts, guests, buildings, objects, and
> machines are contingently brought together to produce certain
> performances in certain places at certain times.[46]

Though pre-*SL*, Massey's articulation of place also helps open up the dynamic and deeply contextualised nature of place, moving it from bounded notions of space to:

> articulated moments in networks of social relations and
> understandings, but where a large proportion of those relations,
> experiences and understandings are constructed on a far larger

scale than what we happen to define for that moment as the place itself, whether that be a street, or a region or even a continent.[47]

For the Dissertation Festival, various elements of pre-existing networks were brought into this space and were part of the development of a sense of place. These included the general ethos of the programme, the previous uses of *SL* (as an informally formal, collaborative space) which influenced the expectations around interaction and practices, and the previous experiences individuals had of *SL*. However, our design intentions, both in building a specific locale in *SL* and in developing the activities of the Dissertation Festival, are not enough to turn a *space* into a *place*. Space turns into place through how people interact with the environment, place emerges from the dynamics of the sociomaterial.

> What struck me about the festival was the fact that I *felt* I was giving a *real* presentation to other people. This was reflected in the fact I felt bothered that my back was to the audience whereas I wanted to have 'eye' contact, even though other people's eyes were very virtual. So there was something quite powerful and immersive about the space and the experience, which was perhaps enabled by purposeful activity in *SL* rather than something more open ended and unstructured.

This response of one of the presenters suggests the successful creation of 'place', while also flagging ways that that 'place' was created – 'real', 'immersion', 'purposeful activity' – in other words a shared space and a shared purpose. We would also add another dimension – a sense of shared time – to explain how space is transformed. While there is clearly a complex interweaving between these three elements, addressing them individually will highlight particular aspects differently.

A. Shared Space

> I think having a shared virtual space definitely helps to give a sense of a shared experience which transcends physical location – something that wouldn't happen if the poster information for instance was simply e-mailed to each student. There is a sense that having a location is somewhere that you can 'hang your ideas and thoughts' which wouldn't be possible otherwise.

As previously mentioned, the space in *SL* was designed to take advantage of various elements of programme experience to act as behavioural cues in this new unique space. The Dissertation Festival area echoed the naturalistic setting of the rest of Holyrood Park, but had distinct elements of its own, such as the bunting and koi kites. This lent the area a sense of authenticity, through its physical and visual kinship with the 'campus' of the MSc in E-learning, but just as crucially, gave it a uniquely bounded space, opening different possibilities for interaction and engagement. The sense of joint discovery of the space, evidenced through the banter around champagne and sushi, sowed the seeds of a shared sense of the space. Though possibly trivial in themselves, these interactions begin to illustrate the multiple ways that *SL* as a platform allowed interaction and expression of self: presentation of an avatar, movement within – and interaction with objects within – the 3D space, and the use of text chat as a backchannel during the oral presentations allowed people more individual freedom and more opportunities to engage than other spaces like the virtual classroom referred to earlier by one of the respondents, Wimba, might allow.

> [F]or me the medium is a vehicle or space where presence can be experienced. If I just log into *SL* and visit, say, the festival space on my own, in that eerie sort of way, I feel no presence at all, but bring others into the space with whom there is some relationship or rapport, and the feeling of presence 'happens'. For me, I think the feeling of co-presence makes a difference to feelings of 'real'.

This echoes the argument that spaces need interaction to become places. While there are cues which suggest particular interactions with the space – informal seating, celebratory signals, past programme *SL* experience – a specifically Dissertation Festival community is not automatically formed by entering the space. Garrison and Anderson suggest that two key aspects of developing a community (in their case, a community of inquiry) are social and cognitive presence; that is, the extent of construction and confirmation of meaning through reflective discourse and the ability to project one's self socially and emotionally.[48,49] It could be argued that the shared experience of 'realness' and 'specialness' participants reported experiencing in this space was not one to do with the environment per se, but in the way the environment allowed for social and intellectual engagement to emerge.

B. Shared Purpose

This combination of intellectual and social interdependence, in which students and tutors came together to collaboratively support the development of meaning making is dependent on 'purposeful activity'. Garrison and Anderson describe this as a community of inquiry, one in which tutors and students transact 'with the specific purposes of facilitating, constructing, and validating understanding, and of developing capabilities that will lead to further learning.'[50] These transactions can function to decrease a sense of distance and increase a sense of community through dialogue, through the amount the learners exercise control over the cognitive space.[51]

In this respect, community is not one bounded by space (though we would argue that the community is still shaped by it), but emergent from the way in which members are connected in their values, interactions, practices and history[52] and in their shared passions and interests.[53] Importantly, community activity is also about enculturating members into the ways of thinking and practicing in that community. For newer members, or legitimate peripheral participants as Lave and Wenger[54] might describe them, learning is not just about engagement in specific events but about 'a more encompassing process of being active participants in the practices of social communities and constructing identities in relation to these communities'.[55] For this specific community, these practices focussed around developing student's confidence, academic interests and connoisseurship, as these students who presented explain:

> Presenter 1:
> Questions from others really helps me thinking about the way I do the study, what analysis I should consider, etc...

> Presenter 2:
> The other thing that was really valuable was finding out what other people were doing. For me, the networking aspect was one of the most valuable bits of the process. Had I not taken part, I would not have made contact outside of *SL* with [student] or [visitor], both of whom share similar interests professionally.

> It's always tempting to think that what you're doing has pretty little value, but other people's feedback was great for confidence building.

Interestingly, unlike Garrison and Anderson's community of inquiry,[56] or Lave and Wenger's community of practice,[57] the community experienced during the Festival was one with a relatively flattened hierarchy. The smooth, informal and amorphous space of *SL* undermined the striated and hierarchical learning spaces one might find in a virtual learning environment.[58] The fluidity of avatar looks (where gender and species changes are just a matter of 'changing outfit') and the ambiguity of avatar identity (where names are rarely linked clearly to 'real life' identities) created a hierarchy that was fuzzy. The focus was not on *who* was saying what, but *what* was being said. One presenter described this fuzziness:

> I found that I like to know who the avatars belong to but after knowing I don't put their faces to the avatar (does that make

sense?) – I deal with the avatar as a 'being' in itself rather than as the real person in disguise. That could be because I'm dealing with everybody during the course as text and discussion rather than as a physical being I meet regularly.

A student attendee noted:

> It's nice to just pitch straight in to talking about interesting stuff, the articles etc. and then the self-disclosure can come in little asides or jokes in the conversation.

As is the nature of smooth spaces, this flattened hierarchy extended rhizomatically,[59] opening up participation in the Festival to those without a clear connection to the programme and inviting them to engage in the community. As one visitor explained:

> I just finished my master's degree and I miss being exposed to the kind of knowledge sharing that I experienced at your festival. Exposure to an intercultural collaborative learning environment was very inspiring.

However, there was an element of risk to this openness, as meeting (or the idea of meeting) other people in the space, on occasion, brought discomfort, particularly out with the scheduled synchronous presentations:

> Reading presentations or leaving comments was always p[r]one to encounters with other presenters, participants or members of the public, and this added an element of risk.

In this respect, the presentation space in *SL* was more exposed than the imagined departmental conference that inspired the Festival:

> The permanence, coupled with the sense of public exposure in the space felt important here, in that the work could be visited at any time, but also that any exploration was itself an anonymous experience.

It could perhaps be argued that the more shared the experience, the more risk may be felt when allowing others into the created 'place'.

C. Shared Time

We have argued that a shared space and a shared purpose come together to create a community, a pre-requisite in the creation of 'place', of 'specialness' and 'real' interactions. There is an additional element threaded through the previous sections which complicates and extends this creation – a sense of shared time. The importance of interaction and community strongly favours synchronicity to help achieve a stronger sense of 'hereness'. In *SL*, a shared time can add to the sense of a shared space, in a way that for instance, simultaneous communication on a discussion forum, may not. Two students explained:

> Student 1: The *SL* meetings and stuff like Skype have all helped me feel I'm occupying the same 'space' as my colleagues and that we really 'know' each other and have met.

> Student 2: [I]t's always good to meet up in a shared synchronous space with interesting people.

Garrison and Anderson also argue that immediacy is key to establishing social presence, and that such immediacy is lacking in an e-learning context.[60] For them, immediacy is key to establishing a supportive social presence, where personal risk is softened by the security of the learning environment. For us, shared time is a great deal more than synchronicity or immediacy, however. We argue that shared time does not necessarily equate with a sense of temporal instantaneity; instead it is associated with the socio-intellectual interdependence aspect of community and meaning making. In this view, shared time becomes less about a clock and more about a sense of continuing social and cognitive engagement. This argument draws on Lombard and Ditton's notion of the 'perceptual illusion of nonmediation'.[61] Here, 'perception' refers to the human sensory, cognitive and affective processing systems and the 'illusion of nonmediation' to the perceptual failure to recognise that a medium exists or is mediating their interaction. Lombard and Ditton argue that although all experience is mediated, this definition particular refers to technology, that which 'comes between' us and our environment. Lee usefully summarises their definition as 'The degree to which users logically overlook the mediated or artificial nature of interaction with an entity within a medium'.[62]

A feeling of being present is what lies at the heart of this definition – how much a person feels as if they are 'there' compared to their physical space.[63] One presenter wrote,

> The questions were also much harder to ignore (if they were difficult) than in Skype or message boards because the person who asked it is sat / stood in front of you

– although, as we all recognise, 'the person who asked it' was many miles away and represented by pixels on the computer screen. It is a subjective perception 'generated by and/or filtered through human-made technology'.[64] While the user may know, in some way at some level, they are not 'there', their main experience is as if they were engaging with the environment, objects and people and the technology was not involved or shaping those experiences.[65]

The aim of shared time is linked to Csikszentmihalyi's notion of flow as 'the holistic experience that people feel when they act with total involvement'.[66] While it might not be as all-consuming as Csikszentmihalyi's concept,[67] there is certainly an element of an engrossed involvement in activity, of focussed concentration where time becomes distorted and the activity is gratifying in and of itself. When the barriers to engagement are low (when the technology runs smoothly, when the participants feel they are competent users of the technology) and the intellectual and/or social engagement is high, participants report experiences that speak of authenticity, specialness and what we might see as 'flow'. The mediated nature of the interactions, even when that mediation is a part of the interactions (such as text chat), seem a part of the flow. Importantly, this flow, or shared time, comes not from one individual being engrossed in their solo activity, but in the engagement of the many, with shared purpose and shared practices.

D. Barriers to Shared Time and Space

One way to examine the importance of shared time is to acknowledge the difficulties inherent in its ephemeral nature. Disruptions to this perceptual illusion of nonmediation or flow were multiple for some of our attendees, undermining their experience of the Festival as a place to 'be there'. For students with equipment or connectivity issues, participation was also seriously undermined. Lack of familiarity with the user interface (it may be have been years since the student had taken a course with a large *SL* input), alongside the complexity of the environment, also created a barrier to participation for some. One student presenter, less practised in the *SL* environment, said:

> ... my machine could not cope with *SL* requirement. And also my familiarity with the control is very poor, so I found it frustrating when I can read the posters/powerpoint properly. So this is nothing got to do with you but just an 'individual error' or 'user error'.

Warburton identified eight barriers to using *SL* in education,[68] and it is notable that the most fundamental, technical, barrier still presents a problem to students on the programme. Though at a more extreme end of the scale, this participant was not the only one who found difficulties: others needed a bit of reminding and coaching on various relatively basic ways of effectively manipulating their avatars within the virtual environment.

Existing in multiple spaces also disrupted the sense of 'being there'. While 'at' the Festival, participants were also in multiple environments simultaneously. One student audience member described how being present in multiple spaces impacted on engagement:

> But using *SL* on a laptop at my inlaw's house was not like that. I
> had lots of inputs from the real world – I could hear voices next
> door, smell cooking from the kitchen, feel the breeze from the
> window and see the rest of the room that I was sitting in etc, so
> in a way the virtual work and the real world were competing for
> my attention. I can see how it is possible to be so focussed on
> what is happening in *SL* (or in a game maybe) that you block out
> all of that, but I think it is hard to achieve...it is hard to be
> completely present in *SL* because the brain is getting other inputs
> from real-life.

As Boellstorff notes, 'In virtual worlds, "virtuality" refers to sociality, not the senses.'[69] yet it is clear that, for this student, the senses performed an important role in how 'there' she could be.

E. Complications Arising from Shared Time

Even if the physical world and technological issues were removed as barriers to a sense of shared time, there is a crisis inherent in its creation. While it immerses the participant more deeply, creating a tighter knit community who feel as those they have been part of something 'special', shared time is, inevitably, fleeting. Indeed, this ephemerality may be part of why it was considered special, but it also made it more exclusionary. One student, who could only attend the Festival asynchronously, noted:

> I was unable to attend the day of the event and suspect I may
> have missed something by not being there for the live
> presentations.

Students living in time zones or with lifestyles incompatible with the timing of the presentation sessions may have felt that the lack of connectedness and non-involvement in the classroom that Rovai argues can lead to feelings of loneliness and isolation.[70] In this respect, the strongly synchronous nature of the Festival risked exacerbating the original problem that it was intended to solve.

9. Conclusion

In a dynamic and participatory programme, the transition from coursework to individual research is one that can provoke feelings of isolation and a lack of a supportive and familiar community. Individual research can also leave students with fewer opportunities to articulate their developing academic arguments and to engage with others' work as part of their growing understanding of what constitutes quality in academic work. The Dissertation Festival was a successful intervention for this particular set of problems, creating a safe community space for the interchange of ideas and the development of academic ways of thinking and practising. As one student presenter said:

> I felt connected to all of the audience, even those I did not know from my studies – it may be that I think of the Uni area of *SL* to be a 'safe place'?

Articulating dissertation ideas multimodally and seeing others' work at different stages of production enabled students to better understand the possibilities for creating and judging good quality academic discourse.

However, the most interesting thing about this intervention was the way it was perceived by attendees (students and tutors alike) as 'special'. One tutor attendee explained their enjoyment of the Festival thus:

> I think for me it was that ever-ephemeral sense of 'being' somewhere. More so than at virtual graduation (though maybe I'm just used to that now). Being somewhere with other people, working on a shared task that couldn't have been done any other way. Lovely.

What made for this particularly engaging atmosphere? We have argued that 'specialness' comes not from a particular moment or thing, but from an approach that opens up and acknowledges all elements, social and material, that turn a space into a place. The Festival took advantage of students' previous experiences with *SL* while creating a new opportunity for engagement based around a familiar but unique shared space. There was a distinct and collaboratively produced shared purpose within that space, and joint sense of immersion and non-mediation bringing the 'flow' of shared time. We suggest that the richness of the Festival cannot be attributed to singular, specific technologies or programme practices, but to the emergent meaning and significance created through the interactions between the material and the social. In this respect, 'specialness' is an enactment any online, distance programme could achieve if it takes this kind of contextualised, sociomaterial approach.

Notes

[1] 'Msc in Digital Education (Formerly Msc in E-Learning),' University of Edinburgh, http://online.education.ed.ac.uk/.

[2] Gunther Kress, 'Gains and Losses: New Forms of Texts, Knowledge, and Learning,' *Computers and Composition* 22 (2005).

[3] Sue Thomas et al., 'Transliteracy: Crossing Divides,' *First Monday [Online]* 12(2007), http://firstmonday.org/htbin/cgiwrap/bin/ojs/index.php/fm/article/viewArticle/2060 /1908.

[4] Seymour Papert, 'A Word for Learning,' in *Constructionism in Practice: Designing, Thinking, and Learning in a Digital World*, ed. Yasmin B Kafai and Mitchel Resnick (Mahwah, N.J.: Lawrence Erlbaum Associates, 1996).

[5] Jerome S. (Jerome Seymour) Bruner, *Toward a Theory of Instruction* (Cambridge, Mass.: Belknap Press of Harvard University Press, 1996).

[6] D. Wood, J. S. Bruner, and G. Ross, 'The Role of Tutoring in Problem Solving,' *Journal of Child Psychology and Psychiatry, and Allied Disciplines* 17, no. 2 (1976).

[7] Velda Mccune and Dai Hounsell, 'The Development of Students' Ways of Thinking and Practising in Three Final-Year Biology Courses,' *Higher Education* 49, no. 3 (2005); Jean Lave and Etienne Wenger, *Situated Learning: Legitimate Peripheral Participation* (Cambridge: Cambridge University Press, 1991).

[8] Lev Semenovich Vygotsky, *Mind in Society: The Development of Higher Psychological Processes* (Cambridge [Mass.]: Harvard University Press, 1978).

[9] Alfred Rovai, 'Building Sense of Community at a Distance,' *International Review of Research in Open and Distance Learning* 3(2002).

[10] Tara Fenwick, 'Re-Thinking the 'Thing': Sociomaterial Approaches to Understanding and Researching Learning in Work,' *Journal of Workplace Learning* 22 (2010); Tara Fenwick, Richard Edwards, and Peter Sawchuk, *Emerging Approaches in Educational Research: Tracing the Socio-Material* (Abingdon: Routledge, 2011).

[11] Glynis Cousin, 'Learning from Cyberspace,' in *Education in Cyberspace*, ed. Ray Land and Siân Bayne (Abingdon: RoutledgeFalmer, 2005), 117.

[12] Martin Oliver, 'Learning with Technology as Coordinated Sociomaterial Practice: Digital Literacies as a Site of Praxiological Study,' in *Proceedings of the 8th International Conference on Networked Learning* (Maastricht2012).

[13] Fenwick, 'Re-Thinking the "Thing": Sociomaterial Approaches to Understanding and Researching Learning in Work,' 105.

[14] Cousin, 'Learning from Cyberspace,' 117.

[15] James J. Gibson, 'The Theory of Affordances,' in *Perceiving, Acting and Knowing: Toward an Ecological Psychology*, ed. Robert E Shaw and John Bransford (Hillsdale, NJ: Lawrence Erlbaum Associates, Inc., 1977).

[16] *The Ecological Approach to Visual Perception* (Boston: Houghton Mifflin, 1979), 129.

[17] Donald A. Norman, *The Psychology of Everyday Things* (New York: Basic Book, 1988), 9.

[18] *Affordances and Design*, Nielsen Norman Group (NNG), 2004), http://www.jnd.org/dn.mss/affordances_and_desi.html.

[19] *The Psychology of Everyday Things*, 9.

[20] B. P. Bloomfield, Y. Latham, and T. Vurdubakis, 'Bodies, Technologies and Action Possibilities: When Is an Affordance?,' *Sociology* 44, no. 3 (2010): 419-20.

[21] Linden Research Inc., *'Second Life,'* http://secondlife.com/.

[22] Michael Sean Gallagher et al., 'Edinspace: New Geographies of Learning,' http://edinspace.weebly.com/.

[23] Kate Caelli, Lynne Ray, and Judy Mill, 'Clear as Mud: Toward Greater Clarity in Generic Qualitative Research,' *International Journal of Qualitative Methods* 2 (2003).

[24] Ibid., 5.

[25] Michael Crotty, *The Foundations of Social Research: Meaning and Perspective in the Research Process* (London: Sage, 1998), 42.

[26] Richard E Boyatzis, *Transforming Qualitative Information: Thematic Analysis and Code Development* (Thousand Oaks, Calif.: SAGE, 1998).

[27] J. L. M. McCoyd and T. S. Kerson, 'Conducting Intensive Interviews Using Email: A Serendipitous Comparative Opportunity,' *Qualitative Social Work* 5(2006).

[28] Roni Berger and Marilyn S. Paul, 'Using E-Mail for Family Research,' *Journal of Technology in Human Services* 29 (2011).

[29] James Holstein and Jaber Gubrium, 'The Active Interview,' in *Qualitative Research: Theory, Method and Practice*, ed. David Silverman (London: Sage Publications, 2004), 152.

[30] G. Cousin and B. Dawson, *Researching Learning in Higher Education: An Introduction to Contemporary Methods and Approaches* (New York: Routledge, 2009).

[31] Ibid.

[32] Jon Prosser and Andrew Loxley, *Introducing Visual Methods: Esrc National Centre for Research Methods Review Paper*, (2008), http://eprints.ncrm.ac.uk/420/1/MethodsReviewPaperNCRM-010.pdf.

[33] SocioCultural Research Consultants LLC., 'Dedoose,' http://www.dedoose.com/.

[34] 'Holyrood Park, Vue South, Virtual University of Edinburgh,' http://slurl.com/secondlife/Vue%20South/135/197/22/.

[35] John Kirriemuir, 'Virtual World Activity in U.K. Universities and Colleges - Virtual Teaching in Uncertain Times,' in *Virtual Worlds Snapshot* (Eduserv, 2010).

[36] Sian Bayne, Michael Sean Gallagher, and James Lamb, 'Being ' at ' University : The Topologies of Distance Students.' (*under review*), http://www.dice.education.ed.ac.uk/?p=483.

[37] S. Bayne, Ross, J., O'Shea, C., Gallagher, M., Lamb, J. and Macleod, H., 'Campus Envy and Being at University: The Geographies of Education on the Internet,' in *Internet Research 13.0* (Manchester, UK, 2012), 15.

[38] Sue Bloxham and Pete Boyd, *Developing Effective Assessment in Higher Education: A Guide* (Maidenhead: Open University Press, 2007).

[39] Dai Hounsell, 'The Trouble with Feedback: New Challenges, Emerging Strategies,' *Interchange* 2 (2008).

[40] D. Royce Sadler, 'Formative Assessment and the Design of Instructional Systems,' *Instructional Science* 18 (1989).

[41] Hounsell, 'The Trouble with Feedback: New Challenges, Emerging Strategies,' 6.

[42] Colleen Mckenna and Claire Mcavinia, 'Difference and Discontinuity: Making Meaning through Hypertexts,' in *Digital Difference: Perspectives on Online Learning*, ed. Ray Land and Siân Bayne (2011); Robin Goodfellow, 'Literacy, Literacies and the Digital in Higher Education,' *Teaching in Higher Education* 16 (2011); Kress, 'Gains and Losses: New Forms of Texts, Knowledge, and Learning'; Madeleine Sorapure, 'Between Modes : Assessing Student New Media Compositions,' *Kairos* 10 (2005).

[43] Fenwick, 'Re-Thinking the 'Thing': Sociomaterial Approaches to Understanding and Researching Learning in Work'; Fenwick, Edwards, and Sawchuk, *Emerging Approaches in Educational Research: Tracing the Socio-Material*.

[44] Ibid., 129.

[45] Reem Al-mahmood, 'Spatialities and Online Teaching: To, from and Beyond the Academy,' in *Hello! Where are You in the Landscape of Educational Technology? Proceedings Ascilite* (Melbourne 2008).

[46] Mimi Sheller and John Urry, 'The New Mobilities Paradigm,' *Environment and Planning A* 38 (2006): 14.

[47] Doreen B. Massey, *Space, Place, and Gender* (Minneapolis, MN: University of Minnesota Press, 1994), 154.

[48] D. Randy Garrison, Terry Anderson, and Walter Archer, 'Critical Thinking, Cognitive Presence, and Computer Conferencing in Distance Education,' *American Journal of Distance Education* 15, no. 1 (2001).

[49] D. Randy Garrison and Terry Anderson, *E-Learning in the 21st Century: A Framework for Research and Practice* (London: RoutledgeFalmer, 2003).

[50] Garrison, Anderson, and Archer, 'Critical Thinking, Cognitive Presence, and Computer Conferencing in Distance Education,' 23.

[51] Michael G. Moore, *Theory of Transactional Distance, Theoretical Principles of Distance Education* (London: Routledge, 1993).

[52] Rovai, 'Building Sense of Community at a Distance.'

[53] Etienne Wenger, *Communities of Practice: Learning, Meaning, and Identity* (Cambridge: Cambridge University Press, 1998).

[54] Lave and Wenger, *Situated Learning: Legitimate Peripheral Participation.*

[55] Wenger, *Communities of Practice: Learning, Meaning, and Identity*, 4.

[56] Garrison and Anderson, *E-Learning in the 21st Century: A Framework for Research and Practice.*

[57] Lave and Wenger, *Situated Learning: Legitimate Peripheral Participation.*

[58] Sian Bayne, 'Smoothness and Striation in Digital Learning Spaces,' *E-Learning and Digital Media* 1, no. 2 (2004).

[59] Cousin, 'Learning from Cyberspace.'

[60] Garrison and Anderson, *E-Learning in the 21st Century: A Framework for Research and Practice.*

[61] Matthew Lombard and Theresa Ditton, 'At the Heart of It All: The Concept of Presence,' *Journal of Computer-Mediated Communication* 3, no. 2 (1997), http://dx.doi.org/10.1111/j.1083-6101.1997.tb00072.x.

[62] K. M. Lee, 'Presence, Explicated,' *Communication Theory* 14(2004): 31.

[63] Biocca (1997) in ibid.

[64] Matthew Lombard, 'Using Telepresence to Communicate Science in Giant Screen Cinema,' in *Presented at the Giant Screen Cinema Association (GSCA) Symposium 'The Greater Potential of Giant Screen Experiences: Connecting Society with Science'* (Jersey City, NJ.2008), 1.

[65] Ibid; Lombard and Ditton, 'At the Heart of It All: The Concept of Presence'.

[66] Mihaly Csikszentmihalyi, *Beyond Boredom and Anxiety* (San Francisco: Jossey-Bass, 1975), 36.

[67] Ibid; *Flow: The Psychology of Optimal Experience*, 1st ed. (New York: Harper and Row, 1990).

[68] Steven Warburton, '*Second Life* in Higher Education: Assessing the Potential for and the Barriers to Deploying Virtual Worlds in Learning and Teaching,' *British Journal of Educational Technology* 40 (2009).

[69] Tom Boellstorff, *Coming of Age in Second Life: An Anthropologist Explores the Virtually Human* (Princeton: Princeton University Press, 2008), 112-13.

[70] Rovai, 'Building Sense of Community at a Distance.'

Bibliography

Al-mahmood, Reem. 'Spatialities and Online Teaching: To, from and Beyond the Academy.' In *Hello! Where are You in the Landscape of Educational Technology? Proceedings ascilite* Melbourne, 2008. Viewed 30 January 2013, http://www.ascilite.org.au/conferences/melbourne08/procs/al-mahmood.pdf.

Bayne, S., J. Ross, C. O'Shea, M. Gallagher, J. Lamb and H. Macleod. 'Campus Envy and Being at University: The Geographies of Education on the Internet.' In *Internet Research 13.0*. Manchester, UK, 2012.

Bayne, Sian. 'Smoothness and Striation in Digital Learning Spaces.' *E-Learning and Digital Media* 1, no. 2 (2004): 302-16.

Bayne, Sian, Michael Sean Gallagher, and James Lamb. 'Being at University: The Topologies of Distance Students,' *(under review)*. Viewed 30 January 2013, http://www.dice.education.ed.ac.uk/?p=483.

Berger, Roni, and Marilyn S. Paul. 'Using E-Mail for Family Research.' *Journal of Technology in Human Services* 29 (2011): 197-211.

Bloomfield, B. P., Y. Latham, and T. Vurdubakis. 'Bodies, Technologies and Action Possibilities: When Is an Affordance?'. *Sociology* 44, no. 3 (2010): 415-33.

Bloxham, Sue, and Pete Boyd. *Developing Effective Assessment in Higher Education: A Guide*. Maidenhead: Open University Press, 2007.

Boellstorff, Tom. *Coming of Age in Second Life: An Anthropologist Explores the Virtually Human*. Princeton: Princeton University Press, 2008.

Boyatzis, Richard E. *Transforming Qualitative Information: Thematic Analysis and Code Development*. Thousand Oaks, Calif.: SAGE, 1998.

Bruner, Jerome S. *Toward a Theory of Instruction*. Cambridge, Mass.: Belknap Press of Harvard University Press, 1996.

Caelli, Kate, Lynne Ray, and Judy Mill. 'Clear as Mud: Toward Greater Clarity in Generic Qualitative Research.' *International Journal of Qualitative Methods* 2 (2003): 1-13.

Cousin, G., and B. Dawson. *Researching Learning in Higher Education: An Introduction to Contemporary Methods and Approaches*. New York: Routledge, 2009.

Cousin, Glynis. 'Learning from Cyberspace.' In *Education in Cyberspace*, edited by Ray Land and Siân Bayne, 117-29. Abingdon: RoutledgeFalmer, 2005.

Crotty, Michael. *The Foundations of Social Research: Meaning and Perspective in the Research Process*. London: Sage, 1998.

Csikszentmihalyi, Mihaly. *Beyond Boredom and Anxiety*. San Francisco: Jossey-Bass, 1975.

————. *Flow : The Psychology of Optimal Experience*. 1st ed. New York: Harper & Row, 1990.

Fenwick, Tara. 'Re-Thinking the Thing: Sociomaterial Approaches to Understanding and Researching Learning in Work.' *Journal of Workplace Learning* 22 (2010): 104-16.

Fenwick, Tara, Richard Edwards, and Peter Sawchuk. *Emerging Approaches in Educational Research: Tracing the Socio-Material*. Abingdon: Routledge, 2011.

Gallagher, Michael Sean, James Lamb, Sian Bayne, Hamish Macleod, Clara O'Shea, and Jen Ross. 'Edinspace: New Geographies of Learning.' Viewed 30 January 2013, http://edinspace.weebly.com/.

Garrison, D. Randy, and Terry Anderson. *E-Learning in the 21st Century: A Framework for Research and Practice*. London: RoutledgeFalmer, 2003.

Garrison, D. Randy, Terry Anderson, and Walter Archer. 'Critical Thinking, Cognitive Presence, and Computer Conferencing in Distance Education.' *American Journal of Distance Education* 15, no. 1 (2001): 7-23.

Gibson, James J. *The Ecological Approach to Visual Perception*. Boston: Houghton Mifflin, 1979.

————. 'The Theory of Affordances.' In *Perceiving, Acting and Knowing : Toward an Ecological Psychology*, edited by Robert E Shaw and John Bransford, 67-82. Hillsdale, NJ: Lawrence Erlbaum Associates, Inc., 1977.

Goodfellow, Robin. 'Literacy, Literacies and the Digital in Higher Education.' *Teaching in Higher Education* 16 (2011): 131-44.

Holstein, James, and Jaber Gubrium. 'The Active Interview.' In *Qualitative Research: Theory, Method and Practice*, edited by David Silverman, 140-61. London: Sage Publications, 2004.

'Holyrood Park, Vue South, Virtual University of Edinburgh.'
http://slurl.com/secondlife/Vue%20South/135/197/22/.

Hounsell, Dai. 'The Trouble with Feedback: New Challenges, Emerging Strategies.' *Interchange* 2 (2008): 1-10.

Kirriemuir, John. 'Virtual World Activity in U.K. Universities and Colleges – Virtual Teaching in Uncertain Times.' In *Virtual Worlds Snapshot*. Eduserv, 2010.

Kress, Gunther. 'Gains and Losses: New Forms of Texts, Knowledge, and Learning.' *Computers and Composition* 22 (2005): 5-22.

Lave, Jean, and Etienne Wenger. *Situated Learning: Legitimate Peripheral Participation*. Cambridge: Cambridge University Press, 1991.

Lee, K. M. 'Presence, Explicated.' *Communication Theory* 14 (2004): 27-50.

Linden Research Inc. *'Second Life.'* Viewed 30 January 2013.
http://secondlife.com/.

Lombard, Matthew. 'Using Telepresence to Communicate Science in Giant Screen Cinema.' In *Presented at the Giant Screen Cinema Association (GSCA) Symposium 'The Greater Potential of Giant Screen Experiences: Connecting Society with Science'*. Jersey City, NJ., 2008.

Lombard, Matthew, and Theresa Ditton. 'At the Heart of It All: The Concept of Presence.' *Journal of Computer-Mediated Communication* 3, no. 2 (1997). Viewed 30 January 2013, http://dx.doi.org/10.1111/j.1083-6101.1997.tb00072.x.

Massey, Doreen B. *Space, Place, and Gender*. Minneapolis, MN: University of Minnesota Press, 1994.

McCoyd, J. L. M., and T. S. Kerson. 'Conducting Intensive Interviews Using Email: A Serendipitous Comparative Opportunity.' *Qualitative Social Work* 5 (2006): 389-406.

Mccune, Velda, and Dai Hounsell. 'The Development of Students' Ways of Thinking and Practising in Three Final-Year Biology Courses.' *Higher Education* 49, no. 3 (2005): 255-89.

Moore, Michael G. *Theory of Transactional Distance.* Theoretical Principles of Distance Education. London: Routledge, 1993.

'Msc in Digital Education (Formerly Msc in E-Learning).' University of Edinburgh, Viewed 30 January 2013, http://online.education.ed.ac.uk/.

Norman, Donald A. *Affordances and Design.* Nielsen Norman Group (NNg), 2004. Viewed 30 January 2013. http://www.jnd.org/dn.mss/affordances_and_desi.html.

———. *The Psychology of Everyday Things.* New York: Basic Book, 1988.

Oliver, Martin. 'Learning with Technology as Coordinated Sociomaterial Practice: Digital Literacies as a Site of Praxiological Study.' In *Proceedings of the 8th International Conference on Networked Learning.* Maastricht, 2012.

Papert, Seymour. 'A Word for Learning.' In *Constructionism in Practice: Designing, Thinking, and Learning in a Digital World*, edited by Yasmin B. Kafai and Mitchel Resnick, 9-24. Mahwah, N.J.: Lawrence Erlbaum Associates, 1996.

Prosser, Jon, and Andrew Loxley. *Introducing Visual Methods: Esrc National Centre for Research Methods Review Paper.* 2008. Viewed 30 January 2013. http://eprints.ncrm.ac.uk/420/1/MethodsReviewPaperNCRM-010.pdf.

Rovai, Alfred. 'Building Sense of Community at a Distance.' *International Review of Research in Open and Distance Learning* 3 (2002): 1-16.

Sadler, D. Royce. 'Formative Assessment and the Design of Instructional Systems.' *Instructional Science* 18 (1989): 119-44.

Sheller, Mimi, and John Urry. 'The New Mobilities Paradigm.' *Environment and Planning A* 38 (2006): 207-26.

SocioCultural Research Consultants LLC. 'Dedoose.' Viewed 30 January 2013. http://www.dedoose.com/.

Sorapure, Madeleine. 'Between Modes: Assessing Student New Media Compositions.' *Kairos* 10 (2005).

Thomas, Sue, Chris Joseph, Jess Laccetti, Bruce Mason, Simon Perril, and Kate Pullinger. 'Transliteracy: Crossing Divides.' *First Monday [Online]* 12, (2007). Viewed 30 January 2013.
http://firstmonday.org/htbin/cgiwrap/bin/ojs/index.php/fm/article/viewArticle/2060/1908.

Vygotsky, Lev Semenovich. *Mind in Society: The Development of Higher Psychological Processes*. Cambridge, MA: Harvard University Press, 1978.

Warburton, Steven. '*Second Life* in Higher Education: Assessing the Potential for and the Barriers to Deploying Virtual Worlds in Learning and Teaching.' *British Journal of Educational Technology* 40 (2009): 414-26.

Wenger, Etienne. *Communities of Practice: Learning, Meaning, and Identity*. Cambridge: Cambridge University Press, 1998.

Wood, D., J. S. Bruner, and G. Ross. 'The Role of Tutoring in Problem Solving.' *Journal of Child Psychology and Psychiatry, and Allied Disciplines* 17, no. 2 (1976): 89-100.

Clara O'Shea is an Associate Lecturer in the School of Education, at the University of Edinburgh. Her research interests are in digital culture and education, with specific interests around how we learn within online spaces.

Marshall Dozier is Liaison Librarian within Information Services, and an Associate Tutor in the School of Education, at the University of Edinburgh. Her research interests are in the area of information behaviour.

Experimentation Not Simulation:
Learning About Physics in The Virtual World

Anna Peachey, Greg Withnail and Nicholas Braithwaite

Abstract
This chapter reports on the evaluation of a study to explore the use of the virtual world *Second Life*™ for conducting real physics experiments, completed as a pilot activity for a new course development at The Open University UK. All HEIs within the UK are currently engaged in some level of activity in virtual worlds. However in such a young field there is a relatively scarce literature, meaning that small scale pilot projects are vital for exploring the pedagogical framework as well as the practical tools for supporting specific subjects within such an immersive environment. This study gave ten participants access to a small range of tools that enabled them to create experiments to explore the physics of *Second Life* using a cognitive learning approach. Data on their inworld activity was collected and compared against their input to a survey at the conclusion of the two-week study period. These results were triangulated using detailed follow up interviews with a smaller sample of two participants. The research found that students look for context and indicators of stability and reassurance during the experience. The majority of respondents indicated that they would be happy to participate in course-embedded *Second Life* activities of this type, albeit also expressing a range of reservations, providing valuable feedback for further development of the pilot tools and module framework.

Key Words: Virtual worlds, science, physics, experiments, immersive environments, cognitive learning.

*****

1. Introduction

The Open University is a pioneering institution for distance learning in the UK, supporting 200,000 part-time undergraduate students. Courses in the Science faculty have traditionally blended distance and e-learning methods with a small number of optional face-to-face tutorials, supplemented with weeklong residential schools offering 10 and 15 credits (100 and 150 hours, respectively) at Level 2. In recent years, only about one third of the target group opted to attend residential schools in science and so, from 2012, the residential options have been replaced by a suite of interlinked distance-learning modules in practical science (S288). S288 will offer subject-specific pathways in physics, biology, chemistry and geosciences, with recommended practical units and an additional mix of online or residential options.

Much of the basic practice of being a scientist is in knowing how to formulate a hypothesis, design an experiment to test and investigate that hypothesis, make observations and process data with rigour and consistency; all skills that translate easily into learning outcomes. A broad range of online investigations within S288 support these learning outcomes through immersion and interaction.

Second Life™ (*SL*) is a virtual world (VW) where users mediate in a three dimensional environment using avatars. In 2009 Virtual World Watch found that all but one HEI in the UK held a presence in a virtual world[1] and The Open University is a pioneer in the field, having owned virtual land in *Second Life* since 2006. The rapidly growing body of literature relating to learning in these environments is almost entirely published since 2006/7 and is in its infancy, with much still to explore and learn.

The S288 Team identified *SL* as a potential venue for one stream of student activities, with a key emphasis on exploiting the physics engine within the environment to conduct genuine experiments rather than simulations. This chapter reports on pilot activity for this inworld module, where students were provided with a small set of tools for experimentation, and their experience was assessed through automated observation and a critical pedagogy of survey and interviews. The S288 Team requested that the experiments in this pilot should explore some of the laws of physics embedded in *SL*, using tools to investigate the environment, rather than following a series of instructions.

This study had four objectives. These were: To collect quantitative data on time spent on tasks, number of returns within experiment period, comparison between students of science and students of other disciplines/gender etc; to collect survey responses from each user; to record interviews with selected users; to triangulate and analyse data, survey, and interview responses. The results are encouraging, finding that despite reservations all the students who responded would be happy to participate in course-embedded *SL* activities. The chapter provides a discussion of these results, paying particular attention to the reservations expressed, and summarises the outcomes with recommendations for further work in the area.

2. Background

The National Physical Laboratory (NPL) has had an active presence in *Second Life* since 2005. NPL co-founded the SciLands (http://www.scilands.org), an inworld region dedicated to Science and Technology based organisations, providing 'shared resources, islands, events and enhanced networking for organisations interested in formal and informal science education, innovation, knowledge transfer and research using *Second Life*.'[2] A number of universities have expressed interest in teaching physics in *Second Life*, but there is currently no literature that reflects on the transferable learning from these specific subject experiences.

There is however a more general body of literature emerging on the wider potential of teaching and learning in VWs. Warburton (2009) reflects on a review of multi-user virtual environments, in particular *SL*,[3] to identify components of the *SL* experience that facilitate innovations in pedagogy through the following: Extended or rich interactions (opportunities for social interaction between individuals and communities, human–object interaction and intelligent interaction between artefacts); visualisation and contextualisation (the production and reproduction of inaccessible content that may be historically lost, too distant, too costly, imaginary, futuristic or impossible to see by the human eye); exposure to authentic content and culture; individual and collective identity play; immersion in a 3-D environment where the augmented sense of presence, through virtual embodiment in the form of an avatar and extensive modes of communication, can impact on the affective, empathic and motivational aspects of the experience; simulation (reproduction of contexts that can be too costly to reproduce in real life with the advantages that some physical constraints can be overcome); community presence (promoting a sense of belonging and purpose that coheres around groups, subcultures and geography); content production (opportunities for creation and ownership of the learning environment and objects within it that are both individual and owned).

Whilst there is potential in all these areas for exploring practical science, it is specifically the combination of authentic content, immersion and content-production that we explore in this pilot activity. Creating content and giving students ownership of that content, working immersed in an individual space, drives a cognitive approach to formalised learning that makes 'learning more conscious in order to enhance it'.[4]

Cognitive theorists view learning as creating associations through inference, expectation and repetition, involving the acquisition or restructuring of the cognitive structures that we use to process and store information.[5] The experiments reported here employ simple tools, in the anticipation that participants will use them to explore and make sense of the physics of their virtual environment. In so doing they will acquire strategies and knowledge that translate directly to the physical world.

The aim is to learn how to specify activities linked directly to learning outcomes for practical science. It is therefore important to understand the processes that lead to the acquisition of knowledge from playing with a limited set of practical tools.

Second Life uses the Havok Physics Engine, a commercial physics engine made by Havoc Inc, which is owned by Intel. Use of a physics engine in a virtual 3D world such as *SL* determines the difference between empty space and full space, enabling an avatar to walk 'on' the ground, walk up and down hills, slide off roofs and be halted by walls. To our particular advantage, the engine also simulates Newtonian object collisions and interactions, gravity, elasticity, and the conservation of momentum between colliding objects. Its behaviour is consistent within *SL*, but not absolutely representative of physical world physics. Hence students conducting experiments in *SL* must either use simulations of physical world behaviour, or understand that they are setting up experiments to explore the physics of the virtual environment.

3. Methodology

Using the graphical user interface and inbuilt Linden Scripting Language (LSL), tools were developed specifically for two groups of experiments to explore *SL* physics within this pilot study.

Distance Measuring Tool

A blue square pyramid forms the start marker, and a pink square pyramid the end marker. When the blue start marker is touched (clicked), the distance to the pink end marker is displayed. Both of these markers can be moved (dragged) around using the standard *Second Life* edit tool – see Figure 1: Distance Measuring Tool.

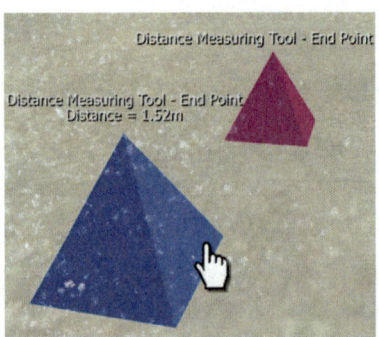

Figure 1: Distance Measuring Tool. © 2013.
Image courtesy of the authors

Angle Measuring Tool

This is a 360 degree protractor, with 0 degrees aligned with *Second Life*'s X-axis. The protractor can be repositioned using the standard *Second Life* edit tool and is a 'phantom' object, meaning that it can be moved through other objects without displacing them. See Figure 2: Angle Measuring Tool.

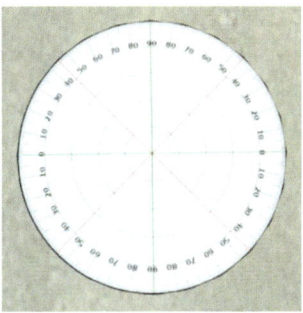

Figure 2: Angle Measuring Tool. © 2013.
Image courtesy of the authors

Gravity/Ball Drop Experiment

This experiment can be used to determine the acceleration due to gravity, and its relationship to the mass of an object

To operate the experiment, users simply 'touch' a green pyramid. This rezzes[6] a ball of either 5.23 Lg or 0.04 Lg 10m above the top of the pyramid, which immediately drops. The ball's fall time is displayed in white text above the pyramid, as in Figure 3: Gravity Experiment.

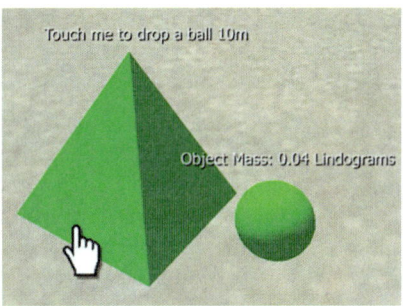

Figure 3: Gravity Experiment. © 2013.
Image courtesy of the authors

Momentum/Rolling Ball Experiment

Two white rolling balls each have a diameter of 0.576m and a mass of 1 Lg. When a ball is touched, a force of 2 LindoNewtons is applied to the ball for 1 second in the X direction. While a ball is moving, it leaves a red breadcrumb marker every 0.5 seconds, indicating its path – see Figure 4: Momentum/Rolling Ball Experiment.

As each marker appears, the ball's current velocity is shown in Local Chat.[7] It is possible to move and position the balls (using edit), arranging for one ball to roll and collide with the other.

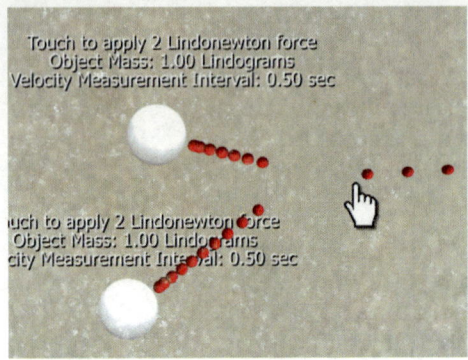

Figure 4: Momentum/Rolling Ball Experiment. © 2013.
Image courtesy of the authors

There are a number of investigations that may be performed with these tools and experiments. Examples, as suggested to participants, include: plot the velocity curve of a ball, perhaps by importing the velocity data into a spreadsheet ; explore one and two dimensional collisions; determine whether momentum is conserved determine whether energy is conserved.

An experiment in action is illustrated in Figure 5: Experiment in Progress.

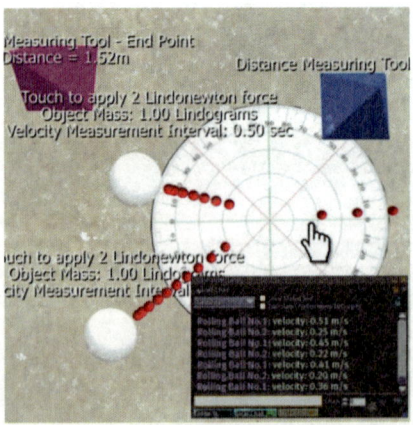

Figure 5: Experiment in Progress. © 2013.
Image courtesy of the authors

Participants were provided with access to these tools in a dedicated space on Open University Island in *Second Life*, with entry restricted to study participants – see Figure 6: Inworld Study Space.

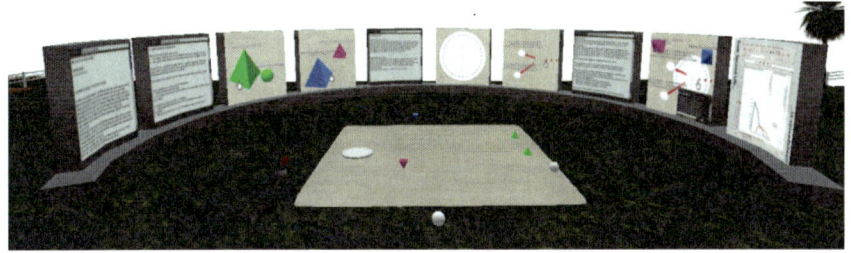

Figure 6: Inworld Study Space. © 2013. Image courtesy of the authors

All participants agreed to wear a device for capturing data relating to their inworld activity during the period of the study. This scripted device, 'worn' as a Heads-Up Display (HUD) by the avatar, captured the following data for each participant: Number of visits (within study period) during which participant interacted with Science activities; number of interactions with Small Ball Drop; number of interactions with Large Ball Drop; number of interactions with Rolling Ball; number of interactions with Distance Measuring Tool; number of interactions with Angle Measuring Tool.

4. Sampling

It is anticipated that the greater number of future students of online practical science at the OU will be following a science pathway, but many will also be taking the course as part of a wider learning experience: At any time approximately 40 000 students with the OU are registered on an Open Degree, allowing them a range of choice between qualifying courses. Therefore the pilot study was not restricted to science students.

In order to focus on the experience of engaging with the experiments in *Second Life*, rather than the learning curve that we already know a new user would face before interacting with the environment, an invitation to participate was issued to the Open University UK inworld group with the expectation that most members of this group would have the core set of basic skills necessary. The ten participants were drawn from respondents to a notice sent to this group, providing a summary of the study and requesting volunteers.

Laurillard writes about how technologies can be used to improve learning, reflecting on a number of evaluative studies on the implementation of new technology that have, she comments, 'predictable outcomes'.[8] It is from this position that we actively exclude issues relating to new users of the environment from this study.

Twelve volunteers came forward within two days of the notice, which was received either live inworld, by forwarding to email or next time the user logged in to *Second Life*, depending on their edited preferences.

All twelve were submitted for OU research approval from the Student Research Projects Panel (SRPP), a process that ensures students are treated fairly and are not subjected to research fatigue, which authorised a sample of ten to participate. Appropriate permissions were sought and granted from Ethics and Data Protection authorities respectively.

5. Research Design

The research has been funded from the S288 course budget and is primarily designed to explore participants' understanding and experience of using the tools provided to test *Second Life* physics, and to explore measures of success in terms of learning. Using both HUD data and questionnaire will enable primarily quantitative data, and observation and interviews will provide primarily qualitative data, enabling triangulation for concurrent validity between sources.

Only people who have participated in the inworld activity were given a link to the questionnaire, ensuring exclusivity of responses, and no questions were mandatory, allowing respondents the freedom to answer as they wished.

Interviews have more emphasis on the participants as individuals, and invite notions of interpretation as well as data. Detailed permission for interviews (including outline questions) was sought from SRPP only after the survey data had been collected and reviewed, enabling the interviews to explore issues arising from that data. Three interview respondents were offered a payment of L$5000 in recognition of the additional time and inconvenience of this further participation. Interviews took place in *Second Life* using text chat.

6. Results (i) Demographic Data

All ten participants demonstrated some relevant inworld activity during the study period but only nine completed the subsequent survey. The demographic data for the nine participants completing the survey is as follows:

5 aged 36-45	2 aged 46-55	1 aged 56-65	1 aged 66-75
5 male	4 female		
All have been using *Second Life* for more than 6 months			
8 have high or higher than average confidence in using a computer		1 has average confidence in using a computer	

Participants were asked to summarise briefly how they spend the majority of their time in *Second Life*. Reponses were grouped as in Figure 7: Time in *Second Life*, noting that some participants offered more than one primary activity.

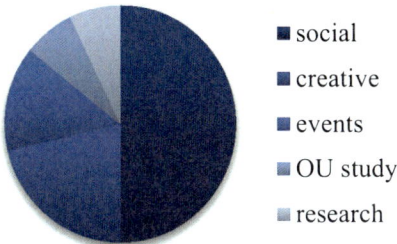

Figure 7: Time in *Second Life.* © 2013.
Image courtesy of the authors

Four participants indicated that they had previously attended some sort of formal learning activity in *Second Life*, of which three were in ICT and one in mathematics.

7. Results (ii) Automated Data Capture
Data on inworld activity was captured for 10 students and is presented for each student in Chart Set 1: Interactions With Activity, showing:

The number of visits within the study period during which they interacted with the experiments
The total number of interactions they made with any significant objects
A pie chart showing the ratio of their interactions with each tool and core experiment

It can be seen that the angle measuring activity was least used, while simpler things like ball rolling were more popular. Interestingly, distance measuring was also a popular activity, despite being one of the less simple tasks.

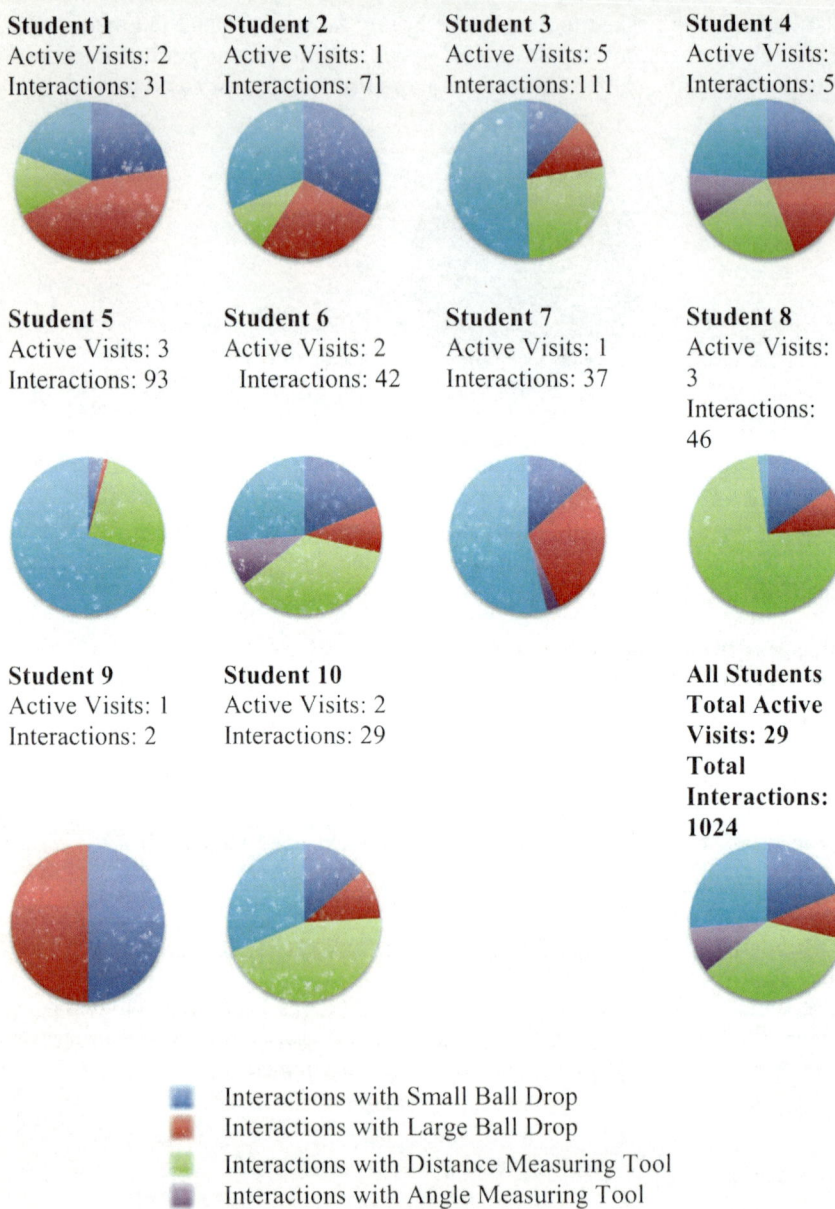

Student 1
Active Visits: 2
Interactions: 31

Student 2
Active Visits: 1
Interactions: 71

Student 3
Active Visits: 5
Interactions:111

Student 4
Active Visits: 9
Interactions: 50

Student 5
Active Visits: 3
Interactions: 93

Student 6
Active Visits: 2
Interactions: 42

Student 7
Active Visits: 1
Interactions: 37

Student 8
Active Visits:
3
Interactions:
46

Student 9
Active Visits: 1
Interactions: 2

Student 10
Active Visits: 2
Interactions: 29

**All Students
Total Active
Visits: 29
Total
Interactions:
1024**

- Interactions with Small Ball Drop
- Interactions with Large Ball Drop
- Interactions with Distance Measuring Tool
- Interactions with Angle Measuring Tool
- Interactions with Rolling Ball

Chart Set 1: Interactions With Activity. © 2013. Image courtesy of the authors

8. Results (iii) Quantitative Responses
The Gravity Experiment
The chart for each question indicates the number of participants selecting each response.

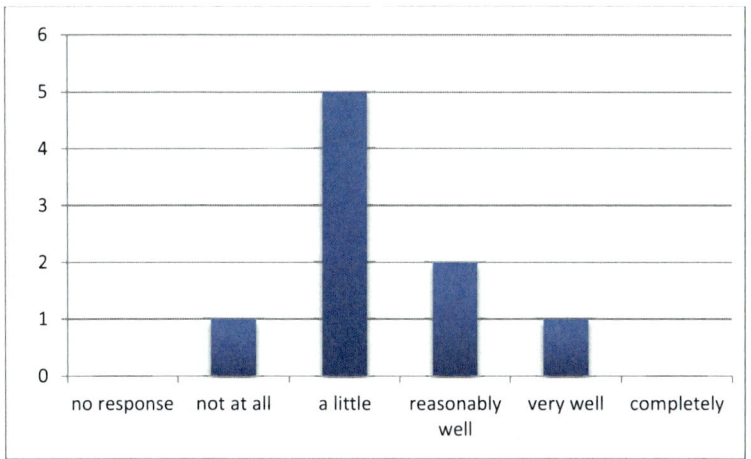

Chart 2: 'The ball drop experiment enabled me to explore acceleration.'

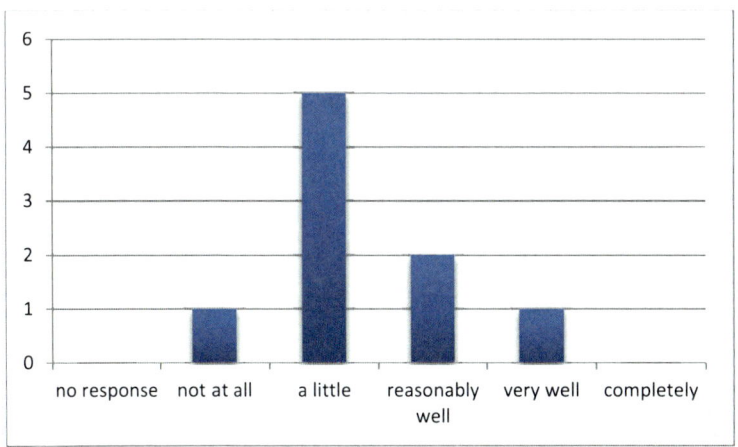

Chart 3: 'The ball drop experiment enabled me to explore experimental accuracy (e.g. by considering the number of decimal places used when timing the ball drop).'

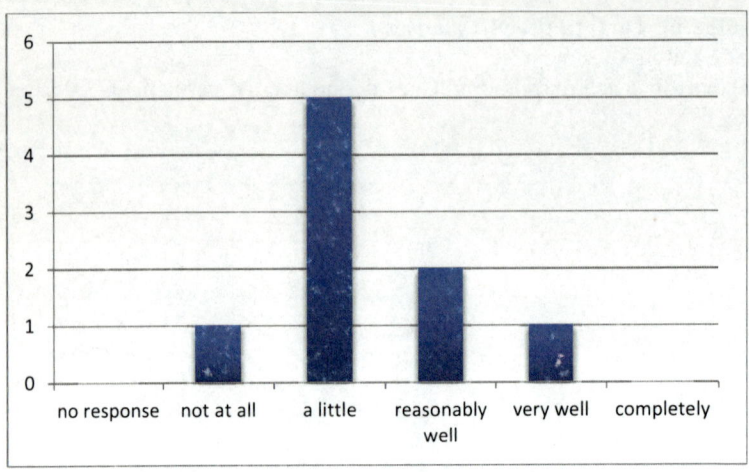

Chart 4: 'The ball drop experiment helped me think about the differences and/or parallels between running an experiment in *Second Life*, and running an experiment in the physical world.'

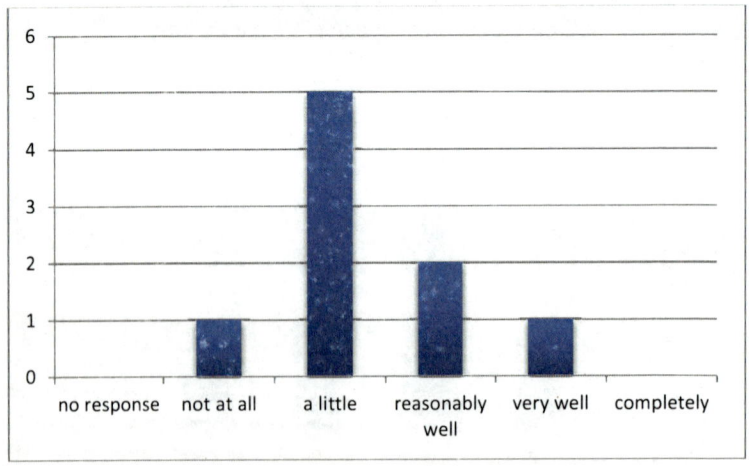

Chart 5: 'The ball drop experiment enabled me to explore the issues involved in setting up an experiment.'

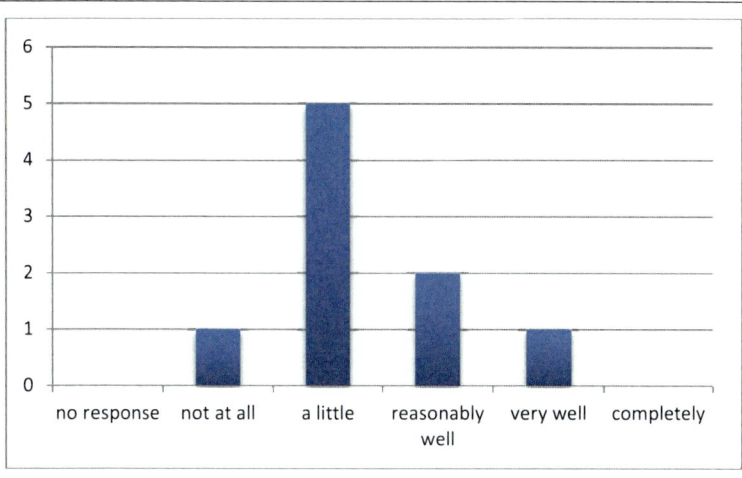

Chart 6: 'The ball drop experiment enabled me to explore the issues involved in capturing data from an experiment.'

The Momentum Experiment

The chart for each question indicates the number of participants selecting each response.

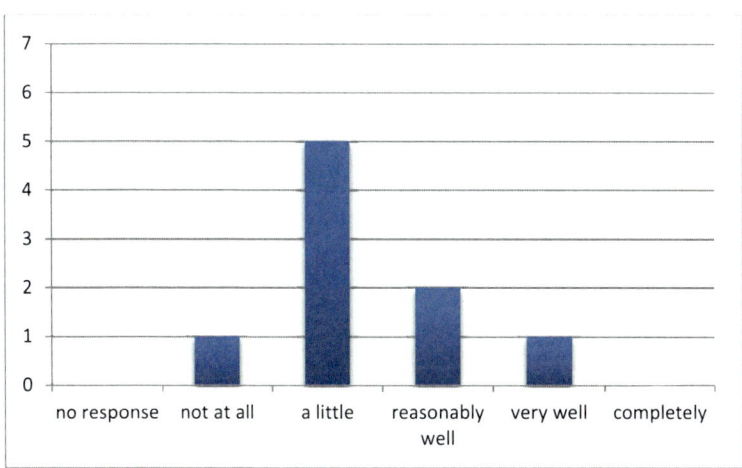

Chart 7: 'The rolling ball experiment enabled me to explore collisions.'

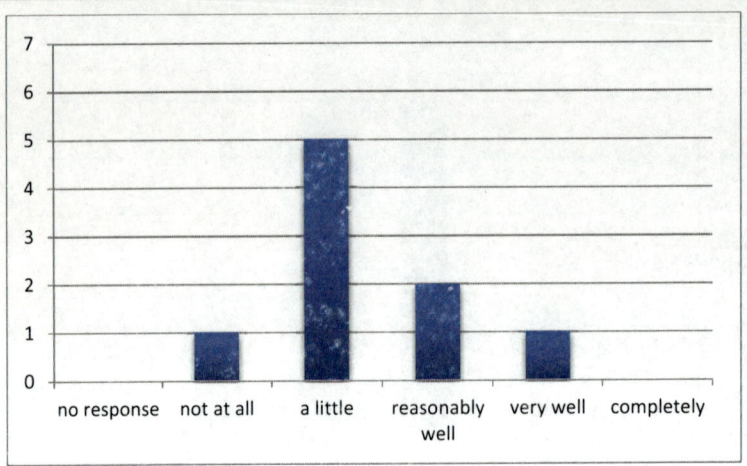

Chart 8: 'The rolling ball experiment enabled me to explore experimental accuracy.'

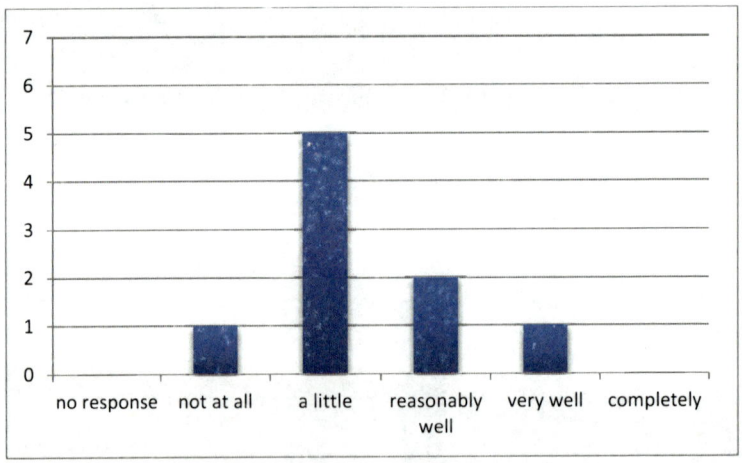

Chart 9: 'The rolling ball experiment helped me think about the differences and/or parallels between running an experiment in *Second Life*, and running an experiment in the physical world.'

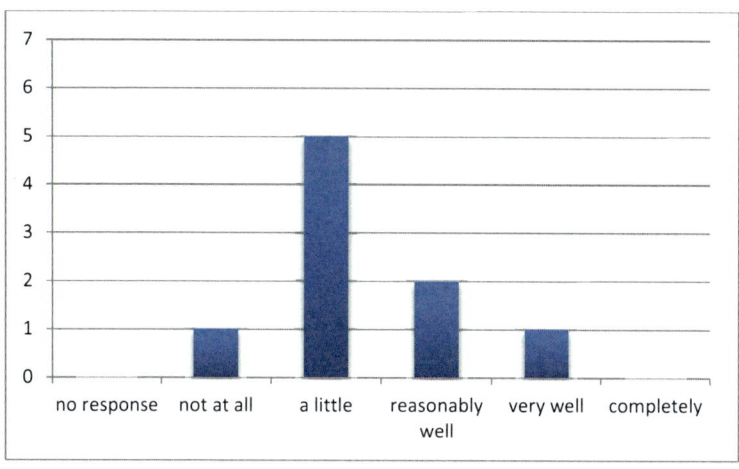

Chart 10: 'The rolling ball experiment enabled me to explore the issues involved in setting up an experiment.'

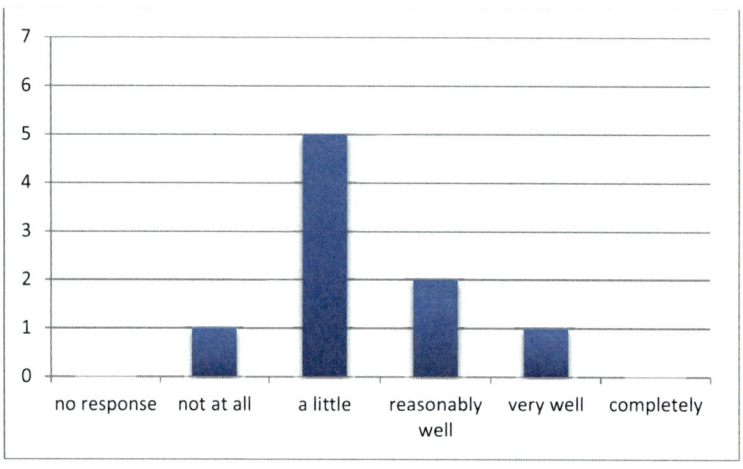

Chart 11: 'The rolling ball experiment enabled me to explore the issues involved in capturing data from an experiment'

9. Results (iv) Qualitative Responses

Participants were asked about their concerns in using *Second Life* for these experiments. Reponses can be grouped as in Figure 8: Concerns, noting that two participants did not respond whilst others offered more than one concern.

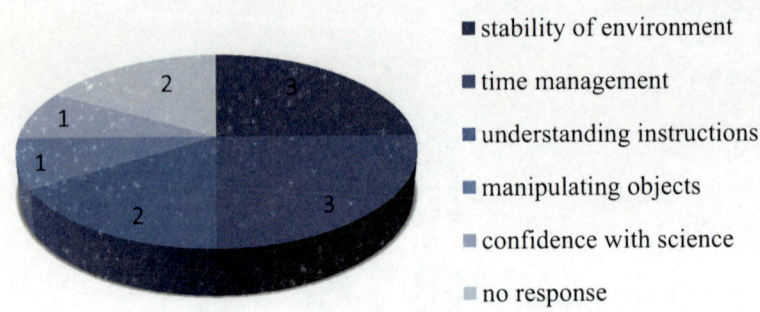

■ stability of environment

■ time management

■ understanding instructions

■ manipulating objects

■ confidence with science

■ no response

Figure 8: Numbers of responses indicating concerns.

Participants were asked about their expectations around using *Second Life* for these experiments. Reponses can be grouped as in Figure 9: Expectations, noting that one participant did not respond whilst others offered more than one expectation.

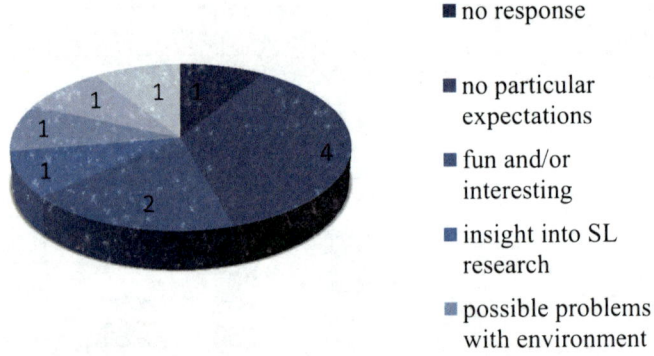

■ no response

■ no particular expectations

■ fun and/or interesting

■ insight into SL research

■ possible problems with environment

Figure 9: Numbers of responses indicating expectations

Participants were asked what they found easy about the experiments. Reponses can be grouped as in Figure 10: What Was Easy, noting that some participants offered more than one expectation.

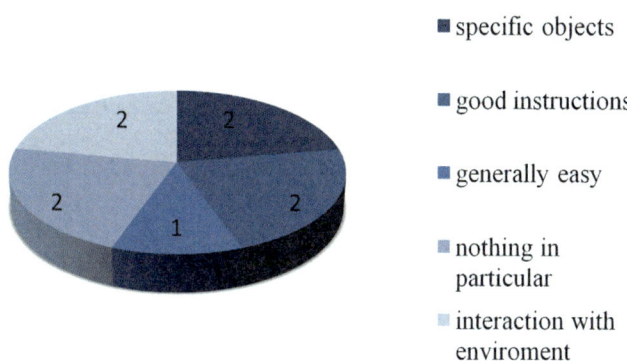

Figure 10: Numbers of responses indicating what was easy.

Participants were asked what they found challenging about the experiments. Reponses can be grouped as in Figure 11: What Was Challenging, noting that some participants offered more than one expectation. Two participants offered detailed feedback about specific aspects of the experiments, which would enable significant refinement if the same experiments were to be offered again. These sets of detailed feedback were each grouped as one instance of specific objects/uses.

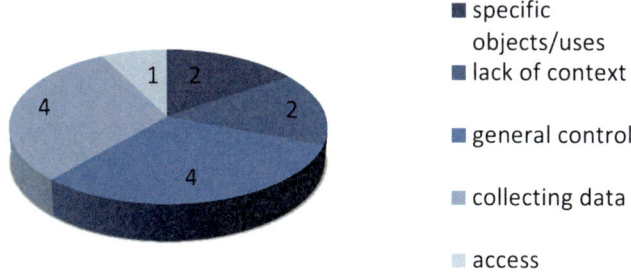

Figure 11: Numbers of responses indicating what was challenging

10. Results (v) Interviews

Student 4 demonstrated a good level of engagement with all the tools, making a total of 50 interactions over 9 visits. She provided positive feedback in the qualitative responses to the survey, and marked highly in the quantitative questions that she responded to, however all the 'no responses' in the quantitative range are attributable to this student. This student was selected for interview and her responses of particular interest (unedited from the original chat text) are listed below:

> *Interviewer: Your activity record shows that you spent most of your time interacting with the ball drop tool in the study. Can you explain what you particularly enjoyed or struggled with about that tool?*
>
> *Student 4: I kept trying it out as I kept getting the same result and thought maybe it should give different results for the 2 balls*
>
> *Interviewer: ah ok, did you do anything outside of SL to explore that theory?*
>
> *Student 4: Only thinking about how objects of different weights would drop at different rates and wondering if the different sized balls in SL had the same 'mass' as each other which would explain why they dropped at the same rate for me. I assumed the bigger ball would drop faster as I saw it as being 'heavier'*
>
> *Interviewer: Feedback was generally more positive for the rolling ball experiment than the ball drop – why do you think this might be?*
>
> *Student 4: Possibly becuse there was more feedback inworld for the rolling ball – the rate it travelled was shown in local chat at regular intervals so you could see how it was slowing. also you could bump into the balls to see how that affected the rate it slowed down etc. I guess you could interatc with the rolling balls a bit more really*
>
> *Interviewer: What do you think about the balance of instruction and investigation in the experiments?*
>
> *Student 4: I think the instructions were very good and clear And for the rolling ball and the measuring experiments you could investigate more 'freely' than you could with the dropping ball*
>
> *Interviewer: and that was better?*
>
> *Student 4: Yes I think so*
>
> *Interviewer: What do you feel that you learned from interacting with the experiments?*
>
> *Student 4: I think I realised how you could use inworld experiments to 'show' people a concept that they may only be able to read about in a book*

Interviewer: What single change do you think would make the experiments easier to learn from?

Student 4: Maybe some kind of results table showing the results people get from the experiments to see if everyone gets the same.

Interviewer: that's interesting, were you thinking about what other people were doing when you were working on the experiments?

Student 4: Yes I wondered if others were getting the same kind of results as me – particularly that drop ball one!

Interviewer: would you have felt more confident doing the experiments with someone else do you think?

Student 4: Not necessarily doing them with someone, but it would have been nice to compare results

Interviewer: How do you think we should test learning from these experiments?

Student 4: Maybe you could check by asking what concept we think the experiments were aimed at illustrating

Student 4: I do think somewhere for the people doing the experiments to discuss their results would be good too – but depends on the situation of course

Interviewer: so if they had something like a tutor group forum where they could each post their results, and discuss them...?

Student 4: yes that would be good I think – do the practical bit (the experiment) and then post results and discuss

11. Discussion

Comparing activity data capture for the participants with their responses to the survey enables a level of interpretation beyond face value, with triangulation supported by the interviews.

For most students the survey data tallied with their inworld activity. Student 9 is highlighted as an exception, with an activity log that shows he did little more than click on a ball drop and drop it. He used no measuring apparatus and made only one visit to the study area. However in his survey responses he marks *Not at all* or *A little* to every question about the experiments, despite having no interactions at all with the momentum tools. Only registered participants wearing the data capture HUD had access to the experiments, so it is not possible for him to have engaged under the guise of another avatar, or to have engaged without his data being captured. This student identified his computer skills as average, but has previously opted in to a group offering OU tutorials in *Second Life* and has sufficient experience within the environment to engage with the simple tools on offer. He did not approve access to his student record for purposes of the study so his wider study history is unknown. When asked what he found difficult about the experiments he commented *Having access*, so it is possible to surmise he was restricted by access issues. Given his lack of engagement, his responses to the quantitative questions should not be given weight. Generally the survey charts suggest that the momentum experiment was better received than the gravity experiment, and the interview respondents both reason that the former allowed more interaction and unstructured investigation, which provides a sensible explanation for the difference. The lowest result for all quantitative charts was shared by the first two questions for the momentum experiment. Both interview respondents felt that they might be doing something wrong with the ball drop experiment as they lacked a theoretical and instructional context for what they observed to be happening, and their interaction with the tool was limited. Neither went beyond the environment, e.g. to the web, to look for an explanation for their results but both were offered the follow up of an email explanation during the interview and both accepted, with Student 4 being so keen as to email a reminder about this as soon as the interview closed. This suggests a limit on how much we might expect students to investigate whilst unsupported, aligning with the cognitive pedagogy and with other practical OU course activities that are embedded in a framework of theoretical material. Both students made excellent observations, but a lack of confidence meant that they didn't follow through to explore the theory independently, and so found the experiment unfulfilling

The most positive quantitative response to the ball drop experiment was to the statement: 'The ball drop experiment helped me think about the differences and/or parallels between running an experiment in *Second Life*, and running an experiment in the physical world.' Only one participant, Student 3, responded *Not at all*.

Student 3 is both a student and tutor, and her qualitative responses are generally supportive of and enthusiastic about using *SL* for study, but express her personal reservations about studying science.

> *I have no knowledge of science. I gave it up as a subject at school over fifty years ago, and athough I think it must be a fascinating subject it is way outside my experience.*
> *I was unfamiliar with some of the scientific terms, and have never used spreadsheets for collecting data.*
> *I would have liked more guidance, but I don;t think this is the fault of the experiments, as if I was in an Arts environment I would not have appreciated being spoonfed. It;s just that Science IS NOT MY THING.*

Student 3 answers *Not at all* or *A little* to all the quantitative questions, and it seems that the experiments were too far outside her comfort zone with the subject matter rather than the context and/or environment, as in response to 'How would you feel about using *Second Life* to access/work with core learning material for an OU course' she replies:

> *I think using SL to access core learning material is an excellent idea. Fun and non-threatening. It would be good to use with a tutor group, so there is more peer input. (as well as tutor guidance)*

Generally the rolling ball experiment was better received, and Student 4's reasoning that this allowed more interaction and free investigation provides a sensible explanation for these results.

The statement 'The [...] experiment helped me think about the differences and/or parallels between running an experiment in *Second Life*, and running an experiment in the physical world', also has a positive response for the rolling ball. Taken together, Student 3 answers the only Not at all, with 7 responses for A little (omitting Student 9's contribution), 5 Reasonably well, 1 Very well and 1 Completely, the last being from Student 1 for the rolling ball. As we aimed to test the more general sense of how students could relate *SL* experiments to physical experiments, this result is encouraging and suggests that ironing out practical issues with the experiments themselves would translate well to this wider context. This is supported by Student 4's comment that

> *I think I realised how you could use inworld experiments to 'show' people a concept that they may only be able to read about in a book.*

Participants expressed concern over the stability of the environment, understanding instructions and over the time required for them to participate in the research. As OU students would have deliberately selected a module of study containing online practical work, time will not be an issue in the same way (although they may have concerns over the time needed to gain *SL* skills). Those who anticipated that they would have trouble understanding instructions went on to comment in response to other questions that they found the instructions clear and easy to follow, so these concerns were abated. Stability of the environment is, however, significant. The specific comments in this group were as follows:

[Student 1]	I had considered changing viewer around the time of the experiment, but decided against it due to wishing to be fully competent in my use of *SL* for the experiments. I also decided to remove anything scripted from my avatar for the experiments as I was unsure if scripts would affect the outcome or not with either client side or server side lag (hope got those terms correct).
[Student 4]	Main problem would have been that if people had problems logging in or 'crashed' they would not have been able to take part.
[Student 9]	Having access

Student 1 is referring to the most recent release of the *SL* client or viewer. A number of viewers and viewer versions exist, and Student 1 is recognising the skills leap needed to move between upgrades. Student 4 reiterated her comments in her interview and noted that the instruction boards never fully rezzed for her. Her concern about logins and crashes is expressed for others as she did not experience either during the study. Student 9 does not elaborate on 'Having access', which could be concern about specific access to the study tools, to the environment generally, to the internet or even to a computer.

Student 1 commented again on the potential for problems in her response to the question about expectations, but generally responses here were blank, said that there were no expectations (these two being arguably indicative of the same answer), or indicated positive anticipation. Student 9 said that his expectations were higher than the actual experience, again a difficult comment to rationalise against his interaction log. Student 2 said *I thought it would take longer than it actually did, perhaps because I rapidly bored with what seemed very simplistic experiments*, although like 6 other participants he did not register any interactions with the protractor tool. Student 1, who also missed out this tool completely despite an otherwise regular interaction pattern, addressed this in her interview by saying that she used one that had been 'left out' by another participant, so it is feasible that other participants did likewise and it was an omission on the part of the data capture to record interactions with an object not rezzed or owned by the avatar. It is also feasible that, like Student 7, they perceived that there were no instructions for use of the protractor.

When asked what they found easy about the experiments participants all responded with predictable variables such as good instructions or comments on tools, for example Student 5: *Activating the objects and experiments* and Student 7: *The green pyramid is straightforward*. The most negative comment was from Student 8, who said: *So a large extent i did not find it easy. I think because i was not really sure of the context of the experiments*. This can be linked back to the earlier comments from the interviews, and would be addressed by experiments embedded in a course framework, providing a context that the students found lacking.

Fifty per cent of all reasons given for the participants' regular use of *SL* could be grouped as social and 8 out of the 9 participants who responded gave this as their primary or secondary reason for being in *SL*, the exception being Student 9. *SL* itself is primarily a social tool; an open VW with no game narrative, bringing together multiple users in a shared space. Participants 1, 3 and 5 reference this social interaction, categorised by Warburton and Perez-Garcia as Community Presence and Extended Interactions, when asked about using *SL* for learning. Students 1 and 4 both talk in their interviews about bringing social content into future developments, although for Student 4 this is about using a context of forums to share ideas and reflections. Previous OU research in *SL* has explored how well the environment supports community (Peachey, 2010) and a socially constructivist pedagogy (Peachey and Withnail, in press). Sfard (1998) argues for the wisdom of respecting a variety of perspectives rather than leveraging acquisition and participation metaphors to enforce a single standpoint.

Five of the 9 respondents expressed reservations about technical issues with the environment should it be adopted for further activity. It is noted that although anticipated these reservations are well-founded and should of course be given due weight and consideration when planning how a full range of *SL* activities might be developed into an online practical science module such as S288.

Student 1 identifies herself as a visual learner and talks about visiting other locations in *SL* to support science learning on other courses, referencing Warburton and Perez-Garcia's category of Visualisation and Contextualization.

12. Conclusions

This research set out to explore participants' understanding and experience of using the tools provided to test *SL* physics. Evaluation found a mix of responses, highlighting specific shortfalls with the experiments (quantitative) but indicating a positive approach overall to using *SL* for formal learning activities (qualitative).

The conclusions are presented acknowledging that this is a study of only ten participants, offering a step forward in development for VW activities, for practical science. Issues are identified that might benefit from further research.

Students are open to relating *SL* experiments to physical world experiments. Students like activities that encourage them to explore and investigate freely but are more confident when activities are set in a theoretical and instructional context, with a range of supporting materials. This aligns well with the cognitive learning approach for activities carried out independently. Students might gain confidence from sharing results and discussing outcomes and there is significant potential for developing *SL* activities into a VLE-based course framework.

The potential of *SL* for distance learning of practical science need not be restricted to cognitive-driven Immersive, Content-rich activities. Students use the environment regularly as a social tool and they are comfortable working within a socially constructivist pedagogy. Community Presence and Extended Interactions therefore present viable options, and use of existing content on virtual field trips as well as bespoke development may be explored for purposes of Visualisation and Contextualization. A milieu of activities, involving a range of pedagogies, would offer a richer learning experience and satisfy a wider range of learning preferences. This study specifically excluded issues regarding access and *SL* skills in order to focus on the experience of the science activities. However participants themselves raised these issues, reinforcing the significance that should be accorded in wider planning for inworld developments for practical science.

Notes

[1] John Kirriemuir, *The Spring 2009 Snapshot of Virtual World use in UK Higher and Further Education* (Bath: Eduserv Foundation, 2009).

[2] NPL Website, *National Physical Laboratory*, 2010, viewed on October 16 2010, http://www.npl.co.uk/commercial-services/products-services/knowledge-transfer/new-media.

[3] Steve Warburton and M. Perez-Garcia, '3D Design and Collaboration in Massively Multi-User Virtual Environments.' *Cases on Collaboration in Virtual Learning Environments: Processes and Interactions*, ed. Donna Russell (Hershey, PA: IGI Global, 2009).

[4] Alan Rogers, *What is the Difference? A New Critique of Adult Learning and Teaching* (Leicester: NIACE, 2003).

[5] Good, Thomas and Brophy, Jere. *Educational Psychology: A Realistic Approach.* (4th ed.) White Plains, NY: Longman, 1990.

[6] In the context of *Second Life*, to rez something is to make it appear (physical) within the environment, for example by dragging out of an inventory folder into the virtual space.

[7] *Second Life* users can converse using text chat, which ordinarily appears on their screen in a format known as Local Chat.

[8] Diana Laurillard, 'How Can Learning Technologies Improve Learning?,' *Law Technology Journal* 3, no. 2 (1994), viewed on 16 March 2009, http://web.archive.org/web/20070322002729/http://www.law.warwick.ac.uk/ltj/3-2j.html.

Bibliography

Good, Thomas and Brophy, Jere. *Educational Psychology: A Realistic Approach.* (4th ed.) White Plains, NY: Longman, 1990.

Kirriemuir, John. *The Spring 2009 Snapshot of Virtual World use in UK Higher and Further Education*. Bath: Eduserv Foundation, 2009.

Laurillard, Diana. 'How Can Learning Technologies Improve Learning?,' *Law Technology Journal* 3, no. 2 (1994). Viewed on 16 March 2009. http://web.archive.org/web/20070322002729/http://www.law.warwick.ac.uk/ltj/3-2j.html.

NPL Website. 2010. *National Physical Laboratory*. Viewed on October 16 2010. http://www.npl.co.uk/commercial-services/products-services/knowledge-transfer/new-media

Peachey, Anna and Withnail, Greg. 'A Sociocultural Perspective on Negotiating Digital Identities in a Community of Learners.' *Digital Identity and Social Media*, edited by Steve Warburton and Stylianos Hatzipanagos. Hershey, PA: IGI Global, 2012.

Peachey, Anna. 'The Third Place in *Second Life*: Real Life Community in a Virtual World.' *Researching Learning in Virtual Worlds*, edited by Anna Peachey, Julia Gillen, Daniel Livingstone, and Sarah Smith-Robbins, 91-110. London: Springer, 2010.

Rogers, Alan. *What is the Difference? A New Critique of Adult Learning and teaching*. Leicester: NIACE, 2003.

Sfard, Anna. 'On Two Metaphors for Learning and the Dangers of Choosing Just One,' *Educational Researcher* 27, no. 2 (1998): 4-13. Viewed on 27 July 2012. http://www.it.uu.se/edu/course/homepage/cosulearning/st12/reading/Sfard_ER199 8.pdf .

Warburton, Steve. '*Second Life* in Higher Education: Assessing the Potential for and the Barriers to Deploying Virtual Worlds in Learning and Teaching,' *British Journal of Educational Technology* 50, no. 3 (2009): 414-426.

Warburton, Steve and Perez-Garcia, M. '3D Design and Collaboration in Massively Multi-User Virtual Environments.' *Cases on Collaboration in Virtual Learning Environments: Processes and Interactions*, edited by Donna Russell. Hershey, PA: IGI Global, 2009.

Anna Peachey spent 4 years researching identity and community in virtual worlds as a Teaching Fellow with The Open University UK. She continues to teach, study and research with The Open University, and established their virtual world project with her company, Eygus Ltd. She has published a range of texts on activity in virtual worlds and is Editor-in-Chief of the Springer book series on Immersive Environments.

Greg Withnail's background is in architectural CAD, GIS and Web Design. As a Project Manager with Eygus Ltd he spent two years working full-time on their *Second Life* developments for the Open University. This involved both managing the technical aspects of the islands (such as permissions, scripting, group management, parcel management etc) and maintaining the social aspects of the islands communities (arranging social events, introducing new members to the communities). He is an outspoken advocate of bringing established Web usability principles to Virtual Worlds.

Nicholas Braithwaite is Professor of Engineering Physics at the Open University, where he has developed modules in a wide variety of topics in science and technology. He is also co-director of the OU's Wolfson Open Science Laboratory that was established in 2012 to present online practical science in a distance-learning context. Between 2009 and 2012 he led the OU team that brought online practical work into the mainstream science curriculum through a suite of modules in Practical Science (S288), His team devised a range of practical investigations based largely on real data accessed through a blend of interactive screen experiments/observations, remote controlled equipment and immersive environments.

Index